When One Door Closes

Reflections from Women on Life's Turning Points

Terri Spahr Nelson, Editor

Sugati Publications
www.sugatipublications.com

I want to acknowledge the individual authors who granted permission to print their original essays and poems in this book. The complete listing of authors is noted in the acknowledgments including the authors who submitted their essays with consent but used pseudonyms or an anonymous byline. This acknowledgement includes any quotes used in the book that are in the public domain or used within fair use copyright guidelines. The credits for all quotes used, when known, are noted at the end of the book.

Publisher: Sugati Publications at www.sugatipublications.com

When One Door Closes: Reflections from Women on Life's Turning Points/
Terri Spahr Nelson

ISBN: 0-9825806-9-X
ISBN-13: 9780982580691
Library of Congress Control Number: 2009910711

With enduring love,
I dedicate this book to the two men in my life
who have enriched me in ways that I never imagined possible:
my husband Pat and my son Josh.
You are my inspiration.
I can't imagine doing this without you.

~

With deepest gratitude,
this book is also dedicated to each of the 53 women
who shared their personal essays and poems with all of us.
Thank you. This book is for you.

Personal dedication or inscription:

Best regards —
[illegible]
2017

*"Whenever I have knocked, a door has opened.
Wherever I have wandered, a path has appeared.
I have been helped, supported, encouraged and nurtured by people
of all races, creeds, colors and dreams."*

— Alice Walker (In Search of Our Mothers' Gardens, 1983)

~

Table of Contents

Part Three: Discovering the Pathways to a Career

Part Four: Facing Unexpected Crises, Challenges and Trauma

Part Five: Coping with Illness, Healing and Loss

Part Six: Moving Forward and Beyond the Threshold

Preface

Writing is the act of reaching across the abyss of isolation to share and reflect.
—Natalie Goldberg

The premise behind the book:

- *All women face turning points or threshold events in their lives.*
- *Each of us has a story to tell.*

We all have significant times in our lives when we find ourselves at the threshold of an important life event or turning point. In almost 30 years as a psychotherapist, I have come to know many people in times of great need, contemplation and suffering. I have also witnessed many women and men who were transformed by these events into a more accepting and loving place for themselves and others. They needed to tell their stories to find a place of peace. For many people, writing opens the door which allows them to tell their story, to reflect, to heal and to connect with others. Writing about these turning points can be a bridge to the other side.

I wanted to create an opportunity for women to share their stories in a way that would allow them to say whatever they needed to say in their own words and for others to learn from their experiences. In addition, I wanted to provide an avenue for women to participate in the process of creating this book from start to finish.

I knew that I had to find ways to include women of all ages, from different backgrounds, different cultures and races, different spiritual viewpoints and different life experiences. I also knew that this anthology needed to become a tapestry representing the diversity of challenges and lessons learned from many women, not just from one perspective or lifestyle. We can learn and grow much more fully from perspectives that challenge us to move beyond our own experiences and perspectives. Therefore, I intentionally stepped outside of the box of traditional publishing to create a book by women and for women which crossed those familiar lines. It was with that in mind that the *Reflections from Women* book project was born. What happened next truly amazed me.

In December 2008, I made a public announcement calling for personal essays from women about significant life events and turning points in their lives. I developed a framework for contributors to participate (submission guidelines, consent forms, deadlines and so on), launched the *Reflections from Women* website and proceeded to send queries across the nation to women's groups, blogs, websites, forums, literary networks and more. Then, I waited to hear if anyone was interested.

When the statements of interest started to pour in, I was elated and overwhelmed. Here is a sampling of the queries that came in:

- *A friend sent me your announcement. My story begins after my marriage ended.*
- *At fifty years old, I finally made peace with the mother I never knew.*
- *I would like to submit a story dealing with loss of a child from stillbirth.*
- *I experienced 15 years of domestic violence and 7 years of stalking after my divorce. I feel it is important to share my experience to let other women know that there is hope and that they can make it through the experience.*
- *After my husband died in 2002, I was numb. Every morning on the way to work I passed a tree. I thought about how easy it would be to go off the road and hit it. Then one day I just knew I would be okay.*
- *I would like to submit a story about deciding to marry my husband who is a female-to-male transsexual.*
- *I am very interested on writing a story about my family and my struggle with culture shock after moving to the United States from Laos.*
- *My turning point came when the man I had loved for years and planned to marry drowned. I hit the bottom of my alcoholic drinking at the same time and didn't believe I had the wherewithal to salvage my life in the face of this loss.*
- *After many years of debate about changing our life style, my husband and I decided to sell our house and live on a boat.*
- *I would like to share the story of the day my best friend died of cancer. She was 30 years old. Her story deserves to be told.*
- *After 11 years of praying for a baby, I was blessed the adoption of a newborn daughter.*
- *I would like to submit a story about trying to get pregnant, including shopping for donor sperm online and using artificial insemination.*
- *I am writing about surviving cancer...I believe that the cancer experience can be a time of renewal of one's life path and a rebirth of one's spirit.*

- *I made a career change at age 40 from a corporate publications manager to United Methodist pastor. Being hit by a trash truck pushed me to make this change—quite a funny and quirky story that has led to deeply meaningful work.*
- *I have recently been in contact with my first love from over 30 years ago. My story is a letter I wrote to him that summarizes the relationships, losses, loves, and crossroads I have faced since he left me.*
- *My story is about my son's lifelong battle with alcohol and drugs, his death and my part in his life.*

Life, death, birth, illness, love found (and lost), faith affirmed (and challenged), career transformations, gender transformations, marriage, divorce, letting go and moving on. I could not have asked for more. In fact, I faced the difficult process of determining which stories would best fit together and which ones simply would not work for this specific project.

The most difficult part of this process as the editor was making the decisions and sending regrets to the authors who did not make each of the three review rounds. There were many great stories that could not be included, and I am sorry that I could not accept them all. I trust you will find that the selected essays and poems provide a meaningful and rich range of writing styles, experiences and lessons learned from some truly remarkable women. To all contributors, whether your work appears here or not, I am grateful and honored that so many shared their personal stories of tragedy and triumph for this project.

In addition to the open solicitation, we also invited authors to submit essays and poems for the *Reflections from Women* writing contest. Once again, the selection process was quite difficult. The top ten works from the contest were selected for publication.

I also decided to donate 35% of the profits from the book to non-profit women's organizations identified by the authors and by the public. Since the essays in this book were written by women who have faced significant life decisions and transitions, this is our way of supporting a few of the many organizations providing assistance to women in times of great need or transition.

The authors and the general public nominated and voted for the women's charities online via the website and blog. The organizations that were selected to receive the proceeds were announced on Mother's Day. These five agencies offer a wide range of assistance to women on global, national and local fronts. As an added bonus, a few of our authors volunteer with some of these agencies.

On July 4, 2009, the final selections for the book and the top ten recipients of the writing contest were announced to the public. The responses from the authors were tremendous, insightful and heartfelt:

> *It was very liberating to write this part of my life's journey. I thought and wrote about things I have never expressed to anyone. For this, I thank you.*
>
> *I am delighted to have my essay included! Our book club is over the moon about it and wants to read the book together as soon as it is available!*
>
> *Oh my goodness! I am so honored! I am sitting here waiting to go into labor with my first baby...and this is just the icing on the cake! I feel so blessed to be a part of this process and especially to share the story of (the death of) my best friend. Between your email and my baby on the way —I feel her all around me today.*
>
> *I'm just thrilled to be a part of this endeavor. Thank you again for selecting my story and including it with a collection of voices I know will be heard around the country and even the world.*
>
> *I'm very happy that my story made the final cut. I have no aspirations as a professional writer, but I have always wanted to share my story in a way that will hopefully touch other lives for the better. I am so grateful!*
>
> *Oh, MY!!! I was holding my breath all night!! I am so honored to be among the authors chosen. To know that other women will benefit from our collective stories is absolutely a dream come true—fills my life with meaning.*
>
> *This has been a huge step in my healing process to have finally acknowledged and shared my experiences.*
>
> *Wa-hoo! That is great news! I'm humbled just to be considered!*
>
> *As I re-read my story, I decided it was too mundane to be included as I expected there would be much more dramatic stories that would have a larger impact. I am honored that it made it!*

This is really amazing for me to see the process of making a book. I'm thrilled to be even a small part of it.

It warms my heart that you were touched. I hope that others will be as well.

Someone in my circle of writers once said how he/she didn't need validation for their work...I sooo disagree!! I'm thrilled...and you bet I'm letting the world know about it!

I told you they are remarkable women—just wait until you read their stories! You will find yourself identifying with some of the authors, laughing out loud at the humor in some of the stories, and finding it difficult to hold back the tears as your heart breaks for some of these women and their experiences.

Their essays and poems are a remarkable collection of stories looking at the many challenges women face in their lives. The works in this book are in the women's own words based on their personal experiences. It was important for the authors' voices to be heard as they told their individual stories. Therefore, you will notice the unique and diverse writing styles in each of the essays and poems truly making this book a woven collection of women's writings.

Prior to publication, the authors were asked to provide a few sentences about themselves including an update to their stories. The authors were also asked to provide feedback, suggestions and preferences on the title of the book. From start to finish, the authors have been an integral part of the project. This book would not be what it is without them!

In the end, I hope that you will find the book to be as fascinating and rewarding to read as it has been for me to develop. This book shines a light on the difficult choices and provocative moments that women face in their lives and on how they carry on despite challenges and uncertainty. The personal stories and experiences shared by the women in this book illuminate connections that all women share on their own life's journey even though the women and their stories couldn't be more different.

If this book reminds you of a woman in your life who you care about, give her a copy and let her know how important she is to you. I have left a place in the front of the book for you to leave a personal message—either for yourself or for a woman who is dear to you.

The tapestry of experiences and lives represented in this book reminds me of a significant insight about humanity from the young author and teen, Anne Frank:

We all live with the objective of being happy;
our lives are all different and yet the same.

I trust you will connect with a story in this diverse collection that will inspire you, or cause you to think about something a bit differently or offer you some comfort as you face your own turning points in life. I hope these stories will help you to realize that, no matter what happens in your life, when one door closes, another *will* open. As one of our authors noted, "*When people listen to one another's stories, peace often prevails.*"

May you be well and may you be at peace.

Terri Spahr Nelson

Acknowledgments

First and foremost, I want to extend a heartfelt thank you to each of the contributing authors. I am deeply honored that they were willing to share their personal stories for this book. I am in awe of their insights, courage, resilience and faith that brought them to this point. Their collective stories speak volumes about the many different turning points that women encounter in life. This book would not have been possible without them! Thank you again to our authors:

- Paula Andresen–Remembering Mary
- Vickie Andresen Sedillo–Paula
- Tamara Bastone–Letter to My Mother
- Michelle Bessette–Extra Baggage
- Rene Brannen–Losing My Religion
- Joy Brubaker–When the Baby Died
- Mary Martha Christianson–David and Mom
- Alice Coggin Bagley–I'm Here
- Cynthia Colebrook–Topaz
- Elizabeth A. Coplan–What's Your Problem, Mom?
- Brenda Dronkers–My Crisis Transformed
- Cara Evans–The Claw Foot
- Edie Fisher–A Letter to My First Love
- Karen Francis–Winter Solstice
- Clara Freeman–Second Time Around
- Doreen Garrigan–The Roundabout Way to Becoming Me
- Maryellen Grady–Transformation
- Katie Hall–Resurfacing
- Emily Harris–Two a Day
- Carol Kabakoff–This Story has a Happy Ending
- Karen Kidwell–Hand Me Down
- Misty Kiwak Jacobs–A trilogy of poems and One White Towel
- Kelli Kirwan–Traveling the Matriarchal Path

- Rebecca J. Love–Shopping in the Sperm Aisle and Class Questions
- Andrea MacEachern–Christmas Heartache
- Jeannie Martinelli–Cheri
- KC McClain–Decision Point
- Marissa McNamara–Heading North
- Minerva–The Turning Point
- Laura Morey–Thank You, Midnight
- Janice Moszynski–Journey into Light
- Marykay Mulligan–The Day the Sun Shined Again
- Melinda Nagle–Life
- Margo Pierce–Ending the Tyranny of 'Supposed To'
- Alicia Powers–The Way of the Wounded Healer
- Anne Richardson–Misery Optional
- Hanan Rose–Departure
- Kate Sheckler–The Mechanics of Destiny
- Mary Scribner–The Teen Years–Can a Steel Stud Look Like a Pimple?
- Nancy Smith–Black Rock
- Laura Sommers–Oops!
- Lana Swearingen–Don
- Linda Tefend–Taming the Monster
- Kelli Trinoskey–Mom, Interrupted
- Nancy Turner–Crash
- Vicki Trusley–Ending the Waking Nightmare
- Va Vang–A New Challenge
- Cassie Walker–Gone
- Erin Wilson–Biology
- Sandra F. Wilson–Reflections of May
- Anonymous–Falling
- Anonymous–true love in the present moment

I also want to acknowledge other individuals who have been a part of this project. To everyone who provided input on the book from the title to the non-profit charity selections—thank you! To my proof readers and copy editors, I could not have done this without you, truly. To Pat, Josh Nelson and Maggie Bertke for their support, encouragement and invaluable assistance with so many details, I owe you (and will do the same when your books are underway!) To Sugati for being a happy and welcome destination time and again.

In conclusion, I want to offer my gratitude. I am grateful to the women who have supported and encouraged me on my journey giving me the foundation to be the woman I am today: my mother whose strength lives on in me; my dear sisters; my faithful friends; and my mentor Gloria Shipley. I am grateful to all of the women who have given me inspiration and to those women whose lives have touched me throughout the years. You have taught me more than you will ever realize. I am also deeply grateful for the men in my world for making my life that much richer. Finally, I am truly thankful to all of the women who have come before me and have opened doors for all of us. I share this book with all of you with much gratitude and loving kindness.

An Introduction to the *Reflections from Women* Series

I am a woman above everything else.
— Jacqueline Kennedy Onassis

The *Reflections from Women* series was developed to recognize and to honor the distinctive experiences of women. The series is built upon a foundation of appreciation and awareness that women's experiences throughout the lifespan are often quite different from those of men. The essays and poems in the *Reflections from Women* series will focus on some of the issues and challenges that women encounter in life. This series offers women an opportunity to tell their story in their own words and for others to learn from, to connect with, or to reflect on the common experiences and bonds that women share.

An important note: The *Reflections from Women* series is not intended to exclude men. In fact, this book is full of essays and poems about men who have been significant and influential in the lives of women. There are stories of true love, deep loss, enduring relationships, lifelong connections, respect, disrespect, betrayal and loyalty. Many of these stories (and women's lives) would not have been possible without men. In addition, I have intentionally included some quotes from men throughout the book to further demonstrate that we all need and can benefit from each other.

Yes, men are important in the lives of women, but this book (and the *Reflections from Women* series) is dedicated to women and girls. As Jacqueline Kennedy Onassis noted, "*I am a woman above everything else.*" From the day we are born, and as we grow and change through puberty, adulthood, menopause, later life and finally until our death, our experiences as women are distinctive. Women have an important place in our everyday lives, in our history and in our future. We have so much to offer the world and the possibilities are endless. This series reflects the inspiration, hope and opportunities open for women in the world.

~

A message to men who might pick up this book or any upcoming books in the Reflections from Women series: If you love, care about or enjoy the friendship of women, I encourage you to read this book and to listen deeply to these women's stories. I truly hope that these stories will bring you closer to understanding or connecting with the women in your life.

~

An Introduction to When One Door Closes

Each of us faces turning points in our lives. They may come as decisions, events, crises or challenges. They can be significant and life changing or simply changes of perspective or different ways of looking at the world. Turning points can happen in an instant, such as getting a phone call that a loved one has been in an accident or learning that a tumor is not cancerous. Or, they can develop over time, such as caring for a loved one with a debilitating illness or discovering your passion and calling.

Many of life's turning points arrive unexpectedly. You may suddenly find yourself facing something that you never imagined, such as losing your job or learning that your partner is having an affair. Crises and unanticipated situations create periods of uncertainty and stress. These are inevitable: All things are impermanent and changing. As contributor Paula Andresen noted:

Life is full of challenges, sometimes one right after another. It really is part of life. People tend to get caught up in the easy, or wore down from the battles, and forget that life is not always easy and can be a real challenge. If you face life's challenges, confront them and deal with them, you can get through them and become stronger in the process... When people try to ignore their problems, they usually resurface later with a vengeance and then bite you in the ass as you try to run from it.

If we are able to face these unexpected turns, we are less likely to get stuck in the past or to become fearful about the uncertainty of the future. We are able to continue moving forward despite the obstacles. No matter what comes our way, we must eventually learn how to accept these situations so that we can live our lives fully and without burden, regret or attachment.

When One Door Closes looks at those times in women's lives when they faced a turning point or found themselves at the threshold of an important decision or a change in perspective. The authors explore a wide range of topics through the lifespan including love, loss, relationships, commitments, parenting, career choices, health and mental health. The women in this book share insights from their own experiences and the lessons they have learned along the way. As one of our authors reflected on her own turning point:

> *It was one of those moments that I can point to and say,*
> *"That's when life changed."*

Using this book as a resource on your personal journey

This book can be a resource on your journey and as a connection with other women facing similar turning points. It is not intended to give you answers, but to offer some insights and reflections from other women, to encourage your own self-discovery and to promote the discussion of these challenging life issues with others.

This book is comprised of 55 essays and poems written by 53 women (two of the authors have two works included). Each chapter begins with an introduction that draws attention to some of the common themes and elements in the stories and concludes with "Reflection Points" including quotes highlighting lessons learned and questions for further contemplation. Consider answering these questions even if you have not faced and are not facing similar issues in your life. The stories reflect a wide range of perspectives and decisions on many topics, some of them controversial; please keep in mind that the questions are not an attempt to promote one perspective or another. The questions are open-ended to encourage thoughtful contemplation and insight. These questions can also serve as a foundation for discussion with groups, classes, or with friends and loved ones.

This book is for your mind and for your heart. It is for you to read by yourself to further your own insights or to share with others for connection and reflection. I hope that these stories will serve as a reminder that *when one door closes, the doors we open can make all the difference in our lives.*

Part One

Standing at Love's Door

And now abide in faith, hope, love, these three;
but the greatest of these is love.
– 1 Corinthians 13:13

CHAPTER 1

Love Found (and Lost)

i carry your heart with me (i carry it in my heart) i am never without it
— e.e. cummings

Love can transform a person, a relationship, a life.

It was no surprise that the most common topic of the essays submitted for this book were about love and the relationships that followed love. In fact, there were so many stories about love that it was fitting to disperse them throughout the book to highlight some of these turning points women face in their lives. The transitions included falling in love, falling out of love, divorcing, having children, parenting, caring for a loved one, grieving for love and saying goodbye. Love and relationships have transformed women's lives in countless ways.

The women in this book shared their heartfelt stories about how love came into their lives: unexpected, cautious, or with an unbridled passion; and they shared their heartbreaking accounts of how love left them: unexpected, reluctant or with a pain so great that some wondered whether they could go on living or whether they would ever love again.

There is nothing like love to move us to sheer joy, complete awe, unnerving frustration or profound sadness. Once you have known true love, you will be forever changed. This is one of the many thresholds in women's lives where most of the stories began—at love's door.

Love found

Who is it for you? Who comes to mind when you reflect on intimate, romantic love?

Pause for a minute and reflect on the person(s) who came into your life and sparked these feelings of intimate and romantic love. For most people, the person's face or name will instantly appear in their mind. If you are have found love with more than one person, you might think of each of them and how you love(d) them.

Whether a first love or your current love, the person of your desire can still make your heart skip a beat if you are open to it. In "A Letter to My First Love," Edie Fisher reminds us that although relationships may come and go, love can endure. Edie's essay is in the form of a personal letter to her first love of decades ago, telling him that she still thinks of him. She keeps a place in her heart for the young man who captured her love but left her unexpectedly all those years ago. Since his departure, Edie has lived a full life with more than her share of ups and downs in relationships. It was a difficult journey but it helped her to realize the importance of reconnecting with her first love. She begins her letter by cautiously telling him, *"I want you to know the person I am today..."* The challenges of the past 30 years have made Edie the woman she is today—stronger, more independent and ready to accept only true love.

Recognizing and accepting love is central to women searching for intimate relationships. However, some women are literally 'looking for love in all the wrong places' when the love of their life was actually there all along. In "Class Questions" you will find an honest and tender love story about a woman and a man who were at the cusp of commitment for some time. Author Rebecca Jean Love (one of the top ten writing contest recipients) tells a poignant and humorous look at her reluctance to commit to the love of her life—a transman (female-to-male transsexual). Although her situation was unique, her dilemma was one that is common to many women: knowing when or if you have found the right person and then trusting your instincts.

The desire for a loving relationship is fundamental. Women want to share their joys, their innermost fears, their days and nights and lives with someone. Without a romantic partnership, some women find themselves consumed in their careers, filling the void with other activities, or finding intimacy through an extended kinship of friends and family. For some women, this connection is enough and they have happy, full lives. For others, however, not having a partner leaves them feeling unfulfilled or alone.

Although loneliness was not a leading theme in any of the stories, it is a strong undercurrent that cuts through several of the essays on the loss of a relationship. You will discover that these are incredible women who are smart, successful and caring, but they are facing a considerable turning point in life: the loss of love.

Love lost

It is often said that *true love* never dies. Perhaps love doesn't actually die, but it can transform over time. Falling out of love, or the path out of love is not nearly as captivating as falling in love, however. Losing love can be tumultuous, painful and often unexpected. The pendulum shifts and your life changes. You may have been at this crossroad yourself. Most likely, you know a woman (at least one, if not several) who reluctantly took this journey when a relationship ended.

This section is about women who fell in love and found what they believed was a fulfilling relationship. If you have ever been in love, you know what I mean. It usually happens early on when you feel a connection with the other person. You enjoy each other's company. You want to spend more time together. You think about each other when you're not together. Perhaps you can even see this person as your life partner. At some point, you make a commitment to this individual, in your head and in your heart.

Then the unexpected occurs: The relationship is over. Sometimes it ends suddenly and without warning: *"I want a divorce." "I'm seeing someone else." "I just don't love you anymore."* When that happens, it can turn your world upside down. Everything changes. In "Second Time Around" author Clara Freeman shares how her life turned the day her husband of 20 years came home and declared, *"I've sold the house. You need to find somewhere else to live."* Just like that, 20 years of a marriage was over. Clara realized, however, that the day that truly changed her life was not the day her husband told her to leave, but the day her divorce was final. That was her turning point and it took her over the threshold into a fresh start.

The ending also came unexpectedly for Kate Sheckler, who wrote in "The Mechanics of Destiny" that her love transformed into *"the worst pain of all."* Yet, Kate later learned that *"it was neither his love nor the loss of it that defined her present nor would it define her future."*

As it turns out, the unexpected and painful loss of love is not a breaking point, but an opportunity for many women to start over. Yes, the loss of a relationship is painful and requires grieving time. It is not easy to let go and to move on. However, with the support of others and a keen sense of self, women can and do move beyond the heartache of a break up or a divorce. They become stronger and in the end, they are often better for it.

These essays remind us that love found and lost are universal experiences that we all share, a common bond integral to humanity. Whatever our backgrounds or histories, we all need love and companionship. Every person deserves a loving, committed, respectful relationship.

Class Questions

by Rebecca J. Love

Reflections from Women Writing Contest Selection

For my husband - I only hope to be as brave as you are.

~

"What does your penis look like?"

"How do you have sex?"

"Do you have an open marriage?"

These are questions my husband regularly fields from strangers. He's an educator at heart and is often invited into college classrooms to guest lecture. He sees these opportunities to speak to psychology, sociology, and human sexuality classes as a chance to correct misconceptions often perpetuated in textbooks or on the Jerry Springer show. As a female-to-male transsexual, he feels it is important to speak to students while they are learning their trades so that those students will become better-informed professionals who can make positive changes in their future work environments.

On the other hand, I am not a guest lecturer. I am, however, regularly mortified that people ask such questions of a stranger in a public forum. I have requested that my husband specifically not talk about my sexuality or our sex life when he lectures. He honors my request and will not say anything beyond the fact that I am a biological, heterosexual woman and deeply in love.

It's difficult to believe that we are so in love after such a rocky dating relationship. We had differing beliefs about children. We wondered if we had enough in common. He was already divorced twice, so how did I know we wouldn't be getting divorced too? And I was having some misgivings about telling my family that I was planning to marry a transman.

I could imagine the dreadful conversations. How could my conservative, 83-year-old Bostonian grandmother possibly understand? Would my mother try to talk me out of it? I knew she would want me to find a nice, normal young man. How would I even begin to explain this relationship to my father?

Then I would have to deal with friends and work. Could I really tell anyone? Would people think we were both freaks? Would someone challenge our marriage of a female-to-male transsexual and a biological woman by saying it was a lesbian relationship and not a husband and wife relationship? Would I lose my job?

Unable to cope with so much uncertainty, I broke up with my husband three times and gave back the engagement ring he purchased for me.

I also returned the engagement ring that I bought for him. Before I chose his ring, I researched various gemstones and found that sapphires were the original stones used in wedding rings symbolizing fidelity in marriage. I found a simple white gold ring with an inset, square-cut blue sapphire for him at our local Ben Bridge store. I returned the engagement ring I bought for him twice. I was too embarrassed to face the sales people to repurchase the identical ring in the same store, so I sought out another Ben Bridge franchise in a different mall to make my re-purchase. I had nowhere to return the third ring, running out of Ben Bridge stores in the area. So, this time, the ring went into the storage cabinets in my garage.

A few days after the last breakup, I was doing laundry while the radio crooned in the next room. It was a Depeche Mode ballad, "Somebody." The tha-thunk of a heartbeat is the framing percussive background in this song. That heartbeat blended with tender words and began to wash over me... *"Somebody to share the rest of my life," "Somebody who cares for me passionately," "Somebody who will put their arms around me and kiss me tenderly..."*

In that single, startling moment, I realized that I truly loved this man. I was breathless. I just couldn't be without him. This truth hit me as I was taking the warm, soft laundry out of the dryer. I crumpled to the tile floor in front of the machine, door swung wide, with the laundry spilling onto my lap. I buried my face into the fragrant cloth and began to cry in great hiccupping gulps. *How could I have pushed him away? How did I fail to realize that I was truly in love? Why was I letting my own fears of what my family might think get in the way of real love?*

Grasping the dryer for leverage, I hauled myself to my feet again, and I tried in vain to stifle my tears. I wiped my runny nose on a sock and threw it back into the washing machine. I had to call him. I had to see him. But first, I had to get his ring out of the garage.

He moved in a few weeks later and proposed marriage formally one final time. We were engaged for a year and then married on New Years Day. This year we celebrated our five-year anniversary. We are deeply in love.

But what the students want to talk about when my husband guest lectures is anatomy and sex acts. They don't ask about the love in our marriage, only what the honeymoon might have been like. They don't want to hear about how we drove home after our wedding, stopping at a Wendy's drive-through in all our finery to get a spicy chicken sandwich and a cheeseburger because we were starving at nine o'clock at night. They don't want to see the picture of me in my white wedding gown eating my sandwich at home in my kitchen smiling from ear to ear because I'm in love and a new wife. They don't want to hear that we were so tired that we draped our wedding garb over the back of a chair and fell into exhausted sleep after a rather chaste kiss. The students just want to know how our organs fit together.

I finally figured out what to say when people ask me how my husband and I have sex–with a great deal of love and passion. It's that simple. And that's really all they need to know.

Rebecca J. Love lives in Arizona and works as a high school English teacher and librarian. She is madly in love with her outspoken husband and her adorable, three-year old son. Recently, Rebecca was accepted into the Creative Writing Certificate Program at Phoenix College. The essays in this book are her first published pieces.

The Mechanics of Destiny

by Kate Sheckler

~

She recognized him at once and stilled, mid-sentence, to consider this stranger who exuded a glow of inevitability. On the sidewalk beyond the broad and slightly streaky window at the front of the restaurant, he was heartrendingly familiar as he stood, lean and windblown, chatting with some chance met acquaintance.

"It's him." The thought had been so absolute that, without intending to, she'd spoken it aloud and the other waitress, lounging against the sill waiting for her next words, had asked, *"Who?"*

Flustered and unable to explain, she passed it off as nothing and then was upset when, turning back, he was gone. She looked for him, even stepping outside in order to peer down the block, but he'd vanished. Reluctantly, she dismissed the incident while still hoarding the sense of illumination he'd left behind.

The next day, he hit her in the face. It was accidental: His arm swung out as he removed his jacket to settle at a table and smacked her cheek. She nearly snapped at him, a bad-tempered rejoinder to the sting. But even before he turned to smile down at her, she had been sure that she should not be rude. His smile was sweet, as was the apologetic hand he reached out to brush the offended cheek. *"Sorry about that."* And once again she thought, *"It's him."*

Just like that, love had come; although later she would look back to realize that neither of them had used that particular word.

Love at first sight—it was a sparkling moment that she had secretly believed in, had always thought might come her way. Their way, for he too had a story to tell about seeing her on the street and turning to some companion to say, *"I know that girl."* It was as if they both had been waiting—watching—for this very meeting.

By the end of the first week it became necessary to spend every possible moment together. There was little time to sleep in order that they might share everything; for life to be fully felt, it must be spent in each other's company. They lunched and dined and kissed. They talked and wandered and made love. They discussed her need of a key to his apartment and how best to tell her roommate that she might soon be leaving in order to move in with him.

Sharing a sense of symmetry, they counted their steps and found the exact center of Union Square in order to settle on that perfect spot upon the grass, knee to knee. There, they traced filigree upon one another's skin, the cells of finger and face imprinting a memory.

For twelve days her life was solved.

On the thirteenth day she used the word love—something that she was sure had been present in every look and touch between them—and watched with horror as it landed, causing his eyebrow to dip and his sweet smile to tighten with what she recognized as fear. He didn't answer, merely patted her cheek, but this time his fingers seemed anxious to depart. As they collected their things, preparing to leave for work, he reminded her to take the sweater she'd left draped over a chair. Despite his presence beside her as he turned the key, the bolt shunting sideways with a clunk, she knew with cold certainty that it was she who was being closed out.

So it slid away and within that silent diminishing it was the physical pain of heartbreak that surprised her. She'd heard the songs; she felt she could imagine the terrible ache. Except that she couldn't. Nothing had ever hurt like this, each muscle a throb or a burn. Lying in bed at night trying to still the twitching of her limbs, she could feel the pain flow in to fill her body, as if from an intravenous drip hanging in the air beside her.

She knew that she would cry sometimes, but in fact she cried constantly. The tears, whether a drizzle or a torrent, always with her. It continued for weeks. Until, slowly, the pain shifted and despite the aches in her body and heart it became clear that the worst of the damage had been inflicted elsewhere: The worst of the damage was in her brain. In her brain this was not a possibility. It was not acceptable that this could happen. She could not accept it.

She explained this to him, standing on his front stoop one hot afternoon. Wandering in his neighborhood, it had come to her that if she could speak to him that very minute she would be able to make him understand; that if he would listen to the words which filled her brain and now lay quivering on her tongue, he'd know that the two of them were meant to be, that each was the answer to the other's life.

The joy that accompanied this epiphany carried her to his door and held firm even at the sound of his voice through the intercom, tiny and distant. It only faltered as she noted the unavoidable discordance of his sweet smile with his closing of the front door, no invitation to come inside in the offing. The brilliant sunlight seemed to dim as she tried to make him understand. Watching his face as she strived to convince him, comprehension dawned: For her, he was vulcanized, Teflon coated. The conversation ended when she asked, hands outstretched,

"But don't you love me?"

"Yes." He was tender. . . remote. *"But that doesn't always make a difference."*

It was unanswerable—inconceivable—and the worst pain of all. On that day the tears never slowed and she walked the streets around her apartment unable to be still, attempting to leave the grinding ache behind. Finally, sitting on her front steps with worn feet and spongy cheeks, she wondered, if love was not a promise that dictated her future, what did? What could?

Gripping the cement edge of the stair, she turned her attention away and considered the sunset. With the pitted surface of the worn cement impressed upon her palms, she counted the colors in that ending of daylight; the cataloguing of them all-consuming. On reaching 23 colors, she stopped counting and, finally ready, turned back to order her confusion and pain instead.

Losing his love was agonizing, irrefutably, but perhaps it was neither his love nor the loss of it that defined her present or would define her future. She tightened her grip and felt the smart of her palm sharpen as a granule of cement broke through the skin of one hand to draw blood, and she considered for the first time what handing over a heart and soul did to the lives involved in the transaction. With a slow breath and then another, she loosened her fingers, keeping her eyes on the setting sun as one color slipped into the next. The ache lessened almost imperceptibly.

What if there was no clear destination? No one in charge? No ultimate solution? What then? Her old ideas seemed to crack and break into pieces that slid away with the last of the sun. In the subtle light left behind, she looked down at her hands, a smear of red across one palm, and shivered with ... fear? anticipation? Her hands looked very small. She wondered if they would be capable.

Truly a believer in the idea that our destiny is our own creation, Kate Sheckler owns a millinery design company and she teaches literature and creative writing at Marianopolis College in Montreal. She also maintains her writing, motherhood and marriage. Her short work has been published in a number of literary reviews. She received an honorable mention in the 2008 CBC Radio and the Quebec Writers' Federation (BBC/QWF) Short Story Contest and is a recipient of a position in the QWF mentoring program.

Second Time Around

by Clara B. Freeman

~

When I was eleven years old, I remember thinking how I wanted to hurry up and become an adult so that I could leave my parents' house for good. At eleven years old, any place away from a world of poverty and seven siblings seemed like heaven.

At the age of eighteen and after graduating from high school, I finally got my wish. I'd had enough of the road leading to nowhere. I packed my older sister's small beat up duffel bag and hitched a ride in the backseat of a car belonging to a distant relative from Chicago. On that day, I said goodbye to life as I knew it.

When we arrived in Chicago, I was left at the doorstep of a half brother, his wife and their three children, ranging in age from 10, 8 & 4. Although I barely knew any of them, I moved in and promptly became their babysitter. That situation lasted longer than I ever anticipated or wanted. When I finally broke away to live with a friend and her mom, I felt like a failure.

One Sunday, a woman at church must have sensed my despair because she approached me after the service. She asked what I wanted to do with my life and I told her that I didn't know. I was 20 years old and living in this big city, but I felt like I didn't belong anywhere—not in Chicago and certainly not in the flatlands of the Mississippi delta. The woman pulled a pad and pen from her purse, scribbling away as she continued to speak: *"There's a training center for adults on State Street. They have a nursing program there that will pay you to go to school. You will have to call to get the registration details, but I'm sure you will be able to get in."* The lady tore the paper from her notepad and handed it to me with a gentle smile. I thanked her profusely and wondered, *where in the world was State Street?*

I got into Nursing School and soon met my future husband. I thought he would be a great dad to our child that I was carrying. We married at City Hall when I was eight months pregnant with our beautiful daughter.

Two years later, our son was born. I was a fulltime nurse, mother and housewife. I worked endlessly to fill in the empty spaces caused by my husband's lack of permanent work. Our marriage had ups and downs in the beginning but as the years passed it became more downs than ups.

The day my life changed sits clearly in my mind. The two of us were staring face to face, strangers on shared turf, when he said, *"I've sold the house. You need to find somewhere else to live."* My heart skipped a crazy sort of beat—not angry, not sad. After 20 years our union was over.

I immediately began to make other plans in my head. *Where would my children and I live? My son had another year of high school; my daughter had already graduated and was now working. How would they take it? How much money did I have on hand? I would have to work overtime to afford rent for a new place. How was I going to make this work?*

My divorce became final on December 31st, 2000.

That night I stood before the festive Christmas tree that my children and I had decorated. I was alone in my new home—a three bedroom apartment on a quiet metropolitan street. I continued the New Years Eve ritual that my ex-husband and I had shared as a couple. On that night, however, instead of a toast with brandy and eggnog, I had a glass of the best champagne I could afford on my nurse's salary. My children were out and busy with their lives. This was my time.

As the countdown to a New Year blared from the television, I joined in with Dick Clark like I was part of the party, *"4, 3, 2, 1...Happy New Year!" "Happy New Year ole girl,"* I whispered, *"Life can only get better the second time around."*

Clara Freeman is happy to be living single, enjoying the company of friends and spending quality time with her children and five grandchildren. She is still nursing part time and spends a great deal of her free time building her freelance writing business. She has two popular blogs—one where she posts interviews with celebrities, authors and filmmakers. She also writes about life as a transitional nurse and woman in midlife. Her other blog is a motivational and inspirational column on women's issues based on her own life experiences. Clara invites you to visit her world and leave comments at her blogs: http://clara54.wordpress.com and http://wisewoman2.wordpress.com.

A Letter to My First Love

by Edith M. Fisher, Ph.D.

Dear John,

Please forgive me for writing after all this time, but I want to tell you about my life through a letter rather than in person. I want you to get to know the person I am today as opposed to the person I was 30 years ago when we were together.

Back then I was 5'5½ and weighed about 125 pounds. My height has not changed but everything else has. After you left, my life became a total mess. My father became increasingly violent and my mom had a break down that drove her to drink. I threw myself into my studies and started school early that summer just to be busy and out of the house.

I met someone that summer who was interested in me but I was not really interested in him. I liked the positive attention so I hung around him. I think I stayed with him because I did not want to be alone again. Then he started abusing me. Once, he even raped me. I felt trapped and became increasingly suicidal. One day I said to hell with it. I walked away, never to look back again.

I threw myself back into my studies at school until I dated another guy who also became abusive. I thought I had genuine feelings for him so I put up with it for about a year. I didn't think I had the right to walk away from yet another relationship.

The next semester I met another guy. He was smart, attractive and interested in me. A year later I became pregnant. I was thrilled but my mom took me to have an abortion. My mom consented to the abortion because I was still a minor. I never got to decide what happened.

After I graduated from high school, I took a job selling solar water heaters. My boss (who was 17 years older than me) asked me to marry him. I married him right after I turned 18 just to escape from home. I got pregnant three months later and that's when he hit me the first time.

He became increasing violent, drunk and possessive. Just two days after my 20th birthday, I walked to the neighbor's house and called the police. They let me take the car and as much of my stuff as I could carry along with our nine-month-old daughter. We went to the women's shelter for about a month. I ended up getting another job and living with my mother and her schizophrenic husband.

My divorce included two long years of custody battles. One night, before the divorce was final, he followed me to the parking lot. I turned to walk away but he picked me up and slammed me into the pavement. Something inside of me snapped. I tore the windshield wiper off his car and repeatedly hit him with it yelling, *"You do not hit girls you stupid redneck."* I got scared of my own rage and didn't get mad again for years.

Three days after my divorce was final I married my boss, who told me he loved me. He protected me during the two years prior to the divorce and he let us move in with him. We stayed together for four more years. During that time, I started taking college classes and worked at my own daycare business about 60 hours each week. When my husband started drinking, I threw him out and started counseling.

I met a nice guy in therapy who had lived through some bad stuff like I did when he was a kid. I felt drawn to him. My family was giving me all kinds of grief for trying to raise my daughter without a father, so I married him. He operated a lawn care business that was his obsession in life. As it turned out, I always came second. I don't do second very well.

My third marriage was a turbulent relationship but never violent until the day it ended. The police ended up arresting him, and then we got divorced.

During the next year and a half I worked at a women's shelter, went to school full time and attended physical therapy three times a week to heal the injuries from the abuse. I graduated at the top of my class with a bachelor's degree in sociology and was accepted into graduate school.

In graduate school I connected with the gay community. I started graduate school and instantly became friends with a group of lesbians there. I dated a few girls and developed a closer relationship with one of the women. I realized I had feelings for her. That messed my world up. I bought a house and she moved in with me. I finished my Master's degree, lost 70 pounds and felt great about myself.

Along the way, I fell in love, hard, with a guy in my class. It was an intense relationship for five years (I lived with the other woman for three of those years). I realized I was in love with him so she moved on.

My mom had a stroke in 2001 and I went back home for three months to take care of her. I lost another 30 pounds and looked like a ghost. I had a miscarriage shortly thereafter and it was an incredibly painful experience for me. The guy and I stayed together until fall of 2002.

Three months later, I married one of my professors. I was finishing my PhD and ready to look for a job when he got sick and nearly died. I couldn't move him right away so I stayed, worked at the local rape crisis center and taught part-time at the university.

Our marriage was rough after the first six months. My husband didn't respect me or my right to say no and he laid his hands on me in anger a couple of times. That was enough to end the romance for me. The marriage was dead but I wasn't going to end it because he needed someone to take care of him—which I had promised I would do. So I stayed. I got into counseling and started taking medication for anxiety and depression. I started getting better but my marriage kept getting worse. Eventually my husband filed for divorce.

Last summer, I got a job at a university. My mom and I moved here together. I still need to lose some of the weight I gained back, but otherwise, I am totally happy with my life. I love my house. I love my job. I love my animals. My relationship with my daughter is very good and I like living with my mom. Life is good.

When I started reconnecting with old acquaintances and friends I thought about my first and most sacred love–you. I wonder how my life would have been different if we had stayed together all those years ago.

Love,
Edith

Edith M. Fisher is an Assistant Professor of Sociology. She is working on her autobiography and enjoys teaching, learning, writing, and living each day as a gift to be shared and treasured. With the help of this letter, she is now friends with her first love and that feels pretty spectacular. The name on this letter (John) is a pseudonym.

Reflection Points

Dignity is a presence, a suffering withheld, a reserve and a patience learned through difficulty, a broken heart held together through acceptance, not bitterness.
— Finding Beauty in a Broken World, Terry Tempest Williams

From the authors in their own words

- *We love each other, mind, body, and soul.*
- *I walked away never to look back again.*
- *Perhaps it was neither his love nor the loss of it that defined her present nor would define her future.*
- *Life can only get better the second time around.*

Questions to contemplate while standing at the threshold of love

What is the most significant question as you face this issue? If you look deeply within yourself and listen to your own inner voice, you will hear the question. Once you know the question, you will realize the answer that is right for you. Here are a few questions to ponder for persons who are standing at the threshold of a romantic or intimate relationship and facing an important decision about that relationship.

- *How does this relationship support you to be your true self?*
- *Does this person treat you with respect? If no (or not usually), what are your reasons for choosing to be with someone who does not respect you?*
- *How do you feel about yourself in this relationship with this person?*

CHAPTER 2

Unfaithful

"I've learned that whenever I decide something with an open heart, I usually make the right decision."
— Maya Angelou

Many women will face a life-changing decision while in a committed relationship. Without any warning, they find themselves standing at love's doorstep—halfway in and halfway out. This is what happens when *another* person unexpectedly enters the relationship.

You will find yourself at this uncertain threshold when your head and your heart are in conflict about love. Your head is trying to be rational while your heart is spinning emotion.

While there are many ways that you might find yourself in turmoil over love, this chapter focuses on those times when women have found themselves face-to-face with an affair or betrayal. The unfaithfulness might be from their partner or it might be their own indiscretion. Regardless of who had the affair, there will be two sides to the story and no one will escape the hurt or the heartache. In the essay "Two a Day" author Emily Harris reflected on her husband's affair and how she started to come to terms with it many months later. She noted, "*What I needed was a shift in perspective, a willing shift on how I experienced the experience.*"

What exactly constitutes an 'affair' is debatable. Unfaithfulness and betrayal can present itself in many forms. There are some relationship boundary crossings that are clearly a betrayal and some that are less clear. Not all betrayals are affairs, yet a one-time kiss can be just as hurtful. Any unfaithfulness in a committed relationship can become harmful. When the unfaithfulness comes to light, the sense of betrayal and violation can be devastating.

"How could they do this to me?"

There is no easy explanation why good people stray from their committed relationships or why some people repeatedly seek out other sexual partners or experiences. Similarly, there are no simple explanations as to why some women stay involved for years with someone who is in a committed relationship with another person. As the anonymous author of "Falling" noted, *"It was harder than I imagined it would be to walk away."* Sometimes there are just no good answers to help us to understand. What is most important if you find yourself at this threshold is that you take the time you need to determine the next best step for you in your life.

The question of whether a relationship can survive this type of betrayal depends on a mutual desire and willingness to commit to rebuild trust and intimacy. Some relationships can survive and grow stronger after infidelity. Some relationships end as soon as the affair begins or soon after it is discovered. Author Marissa McNamara learned that her relationship diminished over time, but when it was finally over, the ending was clear to her. In "Heading North" Marissa discovered, *"Some final thing rose up inside of me–self-preservation, guts, I don't know, but there it was. 'I'm done, James,' I said calmly, no tears, no drama, no pleading, just: 'I'm done.'"* Marissa knew exactly what she had to do. Unfortunately, when it comes to unfaithfulness, solutions are rarely easy.

Women wrote about their painful experiences from both sides of this issue. This chapter highlights three women's stories: two women whose spouses had affairs and one woman who found herself in love and contemplating a betrayal. They each faced and dealt with their situations differently and they each needed to find peace for themselves with their decisions. Their personal and honest stories offer deeper insights to the complexities of unfaithfulness, love and betrayal.

Falling

Anonymous

~

I think I have developed feelings for another man.

Just writing that line sends mixed feelings through my body. I have never actually said it like that before and my first inclination is to delete it—delete the line, delete the thought, delete the feelings—run in the opposite direction because I know that pursuing these feelings will only end badly. You see, I'm married and so is he.

By now, I would guess that some of you who are reading this are having some fairly strong and not-so-kind judgments about me. Maybe you have experienced this in your life—maybe your husband *cheated* on you (ah, that word makes me cringe.) If that did happen to you, I can only imagine how much you must have been hurt by the infidelity. Whatever was going on in your relationship with your spouse, you did not deserve to be betrayed in that way. It is a profound wound to intimacy that some people take a life time to get over. I know because I have dear friends and family members who were married to someone who was *unfaithful* (another one of those uncomfortable words). I have seen the aftermath of affairs that have devastated families, wrecked havoc with the children, and left the other person questioning if it was something about them (Wasn't I good enough? Pretty enough? Sexy enough?) The hits to their self esteem were relentless. If this happened to you, I am sorry. You did not deserve it.

Ah, I diverted so quickly to feelings of empathy for those who have been hurt by infidelities. Then, I am reminded of how I started this disclosure, "*I think I have developed feelings for another man.*" I confront myself with my own shame and guilt for having these thoughts, these feelings, these cravings of passion and excitement. I know it's bad but it feels good. It feels like I'm a teenager in love for the first time, but I'll get back to that later.

I would guess that some of you are identifying with what I am writing. You may be reading this with intrigue, curiosity and with your own secret thoughts flying around in your head. You know exactly what I am talking about if you have ever felt this way. Maybe you are feeling this way right now about someone in your life. I know I am not alone. These kinds of things happen all too often. I am sure most of these kinds of relationships, liaisons, trysts, often start out with just a thought, a flirtation, or an attraction that deepens–and then more thoughts with desire linger. And then, well, you know what can happen if thoughts are left untamed or uncontrolled.

Do you know what it's like to meet someone and instantly feel something different, something special? You may not acknowledge the feelings right away but eventually you realize that this person, for whatever reason (whether it was their physical appeal, something they said, or the way they responded to you) caused you to feel a fluttering of your heart and butterflies in your stomach. Or, perhaps you find yourself smiling, singing out loud, or just feeling better after you see or talk to this person. Or maybe you just find yourself thinking about him. It starts out innocent enough. You were not looking for it and, as in my case, I certainly did not (and do not) feel that I am lacking in my life or my marriage. But, there you are, without inviting it and without intending it, you find yourself with this incredibly wonderful feeling toward another person.

Time goes on and you notice that it is more than just a really good feeling whenever you are around him. You start to wonder if the attraction is real (at least it seems so on your part and you sense that it could be on his part because of how he responds to you.)

You find yourself engaged in thoughts of the next time you will see him, what you will say, how you will act, what you will wear (including the careful selection of your most sexy undergarments, although you realize there is NO WAY that he will ever see them). Yes, reality checks in on a regular basis as does your conscience. But for now, let's stay with the fantasy because that is so much more exciting, more alluring, just more. I just want more of him—even if only in my dreams and in my fantasies.

I think of him regularly—I'm embarrassed to admit how many times a day he comes into my mind. If I didn't know any better, I might think I was obsessed with him, but no, I'm not bordering on the edge of insanity, just on the edge of *desire*. Now that's a word I like. Yes, I *desire* him.

Okay, so I think about him. I think about the last time I saw him and when he told me I looked great or how he gently caressed my arm or the times he looked directly into my eyes and I just melted, right there in front of him—speechless or words jumbled, feeling the heat rise in my body (was my face getting red?) and the butterflies were floating in my belly again. Now, THAT was reality.

Then, there are the fantasies of what might or could happen. I allow my mind to wander to those places where it probably should not go. I think about how it would be if we kissed—just once, nothing more. Just to see what it is like, what it would feel like. It's been years since another man kissed me in that way–on the lips, softly, sensually, every second counting. Just a single kiss. That would be nice. Then, I wonder if it could/would stop there.

Sometimes I allow my mind to go further into a realm of intimacy that is so absolutely fulfilling. It's not always about sex. Sometimes it's just imagining what our time together might be like if we were in a different time—a time when neither of us were committed to other people. I can see us spending time together, talking, walking, laughing, and it feels magical. I feel giddy. I feel like that teenager again finding love for the first time. I just want to be with him.

Then, there are those times when I bring him to me (in my mind) during sex. I think of him and only him when I want to pleasure myself in that way. I imagine that he is there with me, gently caressing me, talking to me about his desires and how he wants to please me. I can close my eyes and he is with me. He touches me. He is gentle and sensitive as he slowly goes down to the place where only my husband has been (for the past 20 years). No other man has touched me in that way, in that place, in that dimension since I made the commitment to my husband. No one in over two decades has made me feel that kind of excitement, passion, warmth and lust (except for my husband). There are now two men in my head and two men in my bed.

I'm a bit embarrassed to say that I think of him when my husband is making love to me—not every time, but I do find that I will come to an orgasm that much quicker and that much more intense when I think of him. I fear that I might call out his name but I try not to say anything, except in the privacy of my very sexy and very off-limits thoughts about him.

In my dreams and fantasies, he is all that. I know I have developed an idealized version of him in my head. In reality, I know he has real life problems and deficits too–but not in my dreams. In my fantasies, he is the man that he is, but he takes our relationship one step beyond where it has ever gone or will ever go, I know.

Therein lies the problem.

I am a married woman with children. My husband and I have been married for twenty years and we have practically grown up together. He *is* my soul mate, my life partner, the love of my life. I would be devastated without him and I am grateful to have him in my life. Our marriage is solid. We respect each other, enjoy each other's company, have a great deal in common, have fun together and have good conversations together. He is a kind, honest, loving man, husband and father. I couldn't have done better. Oh, and then there's the sex. It's not like we're sex maniacs after all these years, but we meet each other's needs and he has touched me in ways that no man has ever made me feel. He is without a doubt, the best man for me in *all* ways.

So, if you were thinking that I have a bad marriage or a non-existent, unfulfilled sex life that is absolutely not the case. In fact, it makes my feelings for *him* (the other man) all the more perplexing and un-excusable. I even feel guilty writing about both of them in the same paragraph as though I am betraying my wonderful husband just by mentioning them in the same breath.

Then what about me? What is going on in my life that I find my thoughts enmeshed with another man? I am clueless. Truly. I am just hitting mid-life, in good health with great friends, a loving family (and children, did I say children?) a beautiful home and a successful career. I am happy, confident and at a great place in my life. I want for nothing. Well, except to be with him. No, scratch that. I don't really want to be with him because I know that if I ever did risk it (that is, if he was even willing or interested) I would be risking all of the above. Yes, I know this is how lives are turned upside down and destroyed. *Why would I risk everything, for just one thing?*

I have tried to figure it out. This has been going on for a few years now. Yes, this affair in my head (or 'emotional affair' as some might call it) has been perpetuated for some time now. I am a reasonable woman but this makes no sense. Whenever I get real with myself I remember that I do not want to hurt my husband. I remind myself that taking this to the next level (or outside of my head) would be devastating for him, for my family and for me. I know that others would think differently of me if they found out I was having an affair (or even contemplating being with another man)—even if there was no sex involved whatsoever.

It is not just about sex. Really, sex is not *that* important to me. I'm telling you, there is something deeper here and I can't seem to let it go. I think we have a bond that goes without words, without actions and without sex. It's a connection that transcends everyday life. I know it deep within my body and I feel it whenever I get the chance to look into his eyes. There is something going on here that I can't explain. Despite all rational thought, all reality checks, all awareness, I can't seem take my mind off of him.

I wonder if it is possible to fall in love or to be intimately in love with two people at the same time? I know that love is limitless and we can have great love for many people in our lives. Is it possible that I actually do love two men? It seems like a remarkable blessing, yet a cruel irony because I cannot have both of these men fully in my life. That sounds dramatic and selfish, but really, I'm just conflicted. This goes against everything I've been taught and my faith as well.

The end of this story is that I have determined I will not give up, risk or hurt my husband to fulfill some fantasy (even if there might be something more to it.) I know that one day I will just have to walk away and say goodbye to *him* (the other man). I know that even with the very remote possibility that he might want to pursue a relationship with me, I cannot do it—not here, not now. I just can't risk it. The hell of it is I want to be with him. I want him in my life. I'm just not quite ready to walk away from him–yet. I long for the next time that I will see him.

Until then, he will be in my dreams and in my thoughts. Until I let go or take the leap. I guess I haven't decided to do that yet. Let go or leap.

~

This author has requested to remain anonymous. She provided the following update since she originally submitted her essay.

I am very happily married, 21 years now with two kids, a dog, a cat and a house in the burbs. I have it all—really. I have recommitted to my relationship with my husband. I would never want to hurt him in that way. It's been a year since I wrote that essay. I can honestly say that I have not made any attempts to stay in contact with him—nor did anything happen beyond my thoughts. The last time I saw him I said goodbye. He offered options to stay in contact. It was harder than I imagined it would be to walk away. I can't explain it, but I think I fell in love with him. I still think of him more often than I should, but I guess that will never leave me completely. Does love ever just go away?

~

Two a Day

by Emily Harris

Reflections from Women Writing Contest Selection

He scatters dark chocolate squares across your windshield with love notes that end with, *"Enjoy your Two A Day."* You find them on the kitchen table one morning and throw them in your purse with the rest of the weeks' "Two A Days." By Saturday you will dump the pile of chocolates in the tall kitchen trash can and tie the bag with a green twisty tie before handing it to your husband to pull to the curb.

The image of your Mother-In-Law stands before you, her calloused voice belittling her husband. She's dressed in green ultra-suede. *"Everyone has their price,"* she taunts you. For a moment you thought she was trying to pay you off. You married her son anyway. Every year, on your birthday she sent you a check which you promptly cashed and blew on something meaningless.

"But we have to keep her, darling. We can't afford to get rid of her now that the practice is for sale. You know how important this sale is. The collapse of the economy guarantees nothing. How else will I sell a business in a dying Midwest town? You know I'm trying to get our money out of it, or I'd get rid of her tomorrow."

He embraces you and tells you he loves only you. It was nothing- it happened long ago.

Anger straddles your shoulders and chokes your neck so you can't turn your head. Anger growls in the pit of your stomach and you can't eat. The close friend on Valium closes in on you across the lunch table. In a confidential tone, she says a quick prayer, *"Dear Jesus, help me find the right words"* and tells you that she has it "*on the best authority*" that your husband and his assistant, "*my, my*," are cheating.

He tells you he's found a young doctor to buy his business but the young man must first finish school—one more year. His voice is so melodic, so charming, you want to believe him.

Bedtime. You shouldn't mix sleeping pills with gin because you wake up sweating panic and dread, out of dreams of wandering through elegant rooms filled with sleeping people. In the dreams you search exhaustedly for a bed, a spot to rest. You crawl into bed with your husband but he snores so loudly that you get up and search for another bed. All you can find is a narrow cot at the end of the room where you sleep alone.

Today you find the chocolate in your car and the note reads *"I'll be your love and support forever,"* and you think you're going crazy.

The assistant is blonde and divorced and reminds you of a kewpie doll with bad grammar. She says, "We was goin' to the show last night but her and I got stopped." You know she's in love with him and will do anything to keep her job.

Everyone is blonde now and everyone has their hands on someone else's husband. *"Affairs at the Workplace—The Most Common Betrayal"* screams the headlines from Oprah's magazine. The article beneath it provides tips on stretching your budget through the current economic recession.

When you express your impatience he becomes annoyed and reminds you that the assistant is efficient, makes money for you, and that keeping everything in place is the logical answer. His words suggest that you should replace anger with gratitude. His expression is sincere and his square hands on your shoulders as he looks into your eyes. *"I have no choice in this, Hon. Look at the people around us who don't have the option to sell, who are forced to just close the doors. I can't hinder this sale. We're buying time."*

Dinnertime. How much does time cost, you wonder? What's the price of time lost, time well spent, time waiting, time stopped while you are eating a year's worth of chocolates, time you regret?

Bedtime. You are dreaming that you are a contestant on a game show called "Wheel of Time." When you spin the wheel your heart is pounding. The wheel choices are One Day, One Week, One Month and One Year. *"I'd like to lose a year, Pat,"* you announce.

Pat's grin turns incredulous. He speaks to you as if you are a child wasting his time.

"Contestants, let me remind you that the goal here is to BUY time- a week, a year, a month–to hold on to your car, your job, house..." He turns back to you. Now he looks ominous. *"You can't afford to give up this year, and you can't LOSE time."*

But you stand there, silently screaming, "YES YOU CAN!" You open your mouth but nothing comes out.

Wintertime. You drink martinis until, head swirling, you fall down in the snow, turning your legs the scorched red of embarrassed cheeks. Your husband picks you up. His hugs twist your arms and legs so that the pain renders you motionless. You stay imprisoned, so fearful of his kindness, so terrified of his charm. His kind words slam you against the wall; his safe kisses bruise your eyes and face. When you look into the mirror, you do not recognize yourself.

Tuesday he leaves two chocolate sticks on your dashboard and a note saying, *"Thinking of you."*

'It's The Economy, Stupid'... Some politician used that phrase as a campaign slogan. Was it Reagan or Carter or Clinton? You wish your thoughts weren't so jumbled. You pour more gin. Oh! What we do to survive. We compromise our self-respect. Corporate managers, dishwashers, teachers, are all one now—all held hostage by the relentlessly plunging economy. We cry, melting into each other like chocolates left out in the sun.

To be trapped in anger is like sitting on top of a volcano, expecting an eruption any minute. You never feel safe or in control. Oh, I was entitled to my 'Year of Anger' and I wallowed in it all too eagerly. As for the two of us: We screamed. We talked. We cried. We counseled. We embraced new awareness. We each willingly accepted responsibility for our contribution to this crisis. I recognized that some of my actions led to a breakdown of communication in the marriage. I had to accept that the betrayal had occurred long ago—years ago—and I had to decide what to do with my new-found knowledge. We reaffirmed that we love each other and want the marriage to endure.

~

Today as I read my narrative I am overwhelmed by the power of anger and pain to engulf me. I was so unhappy living in rage that as my pain deepened, so did my quest for peace. Little did I know that the answer was inside my head. I began searching the teachings of the metaphysical poets, the esoterics, the Buddhists, The Christians, the yogi masters. I began to understand that I was trapped in a common human experience—that of betrayal and pain—and what I needed was a shift in perspective, a willing shift on how I experienced the experience. I needed a different perception of reality based on Radical Love.

I began praying for the willingness to see this situation differently and began to meditate daily pondering the possibility of a shift in awareness based on these questions: What if my conscious intent is to give and receive love? What if I make a conscious decision to give only loving thoughts and to remember only loving thoughts I gave in the past (and those given to me)? What if I perceive only the Holiness in others that the heart reveals?

What if I perceive only innocence within others, rather than guilt? This shift in perception requires constant, focused practice, and much discipline. It requires nothing less than a miracle. But one miracle leads to another, and I have learned that looking through the lens of love can lead to miraculous healing.

Now when I start to feel the volcano erupt I ask: Why am I losing the present moment when that is the only moment there is? Why am I wasting time thinking about what went wrong in the past? Why am I wasting so much time being angry when I could be sharing love? Why am I so unwilling to forgive?

A very liberating experience comes from the knowledge that we choose the world we perceive. If we think of ourselves as limited beings—limited by ego and pain, trapped and controlled by fear and the actions of others—then we are the victims of their control. Frankly, I was tired of feeling like a victim, of being defined by pain. I could choose to perceive my husband's gifts and his apologies with anger or gratitude, to perceive his actions toward me as controlling or loving. The choice remains mine.

Everyday I can choose to perceive my life as one filled with great blessings. I can choose the gift of Love. When I begin my day with a prayer of thanksgiving for all the blessings in my life, I dare to pray for two more—the gifts of perception through compassion, and divine love. Two more gifts in my life. Two A Day.

Emily Harris credits the writing of Marianne Williamson, Wayne Dyer, Gregg Braden, Michael Goddart and Thich Nhat Hanh for inspiration and peace. She travels extensively and meditates daily for optimal joy and serenity.

Heading North

by Marissa S. McNamara

ᔓᔕ

"I am done," I say to him on the phone. I am on my way to spend the Easter weekend with my mother so that I can think and get away from him.

"What's wrong?"

"What do you mean, what's wrong?" I am incredulous.

"Well," he replies, *"You don't want me to sleep with you and when I tried to hug you, you wouldn't let me."*

This is all true. Let me back up. How far do I go? Do I tell you how much I loved him? Do I tell you how he held me while I grieved the loss of my first husband? Or how he pulled me into the back seat of the car during a rain storm to kiss me and then wrote our names in the steam on the window? Or that we made dinner together every night and danced while the pasta boiled? Or do I tell you how funny he was—how he made me laugh doing imitations of people we knew? Do I tell you how smart and passionate he was about his job, about art, or about how excited I was to travel with him, to see the world together? Do I go that far back so you will know the sweetness that we had? Or do I start at the beginning of the end?

ᔓᔕ

A man's back can be comforting. My first husband, who died of cancer, had such a back. I would wake up in the morning and know that I could roll over and fit myself into his back, press myself into it and curl my legs up behind him. My second husband, James, had been like that at first, too, but then we got married and things had changed abruptly.

Let me explain the context of "abruptly." James and I dated long distance for a year. I told him time and again that I would *never* marry a drinker. He obliged, never once letting me see him drunk, never once drinking more than a few glasses of wine at a time in the 18 months before we were married. On our wedding night, however, he was too drunk to open our gifts and passed out without even a kiss. That was the beginning of the drinking.

Over time, I got to know his back well. We went from reading tantric sexual manuals together to him not wanting me sexually at all. When I would try to dance with him in the kitchen while we made dinner (something we used to do nightly) he would dance but turn his face away to avoid kissing me.

Things got steadily worse. I asked what was wrong. As he retreated more and more, I sank lower and lower into desperation. I wanted to work on things. I tried to initiate conversations and tried to communicate while he stared stonily into space and answered only that he didn't know what was wrong. His silence was maddening.

I imagined that all of this was me, that I was too needy. I had married a mere two years after my first husband had died, so I reasoned that maybe I was grieving and not seeing things with James realistically. Maybe I was expecting too much, or maybe I just needed to settle into this new relationship that was different from my first marriage. Or maybe I was too needy because I'd left my job, my career, my friends and my home to move to another city with James. Maybe it was me. I know now that blaming myself was easy because I could change myself. I could not change him, nor could I admit that he was having regrets.

He agreed with my self-assessments. He would say, *"You need to adjust your antidepressants"* or *"Maybe you need to go to Atlanta to visit with friends."* These were his remedies for his lack of desire for me—not talking to me or touching me.

By this time, he was regularly drinking bottle after bottle of wine, coming to bed with a glass in his hand, or passing out on the floor during our parties.

"We're going to be fine. Don't worry," was his mantra. I would try repeatedly to talk with him and find out what was wrong or what we could do to improve our relationship. When I told him I was thinking about leaving, I was met with silence. He would hug me and say, *"We're going to be fine. Don't worry."* He even left me notes in the morning saying, *"We're going to be fine. Don't worry."* But he never had a plan for how we were going to be fine.

I was exhausted. I had nothing left to say.

Then he left for a month-long work trip. He returned on a Thursday night and hugged me unenthusiastically. I was happy to see him and had so much to tell him, but he was too tired to talk. He unpacked and gave me a beautiful shawl and necklace: proof, I thought, that he cared. Then he went to bed. Friday, still tired. Saturday, still tired. Sunday he left for the day to do work with Michelle, a young woman and friend of ours who had gone on the trip with him. He came home tired.

"Oh," you're thinking, *"Michelle."*

Oh, indeed. Only I just couldn't believe that he could be so heartless. I still didn't believe it when I read the phone bill with her number listed for a full page or when I got the credit card bill. When I asked him about all the lunches, he said he had gone out with Michelle.

That Monday night after being gone for a month and being too tired for days to even catch up with me, he went to a work party. He came home at 1am. Tired, indeed.

I confronted him.

Me: *Do you even want to be married?*

Him: *I don't know.*

Later he said he did want to try to work on things.

"Unless you go to counseling, James, then we won't be working on things. Are you willing to go to counseling?"

Standard answer: *"We're going to be fine. Don't worry."*

By then I was weary and deeply hurt, but I let myself hope. I kept thinking that he would not have asked me to give up so much and to move to this city with him if he didn't love me.

We ate dinner together Wednesday night. I went upstairs hoping that perhaps he would join me. Instead, he sat in the back yard on the phone for two hours. Then he came upstairs and spent another hour murmuring and laughing on the phone in the room right next to ours. It was the tone of voice that every woman knows as soon as she hears it—and he was not being discreet.

Three hours on the phone and *then* he came to bed. In response to my inquiry, he told me he was talking to his ex. *"I've been talking to her the whole time we've been married. I thought you knew that."*

Another one of his standard lines: *"I thought you knew that."* This was the exact same thing he said when, six months into our marriage I discovered he had a 14-year-old daughter.

We began to argue, but then he stopped talking. He would not even look at me. He just looked down into his lap.

I had actually considered sleeping in separate rooms for some time but knew that this would definitely mark the end of the marriage. I had not been able to do it. Until now: He had driven me to that point. I believe that he planned it this way. He was too much of a coward to end things himself so he pushed me until I had no other choice. *"Get out,"* I said.

I slept alone that night. I told him the next day that the sleeping arrangements were indefinite. Two days later I packed for my weekend with my mother.

Believe it or not, I was still unsure of what to do. My heart was broken. I knew there was nothing more I could do. I had given up everything for this relationship and for love: a career with tenure, a home and my friends from whom I had now grown apart. I was so busy trying to make things work in my marriage that my friendships had suffered from neglect. My pride had gotten in the way of seeing straight. Everyone else had seen it but me. They saw him for who he was early on. I loved him anyway.

At 38 years old, I had never been alone. I was with my first husband for 15 years and with James for 3 years. I was heading toward a precarious place and I was terrified.

As I got ready to walk out the door, he came to me. Even today, I can't figure out why he tried to be affectionate toward me after all that happened. He was clearly done with me. Was it his ego? I don't know. Maybe he was just testing me to see if I was really done with him. He came to me and put his arms around me.

I stiffened, pulled away and walked out the door. He called as I was in my car heading north, *"What's wrong?"* he asked.

Yes. He asked me what was wrong.

Then something, some final thing rose up inside of me: self-preservation, guts, I don't know. *"I'm done, James,"* I said calmly, no tears, no drama, no pleading, just: *"I'm done."*

I would like to say something symbolic here like I felt free driving on that highway after cutting myself loose from him. I would like to say that I felt a release or freedom, a welling up of confidence, but I didn't.

What I did was to begin the recovery of myself. I had to dig myself out. I am still emerging, but I did it. Here I am. And everything is fine, just like he said it would be–only it's on my terms.

Marissa McNamara is currently teaching English and has moved herself and her three dogs back to Atlanta near her beloved friends. She continues to write and is working on taking her writing—and herself–more seriously. Following the events of this story, the divorce unfolded quickly but her healing to overcome the betrayal has taken much longer. After a year of working hard through yoga, meditation and with good friends, Marissa is now enjoying being single and making her way independently in the South. She hopes she will soon be ready for another relationship, but she has learned that her life and her friendships are more important than she ever imagined.

Reflection Points

"Whatever comes, this too shall pass away."
— Ella Wheeler Wilcox

From the authors in their own words

- *I have learned that looking through the lens of love can lead to miraculous healing.*

- *I know that love is limitless and we can have great love for many people in our lives.*

- *I could not change him.*

- *I had to dig myself out. I am still emerging, but I did it.*

- *Does love ever just go away?*

Questions to contemplate while standing at the threshold of an affair or betrayal

- *Knowing what you know now, how have you been transformed in this relationship?*

- *How can this crisis become an opportunity for you?*

- *What do you need to do to find peace? Is forgiveness an option?*

- *If you are now standing at the threshold, think ahead five or ten years: Will this decision take you down the path that you want to travel in your life?*

CHAPTER 3

Marriage, Divorce and Commitment

"Marriage is not a ritual or an end. It is a long, intricate, intimate dance together and nothing matters more than your own sense of balance and your choice of partner."
— Amy Bloom

There are some people that just belong together: Everyone around them knows they are a perfect union. My parents were one of those couples. They had been married for 57 years when my mom died, but every year after her passing, my dad counted another anniversary. He longed for the day they would reunite. They lived their entire adult lives together and when the time for her to die approached, he told her, *"When you go, I go."* I think that a part of him did go with her when she died, but their marriage lived on. When he passed away five years later, he had been married to my mom for 62 years. He visited and brought flowers to her grave every week until he became too ill to do so. He still went to the cemetery but he stayed in the car while I delivered his fresh bouquet. He was faithful to her and in love with her until the end.

Many couples are not so fortunate. Some have to work a bit harder to keep the relationship going. Of course there are ups and downs in all relationships. In fact, it is the challenging times that can bring a couple much closer together, if it doesn't tear them apart.

This is where our next chapter begins: at the thresholds of marriage and divorce. The authors tell three very different accounts of their personal experiences with love and marriage. One is a poem from a woman about the enduring love with her life partner. The other two essays are heartfelt reflections about couples ending their commitments and their lives together.

The decision to commit to someone for life is one that most women will eventually make; some women will make this promise more than once during their lifetime. Marriage and commitment are usually not chosen lightly, nor is the decision to end the relationship. Sometimes, however, decisions about marriage and divorce do not get the careful consideration necessary. This is especially true when emotions quickly deluge the mind and body with love or with regret.

Generally, most committed relationships do begin with love and a genuine desire to be together. Yet, for some couples, the challenges of staying together seem too difficult to bear. Relationships that were built on a foundation of love and affection can transform into relationships hanging on by a thread. How does a relationship go from "*I want to spend the rest of my life with you—I can't imagine my life without you*" to "*I can't stand to be in the same room with you—I just don't love you anymore*"?

The end of a committed relationship is not always the end of love. Author Hanan Rose referred to the day her husband left her as *"D-Day—Death of Marriage Day"* in her essay "A Departure." She recalled it as *"the day she was dreading for much too long."* She was not ready for her marriage to end, but she knew it was coming and had prepared herself for the inevitable. Hanan poignantly tells the story of that one day in her life and how it forever changed her.

Sometimes, love is not sufficient to sustain a marriage however. The pain of a difficult marriage, from start to finish, is examined in "The Claw Foot." Cara Evans tells the story of her unraveling relationship with her former husband, her anguish ever-present. She reflects on lessons learned, insights gained and empathy awakened despite her suffering.

For some couples, there is no formal ending. They believe that once married, always married: *'til death do us part.* It can be very difficult to reconcile when your values or faith are guiding you one way while your heart or head are pulling you in another direction. The loss of love is not always the end of a marriage however. There are many reasons why women do not leave, even when relationships are void of love or their lives are filled with abuse, fear and control.

Two authors in this chapter recount the demise of their marriages, but they also tell about reclaiming their lives after their divorce. In the essay "Departure," author Hanan Rose realized that "*my marriage was dead, but I was still very much alive.*" The end of her marriage was a new beginning for her. She felt alive again and was empowered to move forward. She later found happiness in a second marriage with a loving husband and children.

Cara E. Evans similarly discovered a renewed commitment to her life after the heartache of a failed marriage. She tells the story of two people deeply in love, newly married and facing the hardship of his deployment to Iraq. Early in their marriage they found themselves struggling to rebuild their lives together after her husband's return from the war. In "The Claw Foot," Evans relays her life-changing discovery as follows: *"The way we react to the unexpected can be equally as important, if not more so, in determining what happens next."* She found that the unexpected end of her marriage led her to a place that she had not anticipated—a place of inner peace. Both women found self-confidence, joy and love again after their marriages ended. For them, the ending of their marriage was a new beginning.

So, what makes a good or happy marriage or relationship? Based on women's experiences in this book, the answer to that question is as unique as the two people involved. There is no single characteristic or personal attribute that will definitively assure someone of a happy relationship. Each person has different needs, wants, wishes and expectations and each union is unique. This is what leads many couples into trouble—when the needs, wants and expectations of each party diverge over time and when consideration or respect for each other weakens.

People change over time and so do relationships. Some couples grow apart to the point of loneliness or isolation, while for others love grows deeper through the years. The tender poem "true love in the present moment," whose author wished to remain anonymous, tells the story of enduring love and the turning points that the couple faced together.

The essays in this anthology remind us that we all want to be loved and most of us want to have someone to spend our lives with. The three women in this chapter remind us that having a partner who truly loves and respects you can make all the difference.

true love in the present moment

Anonymous author, for my beloved

~

the moment we first spoke

the moment we laughed

the moment we cried

the moment we exchanged vows for life

the moment we made love

the moment our son was born

the moment you stood with me at death's door

we have shared a lifetime
and then some.

this moment, like no other,
I am thankful for you in my life.

I am grateful to have every precious moment
with you.

Departure

by Hanan Rose

Saturday, early June, 1992. I have forgotten the exact date, though at the time I was certain it would remain etched in my mind like a memorial, like stones placed in memory of days that live in infamy. I am embarrassed by this forgetfulness. It seems wrong, somehow, to no longer remember the date when my husband left me.

I awoke early to the sound of footsteps above me on the second floor. Darrin had vacated our bedroom months earlier, preferring the lumps in our guestroom's old mattress to my presence in our marriage bed. He was preparing, as usual, for his weekly racquetball game. But this time, he would be taking a suitcase along with his gym bag, and he would not be coming back.

The cold spot I had carried in the pit of my stomach for several months reasserted itself, growing larger and bolder as my groggy mind awakened to full knowledge of what day this was: D-Day. Departure Day. Death of the Marriage Day. The day I had been dreading for much too long.

Surely, I thought, there must be some cataclysm in nature to mark such a momentous day, some karmic symbol that an event of enormous significance was taking place in our community. But when I peered between the slim slats of the Venetian blinds that Darrin had installed on our windows, the world looked typical for June: an occasional puff of cloud dotting the blue of summer sky, squirrels hanging upside down at our bird feeder, a thin yellow butterfly flitting around the garden, sunbeams warming a sleeping cat on our neighbor's driveway. It was just a normal summer day.

But nature lied. It was *not* a normal day. It was anything but normal. I felt queasy and small—smaller even than I'd felt in the months since I had conceded the reality of the impending divorce and stopped fighting the inevitable now unfolding around me.

I crept back into bed and drew the covers tight around me like a cocoon. *"Please,"* I silently begged an impassive world as the tears rolled down my face, *"let this be over with. I don't want to do this. Make it stop. Make him stop!"*

Then something inside me shifted. Something began to rise to the surface, seeping through the wall of hurt, resignation and fear that held me powerless for so long. A voice within me spoke firmly and clearly: *"Do not make this easy for him. Make him look you in the eye before he goes."*

I heard Darrin descend the stairs and enter the kitchen. To my surprise, I pushed myself up and out of bed, shrugged on the robe he'd given me for my birthday only a year earlier, and padded down the hall. I stood quietly in the kitchen doorway, staring at him and pushing away a sudden, foolish wish that I had brushed my hair before emerging from my room. I held his gaze. His expression was grim.

"Why are you up so early?" he asked, breaking the painful, brittle silence. *"It's Saturday. You could be sleeping."*

My voice wavered, but my resolution did not. *"I want you to look at me,"* I answered. *"I want you to have to face me as you leave our marriage."*

Like the actual date, Darrin's reply faded into the realm of lost memory. But that feeling of empowerment has remained. It was a spark of new life, standing up, looking out, having a voice—however tremulous and thin—in my present and my future. My marriage was dead, but I was still very much alive.

Hanan Rose grew up in a small town in southern West Virginia and enjoyed a career as a secondary school educator for thirty years. She is pleased to report that, twelve years after her divorce, she met and married a wonderful man and is thoroughly enjoying life with him, his sons, and their dog. She credits support from her parents, sister, friends, and therapists. They all helped her through the divorce and its' "leftovers," and allowed her to move on with confidence and joy into a truly happy marriage and new life.

The Claw Foot

by Cara E. Evans

To Mom, Dad, Grams, and JK who got me through the worst so that I could be my best.

~

I wondered how long a person could sit in a steamy, hot bath before her skin would soften and wrinkle so much it would literally begin to peel off the palms of her hands and soles of her feet. I loved baths since childhood, but lately I was testing this limit daily. The ridges on my pruney, waterlogged fingers grew deeper by the hour as I soaked away the occurrences of the prior few months. How could I (a 24-year-old, married woman with a mortgage and a job) spend hour upon hour in the claw foot bathtub of my parents' house unable to face the world?

When I finally emerged from my watery cocoon, I toweled off, ran a comb through my hair, and pulled on jeans and a sweatshirt to insulate myself from the December chill. I put lotion on my hands and ran my right fingertips over the smooth, cold shape. Soothing in its familiarity, yet somehow jagged and cutting in the recent days, I slipped off my wedding band. I placed it in the glass dish on the dresser knowing that I would never wear it again. The act was overwhelming. I crawled back in bed hoping to sleep for days.

~

Matt and I met in college. He was a transfer student at the beginning of my junior year. We fell fast and hard for one another, spending much of our time together from the first day we met. We enjoyed being around one another and laughed constantly. I was an art student with a definite direction. I was very involved in school and had many plans for my life. He was a reservist for the U.S. Marines who hoped to study education. He was friendly and well-liked by his peers. America was six months into operation

Iraqi Freedom. We knew that Matt's deployment was a possibility but we chose to ignore it much of the time. Our relationship progressed quickly and within a couple of months we were discussing marriage.

My first experience with the military was when Matt received a call during Christmas Eve dinner. His unit was being deployed soon after the first of the year. They couldn't even give us the courtesy of having a happy, if ignorant, holiday with our families. We had less than a month left before he shipped out. The next few weeks passed too quickly and included a surprise proposal on New Year's Eve. I couldn't have been happier. Committing to our relationship gave both of us comfort and something to look forward to.

Then Matt had to leave for Iraq. He would call me—often at odd hours of the night because of his schedule. I always clung to every minute we had together. We talked about plans, shared stories from our day, and how much we missed one another. Phone calls were brief and sometimes cut off by poor connection or the sounds of sirens in the background. Still, we made it. We survived the eight month deployment.

After his return we moved into a small apartment for my last semester of college. Things were good, but different. He got a job at a local bank. We started fighting but I chalked it up to the stress of planning for a wedding, preparing for graduation, and readjusting to civilian life. The frequent e-mails from the deployment support group for spouses and family stopped right before Matt's return. We were never given much information on what to expect during "readjustment."

Within two months, I graduated with a B.F.A. and started my first full-time job. We got married and bought a small farmhouse. We spent our weekends on renovation projects or with family and friends. Once we married, the fights were less frequent. However, I noticed that when I brought up a serious topic, Matt had a way of joking it off. Initially, I saw this as an improvement from our arguing.

I told Matt that if he ever needed to talk about anything he saw or did during deployment that I would listen or we could find a professional if he was more comfortable talking to someone else. He generally brushed it off, telling me he was more fortunate than others during his time in Iraq. However, within six months of his return it was apparent that all was not well.

He had always been trim but he gained forty pounds in short order. It seemed like he couldn't get enough to eat, plus he often drank several large sodas every day. He seemed to have a hard time limiting his alcohol intake as well. When we went out with friends he would down five or six drinks to everyone else's one or two. I usually ended up driving us home. Still, he was never violent, never missed work, and he wasn't drinking every day.

I talked with his family who were also concerned, but he always assured us everything was fine. I think we all assumed it was just part of him dealing with being back at home from the war and at some point he would start acting like himself again.

My real concern came about a year after his return from Iraq. Matt bought a handgun and wanted to carry it in public. He always enjoyed hunting with his father and brother, so having rifles around was not unusual. One day when we came home from the store he pulled the handgun out from the inner breast pocket of his coat. He told me, *"After sleeping with a gun at your side for eight months, you feel naked without one."* I tried to reinforce that there was no need for him to carry a handgun in our sleepy, small town (not to mention that it was illegal) but again he joked the problem away.

I spoke with his family about it and I felt betrayed when his father paid for a "right to carry" class for both of them. This made it legal for him to carry a concealed weapon. I felt that this only reinforced his unhealthy behavior. Looking back, I think Matt's Dad was probably just trying to be supportive and to make sure that his son was within the limits of the law. Everyone in the family wanted Matt to feel comfortable again but none of us knew how to help him.

Tensions grew that spring when my grandfather passed away suddenly of a heart attack. I struggled to come to terms with the sudden and helpless nature of his death. It was a difficult summer for both of us, but once again we made it through the hardship.

Later that Fall I noticed a definite disconnect between us. I asked Matt about it but he said he didn't notice anything different. He didn't call to talk with me during the day like he did before. Then I discovered an overdraft notice from his personal bank account. We were always very careful with our finances. When I asked him about it, Matt told me it was taken care of and that his account was none of my business. I was extremely hurt and angry that he would hide this from me and then reprimand me when I confronted him. He seemed to be moving farther and farther away from the man I once knew.

By Winter our relationship was even further strained. My family endured another blow in November when my uncle lost his battle with cancer. Matt went on a hunting trip with his father instead of coming to the funeral with me. Then, on my birthday in mid-December my boss suggested that I go home to have a relaxing evening. *"You really deserve a great one after everything you've been through"* she commented. If only she knew what was in store for me that night.

After an awkwardly quiet birthday dinner with no presents and no card, I asked Matt again why he was so distant towards me. This turned into a fight and he denied anything was wrong. Then he told me he needed space and he was leaving for the night. He wouldn't tell me where he was going. I called his cell phone sobbing, but he refused to come home. Eventually, he turned his phone off. I was scared, angry and sad. I wondered how our relationship had reached that point. I wondered how it was my fault.

- *How did I repeatedly allow issues to be pushed aside when I knew they needed to be addressed?*
- *Why didn't I act sooner or more persistently about my concerns?*
- *Why didn't I listen to everyone?*
- *How did I allow my life to get so out of control?*

The next day, everything fell apart when I discovered that Matt was involved with another woman and he spent the previous night with her. He contacted a lawyer to begin divorce proceedings. I was stunned and heartbroken. We never talked about divorce. That night I left my house, my job, and my life as I knew it. I moved in with my parents a few hours away.

In the early days I was reeling. I felt like I had stepped out of my life and into someone else's life. Everyday I woke up soon after my parents left for work and applied for several jobs online. Then, I took the phone and a book into the bathroom and soaked in that wonderful claw foot bathtub for hours every day.

It was white porcelain with gold clawed feet and shiny silver fixtures. I would fill it as full as I could without spilling and slip into the water up to my chin. Some days I read and others I just thought. In the days before I was ready to fully face the situation, that claw foot bathtub served as some of my best therapy—giving me a place to reflect, to heal and to plan. This was my life for nearly a month. Although it seems comical now, it was exactly what I needed at the time.

In a little over a month I had a new job in a new city and an apartment of my own in a quirky, artsy neighborhood. I looked for ways to get involved–at first as a distraction, but soon because I was feeling better and enjoying life again. I worried about being lonely but found that I had so much to do that I spent little time at home by myself. Sooner than I imagined I was feeling comfortable in my new life. I also discovered that I liked spending time alone sometimes.

Some months later I found a therapist to help me deal with the grief I experienced in the previous year. I was still reliving parts of what happened in my head and I wanted to let it go for good. My therapist allowed me to determine the direction we took. I rehashed everything for her—we talked about my fears, my sadness and my anger. Soon I really began to understand. I liked our sessions because I felt a sense of control again. Before I was angry, sad and frightened over the lack of control in my life. I felt victimized by a number of negative occurrences in my life that were out of my reach. My therapist and I were both thrilled when I finally reached that conclusion.

So many of the scariest or most difficult situations in life are stressful because of the lack of control we feel over them: death, illness, divorce, addiction and the loss of job or home. We want to think that we have power over the direction our lives take. Sure, we can do quite a bit to plan and to set ourselves on a good course. However, the way we react to the unexpected can be equally important, if not more so, in determining what happens next.

With that realization, I no longer felt responsible for everything and I was able to let go.

The military did little to prepare Matt and his family for homecoming. I was never contacted again for any reason after Matt returned home from Iraq. I offered help to my husband. I reached out to others for help. I tried to be understanding with him, but ultimately, he chose to make unhealthy decisions that changed the course of our relationship.

I saw my therapist for six months. Near the end of our time together I heard a news story told by a young veteran about the atrocities he encountered in war. This young man also found himself carrying a weapon for protection at all times. He understood that these were unhealthy thoughts but couldn't stop thinking them. At one point he felt so hopeless that he considered suicide. However, he reacted differently. He pushed beyond his comfort zone. He forced himself to interact with people culturally different than himself. He got rid of the weapons he owned and he sought professional help. Ultimately, he found a healthy way to respond to a horrible experience that was out of his control. This man's story allowed me to feel some sympathy toward Matt again despite his hurtful actions toward me. I cannot begin to imagine the things going on inside him that would change Matt so much.

It's been two years since my divorce. I have a new life. I work in a job that I love. I am dating a wonderful man who is caring, kind and ridiculously funny. I have a new set of friends that I would have never known if life had gone the way I originally planned with Matt. I have also been house hunting in recent months. I have a list of 'must-haves' for my new home, among them: a sunny bedroom, plenty of storage space and a great bathtub for coping with life's unexpected turns.

Cara resides in Kansas City, Missouri and is currently preparing to begin a Masters of Mental Health Counseling Degree.

Reflection Points

"Some people think that it's holding on that makes one strong–sometimes it's letting go."
— Author unknown

From the authors in their own words

- *My marriage was dead, but I was still very much alive.*
- *So many of the scariest or difficult situations in life are stressful because of the lack of control we feel over them.*
- *It was a spark of new life, standing up, looking out, having a voice in my present and my future. That feeling of empowerment has remained.*
- *We have shared a lifetime–and then some.*

Questions to contemplate while standing at the threshold of commitment, marriage or divorce

- *When you imagine what your life would be like without your partner, does your heart ache at the thought or does your mind wander with possibilities? What is the overwhelming feeling you are left holding?*
- *How has your partner changed your life for better? For worse?*
- *Would a 'waiting period' before making the decision (to marry or to divorce) affirm or change your plans?*
- *How would your life be different if you do not make this decision?*

Part Two

Contemplating children: To have or not to have?

So much that was beautiful and so much that was hard to bear. Yet whenever I showed myself ready to bear it, the hard was directly transformed into the beautiful.
– Etty Hillesum

CHAPTER 4

At the Crossroads of Pregnancy

"Once in a while, right in the middle of an ordinary life,
love gives us a fairy tale."
— Anonymous

*Decisions don't come easily...*especially when it comes to children.

Second only to love and relationships, the most significant turning point in life for most women appears to be children—whether to have them or not–and if so, when and how many? For women and couples facing infertility or other concerns, the question becomes a more difficult one of *how*, as well.

This chapter focuses on the life-altering decision to become a mother and the extenuating efforts, range of options and barriers that some women face in becoming pregnant. The next chapter (chapter five) continues with the theme on parenting focusing on women who made distinctively different decisions about having children and how their lives have changed as a result of their choices.

As with most other turning points or major decisions, there is no single path that fits everyone on this journey to motherhood. Only you can decide what is right for you. However, there is a greater awareness today that the decisions about pregnancy and having children are dependent on the unique needs, wants and circumstances of the individuals facing the choice.

In the poem "Life," author Melinda Nagle contemplates an unexpected pregnancy. An unwed, teen mother waiting for the pregnancy test result, she weighs the pros and cons of having the baby. *"Decisions don't come easily."* Nagle's words directly speak to women who face unexpected pregnancies as well as for women who are desperately trying to become pregnant, but are unable to do so.

When the decision has been made to become a parent, couples who are unable to conceive naturally are faced with complex and difficult decisions.

Women will often take on great challenges, including physical, emotional, social and economic hardships in their efforts to become a mother. The range of options is limited and most of them are not without controversy, complications, hardships and the need for significant amounts of money. Some of the choices women face in their efforts to have children include fertility treatments, in-vitro fertilization, artificial insemination, sperm donors, surrogate mothers, foster care and adoption. Two women in this chapter (who are now mothers) addressed some of these considerable options and choices.

In her essay, "Mom, Interrupted" Kelli C. Trinoskey tells us about her successful but difficult pregnancy with twins after fertility treatments. She describes the support from her own mother during this pregnancy and she illuminates the parallels between her earlier journey as a single parent and her mom's journey. In this process, Kelli discovered the loving gift her mother had to offer during this challenging time. *"My mom offered me...the reassurance to endure."* Kelli's essay is a touching look at how life and relationships can go on and become stronger even after hardships and obstacles.

A different look at pregnancy is offered by author Rebecca J. Love who wrote in her award-winning essay "Shopping in the Sperm Aisle" about the trials and tribulations of trying to find a sperm donor. She concluded with honesty and humor, *"So much for keeping our intimate baby making to three (Mom, Dad, and Donor)–we were about to add a fourth person to the party."* Her essay gives us a comical inside look at what couples go through when they decide or need to use a sperm donor to have a baby.

In "Biology" another humorous but important look at two sides of having children, Erin Wilson takes us through the decision-making process leading up to a vasectomy for her husband. She reminds us of the reasons for the vasectomy, *"We were so in love there was no room for children."* And, she describes how both biology and emotion play important roles in their ultimate decision.

Whether it is biology or emotion, the desire to create a child is formidable. Difficulties conceiving naturally are a tremendous challenge for many women. For some, the heartache is eased with the eventual welcoming of a child into their arms and into their lives; others are not so fortunate. Although the paths to becoming a parent or conceiving a child are diverse, it can be a very arduous and heart-wrenching journey for many women.

The women in these essays lead us to greater awareness of and empathy for the often difficult journey to motherhood. This chapter is dedicated to those women who are facing this turning point with hopes that they will find themselves exactly where they want to be when their journey is complete.

Life

by Melinda Nagle

~

Here I am.
The green tile floor reflecting,
The basin of the sink shining.
The little white stick says yes
But I am not so sure.

How will I feed you?
How will I educate you?
Should I?
He says yes.
Mother says yes.
What do I say?
I think...

Can I give myself up?
My school
My work
My life?
Decisions don't come easily.

But I made the right choice.
Now you are here-
My heart,
My soul,
My spirit,
One with yours.

I was made for you.
Made to be yours.
My sweetest choice.

∾

Melinda Nagle is a single mother, student, crafter and dreamer. When she is not writing, she enjoys sewing, camping, gardening and caring for her daughter, Kaia, of course!

Update from the author: Kaia is now six-years-old, full of wisdom and the absolute joy of my life!

∾

Biology

by Erin Wilson

～

The room was cold and sterile. My husband cupped the gown around his thighs, trying to eek out a little dignity. There wasn't much to be had—his rooster plucked of every last feather, head bowed in reverence to the upcoming chop. Sterile room or not, we were claiming our own lives. Young and unstoppable, we were clucking out our own path.

We were in our mid twenties, full of love and life, in our rambunctious phase: learning of each other's bodies, suffering nosebleeds in the rough and tumble that is love and learning parameters. We were charting out our days even then, like two wise fools believing we could control where a rooster might run once its head is hacked off. We would work, love, travel, dip hotdogs in salsa, wrap bologna 'round pickles, hike, paint our kitchen, jut up hands at auctions, plant gardens, do puzzles, hold hands and grow old. We were so in love there was no room for children. We were so young there was no room for insight, but we didn't know that then.

He lifted his butt up off the metal table. His skin made a releasing sound. The doctor knocked first but opened the door before we replied and scooted in with his head down reading charts.

V-day. Vasectomy. Control over sex with the slit of a knife.

I'd had problems before, with cell mutation. Not dire, but I was wary. The pill made me anxious, raised my percentages and threatened my health. Other birth control didn't appeal to us. So, being blessed at our early age with love and foresight, a steady revelation of all our days in all our years to come, we thought: snip, control, over.

The doctor raised his head already caught in the drone about procedure and aftercare, hardly thinking about what was pouring from his tired old lips. His words met with our young and eager image. He started, did a double take and then stopped.

"What are you guys doing here?" he asked low and conspiratorially.

"We're getting him a vasectomy." I answered with authority.

"No you're not!"

And then I ceased to exist.

The rest of the appointment was spent with my husband listening like an animal caught in headlights and nodding just a little, as though perhaps this upper head might fall off if threatened with too much motion.

"This wife might not want children but your next wife might. You're too young to make this decision. I would do this for you now if you already had two children but even then, at your age, I would advise against it. I won't do it! No one will!"

I was in shock and silent. The doctor's hand was hovering in the air like a stop sign in my face. I was not allowed to contribute.

"But this is my health!" I thought, *"Our future!"* I railed—but in my mind only. I was cold, freezing really, in the face of my own sterility in the conversation that was going on in front of me but excluded me.

My husband crawled into his underwear and we cussed together behind the closed door about the impossibility of a second wife, and the nerve! And my health and all of those auctions that we were going to go to, dammit! All the places we would travel. We made plans to write letters to that doctor. We promised to harbor rage for years to come and to one day write a note and send it from overseas, because surely our lives would be just that interesting and the letter would tear the doctor apart and make him finally realize that he had been wrong.

Dear Doctor Dumbshit,

I'm sure you don't remember me. I came to you a decade ago for a vasectomy but you refused. You see, my wife suffered from recurring bouts of cervical dysplasia and we wanted to do everything we could to keep her healthy. That was our plan. You ruined it.

You see, my wife did get pregnant, just a year ago, and her cervical dysplasia morphed into cancer. Both my wife and child died. I just thought you ought to know.

Yours truly,
Smarter Than You

Yeah, that's what we planned to do.

Instead, this is what happened:

I was a very efficient daycare director in those days. Well, maybe not that efficient but I had planned to be. I worked forty plus hours a week raising other people's children, tucking their hair behind their ears, cutting their bananas into ever smaller pieces, singing songs of words in books that weren't really even songs but stories. There were fifteen or so teachers that worked for me and with me, saving me from the deluge of so many kids.

I went home in the evenings exhausted, child-satiated, like someone who eats too many sour candies and can't stomach another. I met my husband on the couch, exhausted too. All of our dreams having fallen away from us like tired slippers off our feet as we watched TV and dipped our wieners in salsa 'cause there was no time to cook. Then we hauled our weary working asses up the stairs and slept. No time for rambunctiousness or turnings. Life's movement had solved our fertility issue pretty nicely.

And so this continued. Yes, we did hike through forests and we did read travel books. We did paint our kitchen and go to auctions on Sundays. There might have even been an occasional puzzle. But that was all. And it was good and tasty—my heart was full and comfy. And I didn't know any better. I was tired and adult.

Then there came a day, a naptime at our daycare, with the song on the tape player repeating over and over again. I can hear it even now, a lullaby imprinted deeply in my brain. I even know what I was wearing. I know the posture of my body (my neck slightly bent forward) and the pooling of my eyes in wonder at this thing that I had walked by every day for four years but I was just seeing today for the first time.

There was a four-year-old girl lying on her cot. She was soft and airy, her lips protruding in a pout. Her thin blond hair was wisped back as though she were running even then, in her dreams. Her fingers curled out in a tired cupping of thin air, gentle. Then it occurred to me. It climbed up from within, a stranger pulling itself up from one organ to the next. *"Pssst, hey, you can make one of these."* A simple notion that everybody knows after grade six sex ed, but I didn't know in my body until that afternoon at 1:10 when it spoke to me. My body stomped its foot, *"Well I'll be damned!"* and then it said, *"I want one!"* I was shocked but it was settled, in my soul at least. The rest of the questions that could be asked were never raised. I would have a child. I would make one. She would be of me.

That evening when I went home my husband was in the bathtub. His knees were bent up to his chest. He looked like a gigantic goofy kid. The curtain was half closed on the tub so that as he washed his profile rested behind the curtain. I sat on the toilet and my legs splayed out on either side of me like they would do quite frequently in the making of this baby and then later in the birthing of it. This is what I said *"Babe, let's make a baby."* Only that. No explanation, no begging and no context. No reference to the rest of our lives. No concession to a once wise doctor—only the pull of my body to create.

My husband's face emerged from behind the frosted white curtain with a smile. It was his biology that answered then, too. "OK."

So we rode each other and our uncertain future together, raising arms to the sky like cowboys riding horses, or like Sunday auctions holding our number high when we really, really wanted to win the lot. No other decision that followed this one would ever be as uncomplicated once our egg was hatched.

Erin Wilson is a writer, photographer, wife, mother, daughter, laundress, window cleaner, pet chaser, cake eater–you know how it goes. She lives in Northern Ontario in a ramshackle house with her brood. After giving birth to her first child who screamed for approximately an eternity with colic, it seemed perfectly sensible to have a second – and quickly! Her children keep her grounded and grant her magic every day. Writing keeps her sane when all else fails.

Shopping in the Sperm Aisle

by Rebecca J. Love

Reflections from Women Writing Contest Selection

For my son - You were loved before you existed.

Who knew that trying to have a baby would be so much work? Most people just need a cheap bottle of wine and a night of uninhibited, unprotected passion in the back seat of a car. Not so for my husband and myself. We needed to use a sperm donor to get the ball rolling.

To solve this problem, we consulted the Internet. The myriad of Google results that returned with "sperm" proved both funny and frustrating, ranging from sperm whales to what porn stars have to report about the subject. The sheer quantity of sites was astounding. We shifted through video clips, encyclopedia articles, and unsavory advertisements, trying more specific search terms as we researched. Finally, my husband and I found what appeared to be a few reputable, fertility-centered organizations that wanted to sell us quality sperm. Now the fun really began. We got to design our baby!

Some people take issue with medically-assisted reproduction saying that it is not natural—if a couple is supposed to have children they would have children without outside help. Some say it is against their faith to tamper with the reproductive process. To them, the idea of purposefully choosing certain characteristics is assuming a higher role in the universal order. They condemn organizations like California Cryobank and the Sperm Bank of California, the two companies my husband and I decided we liked the best. We, however, were grateful that a process existed to help us get pregnant with some choice in the matter.

We had fun choosing our baby's hereditary background. Since my husband already has a biological child from a previous marriage, I got to choose most of the characteristics. I wanted blue eyes: Both sides of my family have them, and I wanted to continue that trait. I have dark blond hair, my husband dark brown, so we split the difference looking for light brown hair. My husband is two inches shorter than me at 5 feet 4 inches, so we looked for a donor who wasn't too tall. He joked that he already had to stand on the stairs to be eye-level with his daughter, and if I had a boy (the men in my family tower over 6 feet), he would have to stand on the second or third step to get the necessary physical height a parent needs in a heated discussion with a teenager. We agreed that weight should be proportionate and that we were looking for good physical health and evidence of stable mental health in the donor's parents and grandparents.

My husband and I also agreed about certain traits that did not matter as much. We really didn't have a preference for a particular national or religious background. We both have European family roots, but we mostly consider ourselves to be American mutts.

What did matter, though, was the donor's personality traits. We did not want a donor we didn't "like" on a personal level. We looked for a donor with at least an associate's degree, who had some artistic background, and worked in either an artistic or helping professions career. Of course the traits we looked for mirrored ourselves exactly, even though we knew that developing those kinds of values has more to do with the environment in which the child is raised than in the genes. But we figured it wouldn't hurt to try to "pre-select" sperm with potential tendencies towards our values.

We were shocked by the prices. A dose of quality sperm ran between $300 to $375. *"Look, honey! If we spend $85 more we can get PhD. Sperm!"* On top of that, shipping the frozen sperm in the special medical containers on dry ice overnight with FedEx was going to cost as much as the sperm itself. At $600 or more per cycle, we decided that we couldn't afford the doctorate degree.

There were also varying prices scaled for how much information was available about the donor. The basic package included a three-generational health report, basic physical, ethnic, and religious descriptions of the donor, and a short question/response piece about some of the donor's interests and why he became a donor. If we wanted more information (such as a baby picture of the donor, a sound recording of the donor talking about himself, or a more in-depth question/response survey) we would have to pay additional big bucks, which we didn't have.

At some point, we were down to choosing a sperm bank strictly on price, rather than on the company's philosophical mission statement or breadth of sperm selections. That's when we found the sale aisle.

"This sperm is only $185!" my husband exclaimed.

"What's wrong with it?" I countered.

The sperm was on sale because there was less information available about the donors, and that made the samples less marketable. We considered buying this sperm since we weren't going to buy the add-on information anyway. But we finally decided it was bad enough that we were going to take pictures of the FedEx man holding the shipping container for the baby book, at least we could say that we didn't buy clearance sperm.

By the time we finally narrowed the donor pool down to four individuals, I was frustrated. I was tired of trying to choose who would offer the best biological return for our baby. Also, many of the qualities we were looking for were similar in the remaining candidates. The process and the pressure to make the best choice for my future child wore me down.

"I give up. You're the man. You go hunt some sperm and bring it home. I can't look at this anymore. Your first act as father is to buy the sperm," I told my husband, and I didn't look at the donor information again.

We tried three cycles during October, November, and December. I came home in October to find the shipping container on the front stoop in the rain. I ran to get the camera, and I took pictures of our baby in the rain crooning to the worn, beige plastic container as if it already were a child who could hear me. In November, we were home when the FedEx man made his delivery, and we did make him pose for a picture. In December we missed the sperm drop off, but we have pictures of the container in front of the Christmas tree. Three cycles of insemination at home produced no baby, and the sperm bank was running out of our chosen donor's samples.

After the prolonged stress and disappointment (and over $2200 in fees) we decided we would have to go to a fertility doctor to see if there was something wrong with me. So much for keeping our intimate baby making to three (Mom, Dad, and Donor)—we were about to add a fourth person to the party.

Rebecca J. Love lives in Arizona and works as a high school English teacher and librarian. She is madly in love with her outspoken husband and her adorable, three-year-old son. Recently, Rebecca was accepted into the Creative Writing Certificate Program at Phoenix College. Her essays in this book are her first published pieces.

Mom, Interrupted

by Kelli C. Trinoskey

For my mother, Maureen "Mickey" Christiansen

My mother, who recently broke her ankle and is walking around with a boot cast, is painting the nursery–well, she's gearing up to paint the nursery. I'm in bed incubating twins. Let me explain.

The rollercoaster of infertility treatments finally yielded success but I have been stopped in my tracks and on strict bed rest until delivery. The girls are due in three months and I can't do a thing to prepare. I can't go to Babies R Us to stroll the aisles, marveling over the tiny onesies or matching outfits. I can't nest by cleaning every corner of my house, including wiping out dust bunnies that now mock me from the corners. I can't cook pans of lasagna to freeze in anticipation of those first few weeks when I won't have time to brush my teeth, let alone prepare a meal. I can only stay in bed, and wait, and watch.

My husband prepared another bed for me in the living room (a futon mattress on the floor) so I can feel a part of daily life in our house. I pass time reading, writing, and sleeping while he rushes around frantically, working, cleaning, cooking and holding down the fort. Today, I am camped out in my bedroom upstairs so I can be near the nursery painting project and "direct it" from my bed. It helps me to feel a little bit involved and have some control of the project.

"I forgot the paintbrush in the kitchen," Mom calls as she descends the uncarpeted stairs. *Clump, clump, clump.* Each measured step of her cast boot echoing my desperation and reminding me that I'm stuck in bed. I can't fetch the brush for her to speed the process. I just lay and listen and roll my eyes.

Five minutes later, she decides she needs an old rag to wipe up potential spills. *Clump, clump, clump.* Again, her painful descent. My mother is not one to plan, gather all her supplies and then jump into a project—a fact made even more obvious when she descends once again to find a screwdriver to unscrew the outlet cover. I'm sure my girlfriends will laugh when I retell the events of the painting project, complete with the sound effects of her boot hitting the stairs, slowly, maddeningly. I will coin the incident, "Das Boot." Her unconventional mothering has been a source of many discussions, laughter and tears over the years.

She paints the base coat a pale pink that I picked out months ago. We decide on a stripe motif on the largest wall, pale pink and pale blue. When it's time for my mom to figure out the math behind the stripes, she panics. I lay down on the carpet in the empty room, always on the left side to ensure good blood flow to the placenta. I feel a sharp kick upon resettling and smile.

"Do I calculate from the center or one end of the wall?"

I never saw my mom as a perfectionist. A procrastinator, yes, but I didn't see the perfectionism. It makes sense, though. Perfectionism was the reason her dissertation was started and stopped so many times and it's the reason she's hell-bent on getting these stripes absolutely right. I don't know if she's more flustered by her many trips downstairs or by the task itself.

"How wide should the stripes be?" She wipes sweat from her brow and goes in search of painter's tape.

Clump, clump, pause. There's a quiet desperation in her steps now. I know she will be a while. I appreciate her fastidiousness. I can often be fast and sloppy with paint. I would have smothered the white base board in pink dribbles had I been the one wielding the brush. Of course, I would've cleaned them up but my swiftness often slows me down in the end.

She probably found all of my fuss over this paint job silly. I know she didn't paint a nursery in preparation for my arrival. There was no preparation, period. She conceived my sister in college after finally succumbing to my father's relentless pursuit. They were married by the Justice of the Peace but separated four years later. She didn't tell anyone she was pregnant with me. I was born ten weeks early. After a month in the neonatal intensive care unit, I went 'home' to foster care while she contemplated whether she could raise two kids alone. My uncle Jack offered support and advice. He assured her that she wouldn't have to raise her kids alone because he and her sister would help. She came to get me and the rest is history—my history, our history. As I lie on the itchy carpet, I try to reconcile her unlikely road to motherhood.

I realize that my own path has been less than traditional too. I got pregnant unexpectedly at age 26 with my first child, Gracy. I had a history of menstrual difficulties and was told by a doctor that it would difficult to conceive. So, I wasn't as careful as I should have been. I was unmarried but quickly remedied that by planning an outdoor wedding in the stifling June heat of Atlanta, Georgia. I wanted to ensure that my baby wouldn't be fatherless.

My husband and I separated two years later. I took on the role of single mother in a very matter-of-fact way. I knew the difficulties of single parenthood intimately from my own upbringing. However, I rationalized that because I had something my mother did not have (a college degree and a good job) it would be easier for me. Gracy would always come first.

The realities of work deadlines, relentless household tasks and the stress of single parenthood emerged. Soon exhausted and frazzled, I sought outside support. I found a great therapist and I started calling my mother more. Over the phone, our shared experiences of single parenting forged a common ground. We inched closer.

Gracy and I traveled to Wyoming for a visit. I was a wreck, physically and emotionally. In a late night conversation, my mom offered me what my uncle Jack gave her at her time of need: the reassurance to endure. She rightly pointed out that I was better off raising Gracy as a single parent without an emotionally abusive husband in the picture.

I began to make peace with my decision and with my shame over following in my mom's footsteps. I still didn't agree with many of the decisions she'd made over the course of my childhood, such as never taking her ex-husband to court to get child support. The fact that she got out of bed every day and went to work to support us became stronger evidence to me of her devotion. She did the best she could at the time, just as I was doing every day.

Then there was another time of need: My daughter developed some chronic health issues. I struggled to care for her and hold down my job. My mom stayed with us for nine months to help out. At 30, it wasn't easy living with my mother but it really made a difference. She stayed home from work when Gracy was sick, since I had already missed too many days of work. Her presence also allowed me some time for myself. I took a dance class and every once in a while I went on a date. Even if living under the same roof again was challenging, her mere presence helped me to realize that I was not alone.

൬

Two years later I met my future husband, Mark. After a year as newlyweds, we tried for a baby. Everything was in place. I was married. Gracy flourished in our solid home life with two loving parents. I left my demanding job as a television writer/producer to be a stay-at-home mom.

After a year, it became evident my problem was quite different from my mother's—I couldn't get pregnant. If I inherited my mom's genes and propensity towards high blood pressure and high cholesterol, why couldn't I inherit her propensity for fertility? She claims she got pregnant the first time she had sex with my father. She was a farm girl who made it to college despite great odds. Her dreams consisted of advanced degrees, not diapers and more poverty. Why do some pregnancies happen by accident or at inopportune times when you're not ready to have a baby, but when you're ready and everything is in place, there's no pregnancy?

We looked at adoption after a miscarriage ended my pregnancy by artificial insemination. I was comforted by the idea that maybe it was my destiny to love a child from a single mother who believed that having someone else raise her child was hope for a better life. However, I was not quite ready to give up on my chances for another biological child yet.

The in-vitro fertilization procedure that loomed ahead was as far as I would push my body to perform. To our great relief, it worked! Seven weeks later, two strong heartbeats pulsed from my womb.

When the required bed rest began at six months into the pregnancy, my mom came to help me again, to keep my family going and to prepare for the twins arrival. This time, she painted the twins' nursery.

I may never know all of the details of my early childhood nor what it took for my mom to keep things together as a single parent of two children. What I do know, however, is that when I need her, she comes. She offers her presence. She never remarried or found a life partner. I believe in all those years, she needed to know she wasn't alone.

൬

When I wake up, the sunlight that once flooded the room has muted and fallen to the floor where my body still lays on its left side. Drool cakes the carpet in front of my face. I rise up on my knees, making the slow ascent to standing. I need to pee.

Then I notice that my mom has finished the stripes while I slept. She must have tip-toed around my rather large, snoring body and taped the linear lines, filling them in with blue paint. The lines are perfect, with only an occasional smidge of blue migrating onto pink's side. It looks mechanically reproduced.

"There are a few places I want to touch up." Mom stands in the doorway with pink paint on her left cheek.

She limps past me and grabs the open can of paint. I think for a while before I answer. I know I will soon sit in the rocking chair and see the imperfections in the lines. I know my obsessive- compulsive nature will propel me to fix them. But I vow not to change a thing. My mom did this for me and for the babies. She did this to celebrate their arrival and in her quiet, wordless way, to celebrate me. How could I change anything?

I hand her the top to the paint can that is threatening to leak onto the carpet. The smooth blue liquid pooled on the surface beckons for my finger. I work the tactile goo through my fingers and say, *"It's beautiful."*

Kelli C. Trinoskey's twelve weeks of bed rest paid off and she delivered healthy twin girls in October of 2004. Molly and Tess will soon be five years old and Gracy will be thirteen. Kelli shares her time with her family in Columbus, Ohio teaching creative writing classes to young writers ages 12-20. She recently edited and published a teen literary magazine, Flip the Page. Her mom, Mickey, is now retired and lives in Minneapolis but visits often.

Reflection Points

"Only do what your heart tells you."
— Princess Diana

From the authors in their own words

- *Why do some pregnancies happen by accident or at inopportune times when you're not ready to have a baby, but when you're ready and everything is in place, there's no pregnancy?*

- *Who knew that trying to have a baby would be so much work?*

- *No other decision that followed this one would ever be as uncomplicated again.*

Questions to contemplate while standing at the threshold of having children

- *How do children factor into your dreams for your future? How do you see yourself in five years? Ten years? Forty years?*

- *Do you have people in your life who support your decision? Go to them when you need their love and support.*

- *What if the plans to have a child do not go as expected? Which options are you willing to consider? Which are you not?*

CHAPTER 5

Perspectives on Children and Parenting

"To live in this world you must be able to do three things:
to love what is mortal;
to hold it against your bones knowing your own life depends on it;
and, when the time comes to let it go, to let it go."
— Mary Oliver, Blackwater Woods

Motherhood is not a role that should be entered into lightly, as the challenges of raising a child are considerable. However, it is a title that once earned is forever held. Once you are called "mom" you will always be a mom—no matter how old your kids become, how they came into your life, or if they die before you do. Even parents who relinquish their rights are often still seen as mom or dad by the adult children who may later try to reconnect with their biological roots. Once a mom, you will always be a mom in your heart–even if not in your daily role.

"To hear people talk, having children is the ultimate life experience," remarks author Laura R. Sommers. Many parents would wholeheartedly agree. However, after much thoughtful consideration, Laura opted not to have children. Instead, she has found great value through supporting and mentoring the children of friends and family. She has become a role model and confidant to these children, enabling her to be at peace with her decision. In her essay *"Oops!"* Laura recounts how she found meaning in life through her relationships without having children.

The decision to forego motherhood can be hard to understand for women who are mothers or who desperately want to be mothers. Laura brings to light an important aspect of being a woman who opts out of having children. Her essay offers a perspective on mothering that is often misunderstood. Too often, women are judged for their decision not to have children, or they are repeatedly asked when they intend to get pregnant. For these women, the constant questioning and efforts to persuade them to have children are often experienced as judgmental.

There are numerous ways to make a difference in children's lives, and many women have meaningful and fulfilling lives without having children. Consider Oprah Winfrey: She has been very public about her own decision not to give birth to children. Would anyone be critical of Oprah for not having children? Like Oprah, Laura is a woman who has meaning in her life without rearing children, while still having a positive influence on the lives of other children. As with many other turning point decisions in women's lives this path is uniquely personal.

After the decision to have children is made (whether the pregnancy was planned or not) come the inevitable challenges of raising them. Some of these challenges are explored in Elizabeth Coplan's touching essay *"What's Your Problem, Mom?"* Elizabeth eloquently sums up her expanded view of being a mother: *"My motherhood does not begin and end with raising my own two sons. It continues indefinitely as other mothers' children go off to war, experience debilitating disease or illness, remain uneducated, starve or die."* The practice of caring for children in the world beyond our own family is something that could benefit all of us.

Another perspective on parenting is found in Mary Scribner's humorous essay, *"The Teen Years – Can a Steel Stud Look Like a Pimple?"* where the author offers a refreshing look at a teenager's developmental tasks and challenges. Her dilemma was to help her son to navigate through some difficult decisions in a way that optimized his self-confidence and supported his eventual independence. She reflects, *"The best thing that came out of this is that our son felt respected while continuing to march toward individuation and autonomy."* Mary models an approach to guiding teens that shows regard for them and recognizes the developmental tasks that they will inevitably encounter.

The turning point for Mary was not in the significance of the event; it was about successfully working through yet another adolescent hurdle with her son. Some of our most memorable turning points happen in the everyday decisions that we make with our families and affect us for a long time to come.

The approaches to parenting are as unique as the women in this book. Each of the essays in this section helps us to better understand and appreciate the different choices about motherhood and mothering. They encourage us to respect the choices that women make about having children and raising them, even if their decisions are different from our own values or experiences.

What's Your Problem, Mom?

by Elizabeth Coplan

Dedicated to my "good sport" son Spencer whose adventures (and misadventures) provide me with unlimited essay topics.

~

I searched the crowd for my son Spencer. First, I saw the signature baseball cap, and then I noticed the familiar walk, a proud, self-confident walk that reminds me of my father. Finally I saw Spencer's face happily talking with a fellow traveler and I felt a surge of excitement.

When Spencer saw me, he beamed with the look of a man glad to be home yet proud of his accomplishments. As one of twenty high school students and six chaperones, Spencer had spent the past two weeks on Ometepe, a remote island in Nicaragua. At that moment I realized that I had really missed him and his smiling face.

Tears trickled down my face as I gave my son a long hug. After a few moments, he pulled away, looked at my tear-stained face and said, *"What's your problem, mom?"*

Stop! Rewind the scene twenty minutes.

~

Just as the plane from Houston landed at Sea-Tac airport, the parents of the Ometepe delegates began to congregate at the entrance to baggage claim. We discussed our excitement to see our children, and the improbable possibility of catching the next ferryboat back to our own island at the end of Spring Break with Friday traffic already slowed to a crawl. I stood talking with other parents about how quiet and peaceful our homes were with one of our children gone.

At the plane's scheduled arrival time, the number of anxious parents swelled. Off to the right I noticed another group forming. They were of all ages carrying red, white and blue balloons, and Mylar balloons shaped as American flags. Some carried roll-up banners. Their excitement reverberated throughout the waiting area. They exuded energy of relief, mixed with giddiness and held-back tears.

And then they saw the soldiers walking down Concourse B and toward the waiting group. One soldier, a young man, looked somber in expression but proud in his uniform. At his side, the other soldier was older and weary-looking, but also somber, also proud. Then the frenzy of their welcoming party climaxed as the children shouted their names and the tears were held-back no longer. One boy opened his banner: Welcome Home Uncle Joe!

Without slowing his pace, the younger soldier went to his wife, gave her a quick kiss then fell into a long embrace—a desperate, I'll-never-leave-you-again-if-I-can-help-it embrace.

Minutes ticked by, but time seemed to stop. The baby in the stroller began to cry. The soldier scooped up the child and held him close in one arm, his other arm around his wife's waist as she put her head on his chest. Not a word was said. The baby choked back sobs while he studied the face of this man holding him.

I turned away, sensing that the moment was too private. My gaze turned momentarily to the older soldier who held a man and a woman close to him—a brother and his wife or his parents? No one spoke. Clearly words don't come easily at a homecoming such as this one. What do you say to someone who has seen too much and has experienced the unimaginable, traumatic events of war?

The frenzied anticipation of the crowd gradually gave way to measured interaction. Other family members came forward for their turn to show their love for the returning soldiers. I wanted to add my "thank you." I wanted to surround them with a protective light that would keep them from harm. They had come so far but now they were home again.

When I saw my son walking towards me, I still felt the combination of love and sadness from the soldiers and their families. My own son did not look particularly excited to see me. I am sure I represented the end of his amazing journey.

He had a new family now, one in a tiny village on Ometepe in Nicaragua. During the past two weeks, he'd witnessed a birth and dug fence pole holes with sticks that only remotely resembled shovels. He'd built piñatas and entertained village children. He'd climbed a volcano, fought off colonies of ants, eaten rice and beans at every meal. He'd lived in a shack without water or electricity. He'd seen the smiling faces of children with so little and yet so much. I'm certain he was glad to be home but could not wait to go back.

What's my problem? Sorry Spencer. These tears are not for you. I predict that you'll travel to other amazing places and will meet friends wherever you go. Today "my problem" lies in the feeling that my motherhood does not begin and end with raising my own two sons. It continues indefinitely as other mothers' children go off to war, experience debilitating disease or illness, remain uneducated, starve and die. My heart feels full with love and sadness. I close my eyes and send this love to these children of the world.

What's my problem? I appreciate now that I have no problems. In fact, as you chat amongst your friends, unwilling to let the trip end just yet, I realize that I am standing at the happiest place on earth.

Elizabeth Coplan began her marketing and public relations career in New York and Los Angeles over 30 years ago. She is now CEO of COPLAN AND COMPANY based in Seattle. Elizabeth focuses on business development consulting and her most important jobs as a wife and mother. She is also co-creator and author of A Wild Ride (www.awildride.net), a website for parents of challenging children. Six months after writing "What's Your Problem, Mom?" Elizabeth sent her son Spencer to college on the East Coast. During his freshman year, Spencer found himself penniless in Manhattan and called his mom. As soon as Elizabeth heard his voice, her heart was full of love. She closed her eyes, sent her love and then she wired him money. The next day Elizabeth began her newest essay on the problems that can arise when rescuing a son via the Internet and text messages!

The Teen Years – Can a Steel Stud Look Like a Pimple?

by Mary Scribner

൴

"No, absolutely not! Not while you are living under my roof" were the first thoughts that exploded out of nowhere into my mind. Somehow I was able to suppress the verbal output that would have taken my son and me into a power play of who's right, who's got the upper hand here, etc, etc.

"I'm 16 and legally I can do this if I want to!" I was informed.

OK, Mary, you need to take a deep breath, I coached myself. I suddenly realized that my son's stand was about more than the physical act of sticking a steel stud into his virgin skin. I wasn't sure what though. Finally I was able to muster the words, *"I'm curious and want to know more. Let's talk about this later."*

I needed distance from my first reaction, needed more information, and needed to talk to my friends who had already weathered this teen right of passage. My first impulse was to control, then I just wanted to escape: Beam me up Scottie. Why did my beautiful, sensitive son want to staple a steel stud into his lower lip? I'd already accepted the long hair and baggy clothes that I thought would characterize his teen years. Silly me, I'd thought that I was out of the woods. I should have known better. I just got comfortable with one developmental stage and got hit in the face with chaos as the next one asserted itself.

Two days later with my son and husband I prefaced our talk, gently addressing my son's worries: He had not done anything wrong. We weren't there to criticize him. I stayed curious and began with innocent inquiry. *"So, we wanted to learn more about the lip piercing that you're thinking about getting." "Who would do this for you? How would you take care of it? How would you pay for it? What if it got infected? What would it feel like?"* Each question was answered maturely and without defensiveness. We took our time and allowed some silence and thoughtfulness to spark the next inquiry.

I was actually getting into the "feel" of having one of these studs as my tongue slowly slid across the inside of my bottom lip. I imagined tongue and steel colliding in an unnatural sensation. *"How would it feel in your mouth?"* I could see my son's tongue also investigating his soft tissue.

Thoughtfully he remarked, *"Well you know, I'm just thinking about this. I didn't say I was actually gonna do it!"* As he got up to leave I breathed a sign of relief knowing that today we had all navigated this potential battle pretty darn well. Tomorrow could be another story.

On reflection I learned that with enough information I could actually entertain the idea as a possibility rather than a reactionary "NO" that would shut down communication. One of my friends talked about these piercings as rights of passage for boys in a culture where there are few. Another mentioned that these piercings were similar to getting our ears pierced (this is really going to date me!).

The best thing to come out of this is that our son felt respected while continuing to move toward individuation and autonomy. His choice might not be one that I would make, but this is his life, not mine. My job is to keep him safe, foster a loving relationship, and respect him as he zigzags toward adulthood.

Who knows what decisions he will make in the future? I hope that whatever decisions he faces, he will feel free to share his thoughts with us as he processes his way through the teen years.

Mary Scribner, is a registered nurse and Parent Coaching Institute-certified parent coach with SOUND PARENT. Over the past 25 years Mary has helped parents remain sane in the face of overwhelming parenting challenges. Out of a strong passion and devotion to parents of spirited children, Mary co-created and writes for A Wild Ride, a Web site dedicated to parents of children with unique needs. Update from the author: Thus far, the piercings are resting back stage.

Oops!

by Laura R. Sommers

Reflections from Women Writing Contest Selection

~

"Once you've been a mom to six children, there's not a whole lot else."

A 67-year-old woman said this to me recently. At first, I thought maybe she was talking about her uterus and I felt pity. But no, she was talking about having confidence in a job interview!

To hear people talk, having children is the ultimate life experience.

"Raising children is the most important thing I've ever done," a long-time friend said at a dinner party. The heads around the table nodded vigorously. Others chimed in with the same sentiment. All the couples, except us, had that look that only younger parents seem to get.

I kept my mouth shut. But I thought, *"Next stop, sainthood? Is having children really the be-all, end-all that everybody says it is? And why am I talking to myself in such an angry tone?"*

And then I realized— Oops! I forgot to have kids.

Well, I didn't exactly forget. There came a time when the natural means of getting pregnant didn't work for us. So, it was time to pursue artificial means and that made us nervous. We're not deeply spiritual people, but we do believe in cosmic irony. If we meddled too much in our own fertility, we might be asking for it. We worried about Down's Syndrome. We pictured our home crawling with octuplets. Getting in bed with science was clearly not for us.

Still, we continued to waffle for a long while. "*Maybe*," we told ourselves, "*God has another purpose for us? Maybe it's not up to us to decide?*" We reminded each other that it's not about making ourselves happy. It's about making another life.

Then I turned fifty and menopause made the decision for us.

Now I feel free to admit that I never felt pulled toward babies anyway. To me, the ideal child is nine years old, well-read, and politely talkative until it's time to go to bed—punctually, with teeth brushed and ready to tell *me* a story. My friends with grown children tell me there's a brief shining moment when this happens and then it's over.

So—Oops! I didn't have kids.

You might imagine, with so much free time that I have tackled all the things that are out of a busy mother's reach.

Oops.

I haven't cured cancer. Never ran for public office. Will not make the short list when they pick someone to walk on Mars. Haven't written the Great American Middle-Aged Childless Feminist Baby Boomer Novel (I'm still working on it.).

I also didn't win a major peace award, invent a dance craze, write my generation's rock anthem, start a religion, create a cutesy handbag company financed with credit cards, coin a catchphrase, lead a movement, become the first woman to do something only men did previously, or play a quirky, beloved character on a TV show.

Oops!

Don't get me wrong. I've been busy. Really busy. If there was a major award for just plain busy, I might have won it. But have I really done anything as important as having children? Since I'm prone to the occasional George Bailey-style meltdown when I measure my achievements against my dreams, maybe it's time to make a list. The following are the most important things this childless woman has ever done:

- Learned to swim at an early age (which prevented me from drowning at an early age). Became a lifeguard as a teenager, although I never pulled anyone out. Much later on a Caribbean vacation I actually did pull a child out of the ocean and saved him from drowning. I like to think it's because of all the early training. And because I didn't have my own children to watch.
- Almost made it to the state spelling bee in eighth grade. Important, because I like to think that losing kept me from being pegged as a total geek in high school.
- Made it into the Eastman School of Music as a performance major; a big accomplishment, achieved over the objections of my parents and high school teachers, who thought I should pursue something more intellectually challenging or become a doctor. OK, still a geek.

- Dropped out of the Eastman School of Music (over the objections of my parents and music teachers) when I realized that I needed something more intellectually challenging.
- Became an English major (over the objections of my parents) because it was clear to me that all along I wanted to be a writer. Although "English major" used to be a nice way of saying "unemployable," it's still a decision I've never regretted.
- Found and left the "love of my life" (the same guy, twice), which freed me to find and marry the Real Love of My Life (the perfect guy, once).
- Visited my grandmother often, and got to know her in a way I never would have otherwise, when Lou Gehrig's disease turned her into a housebound invalid.
- Spent time with my stepmother while her health failed, and was there with her the moment she died.
- Finally made peace with my anger and guilt about not being there for my own mother's death from cancer.
- Created a business, served clients with dignity and integrity, and helped feed, clothe and shelter the families of my employees, vendors, and clients as well as my own.
- At the age of 49, finally started planting trees.
- Moved near my hometown to live and was here last month to drive my 80-year-old, widowed father to his latest doctor's appointment.

And there *have* been children—those whose lives I've touched. There's the daughter of one of those dinner party friends I've known since her birth; I recently helped to see her off to college. There are my nephew and niece in Toledo, who are the brightest, most interesting children God ever put on this planet (with the most doting aunt). There are the older nephews, who upon entering college suddenly realized I was highly relevant because I have always worked in their chosen fields of writing and design. I like to think they find me interesting. I'm someone they can talk to in a way that's different from talking with their moms or their friends' moms. I hope to be an influence for them for the rest of their lives.

If I haven't done the most important thing yet in my life yet, well, I figure I still have 30 or 40 years ahead of me—in which I won't be distracted by the dreaded teen years, underage drinking, paying for college, my children's poor marriage choices and subsequent unhappiness, the threat of chickens coming home to roost, and babysitting grandchildren, because it's assumed I have nothing better to do and must miss having children around.

I don't have children, and that gives me all the time in the world to find something important to do.

Oops! I forgot to have kids, but because of that, the best is yet to come—I hope.

Laura Sommers spends most of her time as co-owner of a retail design firm, Whole-Brained Creative, which does environmental design and brand expression for prominent global brands. In addition, she publishes articles and personal essays, works on a historical novel about the wife of a fictional American Impressionist, takes tennis lessons, studies Italian, and generally gets eight hours of sleep a night. She lives and works in idyllic Granville, Ohio with her husband and three Great Danes. Still no kids at age 52. Still no regrets.

Reflection Points

"One needs something to believe in, something for which one can have whole-hearted enthusiasm. One needs to feel that one's life has meaning, that one is needed in this world."
— Hannah Senesh

From the authors in their words

- *My job is to keep him safe, foster a loving relationship, and respect him as he zigzags toward adulthood.*

- *My motherhood does not begin and end with raising my own two sons...*

- *There have been children—those whose lives I've touched... I hope to be an influence for them for the rest of their lives.*

- *The best is yet to come–I hope.*

Questions to contemplate while standing at the threshold of raising children

- *Are you at peace with your decision about motherhood—whatever it is?*

- *How has having children or not affected your life?*

- *Do you know someone who has made a decision not to have children? How can you better understand and support their decisions?*

- *Do you know someone who is having some challenges as a parent? What support can you offer? Who has been most helpful to you? How were they helpful?*

Part Three

Discovering the Pathways to a Career

Let the beauty of what you love be what you do.
– Rumi

CHAPTER 6

Your Life's Work and Passion

"Your work is to discover your work and then, with all your heart, give yourself to it."
— Buddha

The message from women who wrote about the pathways to their careers was clear: Trust your heart and the work will follow. Unfortunately many people do not have the luxury of finding work that ignites their passion and gives them a sense of purpose or meaning. Countless women find themselves in jobs that are far from what they would *like* to be doing, but the employment meets their needs in other important areas (finances, proximity, schedule...). This is especially true in a difficult economy when many men and women are grateful for whatever work they can get just to meet their basic needs.

Women face other realities and obstacles in the labor force as well. Women make less than their male counterparts, get promoted less than men and have less professional and leadership opportunities in the job market. Women are more likely to take time from their jobs or from their career to care for their children. Thankfully, there have been noteworthy gains in laws and shifts in viewpoints over the past three decades, but many challenges for women and work remain.

Although the paths to a career or long term employment can be significant turning points for women, many often look beyond their jobs for their life's work or passion. The essays in this chapter illuminate some of the different ways in which women have found their life's calling through work or service and how it has transformed them.

Women discover their life's work at different points throughout the lifespan; however, there seem to be three times when this realization is most likely to surface: young adulthood, mid-life and later life (pre-or post retirement). While many women in our society start on their career paths soon after high school, it is not always a smooth transition. Author Sandra Wilson experienced a painful and confusing period following the death of her mother just before her high school graduation, *"There I stood at the crossroads of my life, at the onset of adulthood but without my mother."* In her essay, "Reflections of May," Sandra tells of her uncertainty and grief as she leaves for college without her mother's guidance, not knowing what will be ahead for her.

About twenty years later and at mid-life, Nancy Turner knew that she needed to make some changes in her career, but she did not know what or how. *"I realized that I was facing a life transition as I was approaching 40 years old."* Other women are nearing or at retirement when they find themselves wanting to do something more or something different in their lives. For some women, their calling leads them to volunteering, ministry, or community service. Others will discover that changing to a totally different career path (e.g., from service worker to business owner) provides newfound excitement and fulfillment.

The ways in which women discover their passion or their life's work can come unexpectedly or with much deliberation. It was an unanticipated and unusual event that helped Nancy Turner to realize that she had known her life's calling all along but had never pursued it. *"I was hit by a trash truck,"* was her reply to a young woman about how she became a minister, validating a passion she had felt since high school. Similarly, Misty Kiwak Jacobs knew her calling was connected to her faith. In her essay, "One White Towel," Misty noted, *"I was so sure I was staying, so sure I was called to this."* Like many women, Misty and Nancy knew their callings early on and they pursued them into their adult lives. They both continue to follow their passion.

For others, the discovery of their life's work is not readily realized or it shifts along the way. In "Decision Point," KC McClain tells about her reluctant entry into Officer Training School. When someone initially suggested the military to her, she responded, *"I might also jump off the building!"* She started her career as a public school teacher, but four years later she found herself surprisingly considering the military. *"I never expected just how different my career change would be,"* noted KC McClain after over 30 years of distinguished service in the U.S. Air Force.

Sandra Wilson also took an unforeseen turn to the military when she was in college and facing an uncertain future. Wilson was so ambivalent at the time about the military that she realized months later, *"I still had not discussed this with most of my friends, since I had an uneasy feeling that they would not approve."* Following her retirement after 24 years in the military, Sandra proudly reflects, *"Serving my country gave me meaning, purpose, and a sense of duty... It became my life but more importantly gave me back my life."* Both McClain and Wilson followed their instincts despite some initial hesitation or reactions from others and it led them to successful, fulfilling careers.

An unexpected shift in career and a life transformation occurred for Brenda Donkers when she became seriously ill. The owner of a successful 70-million-dollar-a-year company with over 200 franchises, Brenda found herself stressed, sick and unhappy. In "My Crisis Transformed," Brenda describes her discovery of what was behind her illness and how she found a way out of the emptiness she was feeling. Brenda crossed the threshold and took a leap of faith by leaving her prosperous business and moving across the country. Her healing journey has allowed her to find better health, renewed energy, a commitment to her relationships and to her spirituality as well as a new career. Brenda noted that with these important changes, *"I am growing and excited for the future again."*

For Brenda and many other women, sometimes it takes leaving something behind before you can find what you are missing in your life. To find your niche in this world requires listening to your instincts as well as your heart. Only then will you discover your life's work and be ready to take the path towards your passion.

One White Towel

by Misty Kiwak Jacobs

Reflections from Women Writing Contest Selection

~

It was a thick, white Ralph Lauren towel, bath size. It was on the list: one white towel, a hairbrush, two navy blue skirts, two long-sleeved white cotton shirts, one slip, three pairs white cotton underwear, twelve cotton cloths (diapers worked), two large safety pins, one long white nightgown, a Bible—Oxford Annotated with the Apocrypha, Study Edition—and a set of "The Liturgy of the Hours." For some reason I chose a thick, white, Ralph Lauren towel. I was 23. It was the first towel I ever bought.

Sister Annie George went through my possessions, my dowry, on the second day. She was young and Indian and cruel. Her face was placid and round. I laid everything on the cot: striped ticking floating over a seascape of shifting lumps. She glanced over my things quietly, my collage of cotton and simplicity—no longer even my things but now the community's. She paused at the nightgown and held it up to the light of the window. It was not new, and it had been worn to the edge of transparency, of immodesty. She seemed to consider it for a long time. Neither of us spoke.

I would wear the gown only at night during Grand Silence and only between my cell and the bathroom. I would be seen only in the candlelight which slipped into the hall from the other sisters' cells. I would wear it for only six hours 40 minutes a night for the rest of my life. While we stood silently, gazing through my nightgown towards the light, I thought about the rule against particular friendships and the temptations the nuns promised that we would have. Finally, Sister laid the gown on the bed.

She told me to cover the prayer books in brown paper. Then she picked up my white towel. She held it up, weighed its heavy excess, its ostentation in this place of cleanliness and prayer. "*You will have to cut this*," she said. "*Bring it to the refectory during recreation. I will hem it for you then.*" It was my second day and this was my first obvious fault: An offense against poverty and simplicity, an attachment to the things of the flesh.

༺༻

In our first days removed from the world, a passage was dictated to us. As the sister paced the length of the refectory table, the chink and jangle of her rosary was the rhythm in which we wrote. As she paused between each line, the other aspirants and I would raise our gaze to one another's faces, to the nun in her white sari cradling a holy book, to the sunlight passing through the thin homemade curtains, a literal heavenly light. We were nine women relinquishing every past and future physical touch and every person we loved. Yet happiness like sex was blooming in us and making our faces hot.

As the sister read, I was mindful of the pencil's benevolent movement, of the paper's openness. This is what I wrote:

> *Nothing is so glorious to God nor so useful for our souls as to unite the offering of ourselves, absolutely and without condition, to the offering which Jesus made at the moment when he gave Himself up to the executioners to be stripped of His raiment and fastened to the cross.*
>
> –Dom Columba Marmion, The Way of the Cross.

༺༻

I wonder if Sister Annie George knew that I would not be staying. I wonder if she somehow saw it in the towel she intended to split, if she had the insight of King Solomon when he raised his sword to divide the harlot's child. I was so sure I was staying, so sure I was called to this. When I did leave, I did not know why I left. But it was not for thick towels or chocolate or noise or sex.

There is a keen exchange for escape from the world—distraction for psychic discomfort, certain and inescapable, a sort of mystical mirror constantly before one's face. There are no diversions in a contemplative convent, no television, no novels and no slow, unraveling chats. There are only the ancient, silent rhythms of prayer and work and prayer and sleep. It is the most beautiful thing I have ever experienced, a timeless, incensed, circular flowing lit by flickering candles and chaperoned by chalky saints. And it is the coarsest thing I have ever experienced—the unbearable, unceasing encounter with myself.

I could leave, and so I did. I could lose myself in marriage and children, in a tract home, in decorating and redecorating it, in cooking too well and in excessive sleep. But I committed myself to an exile's sadness. I wed myself to Loss, to be renewed on every holy day and during every Lent.

Before I left, I sneaked to the supply room on the third floor and found the lost half of my towel tucked away on a bare wood shelf. I found it shining as bright as the "final vows" saris in their tidy stacks, laughing at the pile of barbed wire belts. I reclaimed my raiment, my severed towel. It was the last earthly thing I had surrendered beneath the cross and the first thing I seized before turning back.

Then, one night under cover of darkness, two nuns raised the steel bar from its rests and led me out the portal into a South Bronx street.

Misty Kiwak Jacobs was born in Scottsdale, Arizona. She is a graduate of Sarah Lawrence College in Bronxville, New York, and has studied at The Russian School, Norwich University, The Summer Institute of Linguistics, University of North Dakota and the Maurice Thorez Institute of Foreign Languages, Moscow, Russia. She has studied poetry under Norman Dubie at Arizona State University. In addition to many local publications, Misty's work has been published in The Sarah Lawrence Review and The Red Rock Review. Pulitzer winner Gary Snyder placed one of her poems among the top three in the Tucson Poetry Festival Statewide Contest, 2002. Currently, Ms. Kiwak Jacobs classically home schools her two children in her native town. She is an aspirant of the Order of Carmelites Discalced Secular.

~

Decision Point

by KC McClain

For my daughter-in-law Ashley McClain, the strongest woman I know

I taught junior high and high school for four years and knew it was time for me to do something different. I never expected just how different my career change would be.

As I was considering my options, one of my fellow teachers recommended the military, to which I replied, *"I might also jump off the building!"* However, as she explained the opportunities available with the military, I warmed to the idea.

I began the application process and it wasn't long before I was in San Antonio Texas in August as an Air Force officer trainee. There was no military background in my family (other than my father serving in WWII) so I had little concept of what to expect.

There were many factors in play when I began the 12 week training experience. I left my seven-year-old son for our first extended time apart. I was stressed to the point of having severe stomach pains. My shoes didn't fit (but I didn't want to complain) so my feet soon resembled hamburger bound with adhesive tape. We were out of bed and already running before the sun even thought about rising and it was hot…stinking hot in Texas in August. All of these factors caused me to doubt the wisdom of my decision. To say that Officer Training School (OTS) started out as an out-of-body experience—seemingly plucked off the planet earth and set down in some completely alien environment—was truly not much of an exaggeration for me. It was miserable.

At about the third week, I was beyond miserable. I missed my son, hated running, wasn't good at marching, my feet were hurting and did I mention that it was hot? On that day, we were marching most of the morning, dressed in dark blue and black shoes in the blazing Texas sun.

My toes were sizzling. Then, we lined up outside the dining hall to wait our turn to eat.

Due to my stomach condition I was swigging Mylanta straight from the bottle and eating only soft foods such as mashed potatoes and Jell-O. I was worried that if I told anyone about my pains they would make me leave the Air Force, so I dealt with it on my own.

As I went down the serving line, I must have been a sorry sight because one of the serving ladies asked me if I was okay. Although I nodded yes, I really wasn't okay at all: I was at my breaking point. She asked me again but I could only nod. The next thing I knew, she came around the line and asked me to sit with her in back. I shook my head no, still unable to speak. She tried to persuade me but I shook off her hand and proceeded down the line. I knew that if I went with her, I would leave OTS. I also knew that I had a child to support and I'd made a commitment to the Air Force. As much as her kindness (and my discomfort) pulled at me to walk away, I didn't go.

At this point in the training we had "tight" meals which meant no talking, no looking around, just stare at your plate and eat. This was also difficult for me since meals had always been social occasions. So, I was sitting at the table with three men from my unit and we were all staring at our respective plates. Suddenly I realized that I was going to cry, which was mortifying. To paraphrase Tom Hanks, *"There's no crying in the Air Force!"* Plus, I certainly did not want my teammates to label me as the "crier."

I thought that if I just sat quietly, no one would know since we were all staring at our plates. So I sat, watching my tears plop into the mashed potatoes and gravy which made an interesting splatter pattern. I was certain that once I got myself under control, my cohorts would be none the wiser. Just when I thought I was home free, out of my peripheral vision I see a hand sliding a napkin towards me. Again, I was mortified, but I took the napkin and got myself under control. As we walked out of the dining hall, the man who slipped me the napkin simply nodded and I nodded back. Surprisingly after that my stomach quit hurting and that's when I knew I was going to make it.

I tell this story to let you know that there are decision points in every difficult situation. If we do not recognize the decision points when they present themselves, we can end up making a significant life decision without any awareness of the impact. At the time, I did not consciously know that if I accepted the kindness of the woman in the dining hall that I would leave OTS, but I sensed it. My gut told me to stay regardless how much I wanted to go. It was a turning point for me in that I had an opportunity to leave and I didn't take it. I believe that is why my stomach settled down and the whole experience became much easier for me. It was at that moment that I truly made my commitment to the Air Force.

I finished training and was commissioned as a Second Lieutenant. Since then, I have served over 30 years in the Air Force. The opportunities and experiences were innumerable, including standing on the Berlin Wall and on the line dividing North and South Korea. There are many people I owe for these opportunities in my career. There are those who have mentored and assisted me, of course. But there was also the woman who reached out to me that day at Officer Training School. I wish I knew her name. Although I chose not to go with her that day, her offer was indeed a turning point for me. I think of her often and thank her for her kindness.

K.C. McClain was raised in Oklahoma and graduated from Oklahoma State University. She taught public schools for four years prior to joining the military in 1977. She continues to serve as an Officer with over 30 years of experience in the U.S. Air Force.

Reflections of May

by Sandra F. Wilson

Dedicated to my mother and father, Margaret "Marge" and Fred Butler

~

May 1976, Memorial Day: My mother died of breast cancer. It would prove to be one of the most devastating days of my life. It would also prove to be one of the most profound and critical turning points in my life. This would become a time in my life that would define all future endeavors and decisions—both conscious and subtle. In many ways, I still live with the gut-wrenching realization that my life changed forever on that day.

My mother was my best friend in so many ways. I knew she loved me and was proud of me. I loved her deeply. When I heard that she died soon after I visited with her in the hospital, I cried until there seemed to be nothing left in my body. I hurt to my core. I could not be there for anyone else—not even my father. I was only 18. This was not supposed to be happening. Not like this, not now.

My life was built on the idea that I was supposed to be the promise of a better future for my family. I was going to make my parents proud. We struggled so much and I knew my future depended on a good education. This would also give me the opportunity to help my family realize a better way of life. I was accepted at the University of North Carolina at Chapel Hill. I was going to be the first person in my family to go to college. There was so much excitement and promise in my family surrounding this major milestone. My mother laid the foundation for this to happen in our lives, but she was not here to bear witness to her promise.

~

My senior year in high school was *everything but normal*, especially in the last weeks of my mother's life. Unlike most of my friends who were worrying about which dress to wear to the prom, I spent my time with my mother.

As she received her chemotherapy treatments, I sat in the car studying in the parking lot at Duke University Hospital. My mother insisted that I do my homework and get ready for college instead of accompanying her into the hospital waiting area. While I was reading and studying, I had no idea that these would be some of my last days with her. I thought she was getting better. Then, on Mother's Day weekend, she went into a coma and she never fully recovered.

On Memorial Day, two weeks before I graduated from high school, my life changed when my mother died. There I stood at the crossroads of my life at the onset of adulthood but without my mother. I felt that everything I did from this point on should make my family, my mother, proud of me.

My freshman year at college was really tough but I tried not to show how bad I really felt.

During my sophomore year, a friend of mine in the ROTC program invited me to come by to learn more about the program. I ended up talking to a Captain about the opportunities and soon found myself agreeing to take the officer qualifying test. I showed up at 6:45 am for the test thinking that the worst that could happen is that I would never hear from them again. I didn't even tell my friends what I was up to. I knew they would think I was crazy for even considering it.

I did well on the test and was asked whether I was interested in taking the physical exam. After going through all of the medical exams and paperwork, I was notified that I passed the physical, too. Soon, I was scheduled for an interview with the Colonel of the detachment.

In subtle ways, this process was a distraction from the grief I still felt. It was as if something was propelling me down this unfamiliar road. I still had not discussed this with most of my friends, since I had an uneasy feeling that they would not approve. I was not even sure what I was doing myself, so how could I explain it to others? Then in May 1978, two years after my mother's death, I received a phone from the ROTC detachment officer to advise me that I was scheduled for the summer training class in Florida.

When I showed up for training that summer, I did everything wrong. I was exhausted at the end of each day and wondered what the hell I was doing in this place. After several weeks, I began to get into the rhythm of this new world and I made fewer mistakes. Several weeks later, there was a guest speaker who had been a prisoner of war in Vietnam for five years. I could not believe how much this man had sacrificed for our country.

He impressed me so much. I knew then that I wanted and needed to be part of something that was much bigger than me.

At this point I began to take the training more seriously. I had found my calling but did not realize it yet. I still had to make a decision as to whether I was going to go into the military as an officer or move in a different direction. By the time we returned to training in September, I knew my decision. That summer at the Air Force ROTC training camp proved to be another turning point in my life. It gave me hope in a way that I thought would never be possible again.

Sometimes I say that I wandered into the Air Force, but it was actually the Air Force that anchored me when I was adrift. It became my life but more importantly, the Air Force gave me back my life. Serving my country gave me meaning, purpose, and a sense of duty. My life became intertwined with the service and preservation of our nation in a way that I could never have imagined. It was a privilege to serve with honor and it was the biggest adventure of my life.

I thought I would never find my way home again but the Air Force helped me to pave a path to my own destiny and to find my self. In the end, the Air Force brought home to me.

In the summer of 2004, after 24 years of serving my country and 28 years after my mother's death, I made another turning point decision. I decided to retire from the Air Force. This decision was based on a promise and a celebration—knowing that I had lived my life in a way that made my family and my parents proud. For this, I am grateful and at peace.

Sandra Wilson is a retired Colonel. She served in the United States Air Force for 24 years. She currently works as a Senior Executive for the Federal government and is on special assignment in Florida. She resides in Tampa, Florida.

My Crisis Transformed

by Brenda Dronkers

To my wonderful family, Ron, Jenelle, Matt and Jake for supporting me through the toughest time in my life. I love you all so much, and I cherish each one of you.

~

I am a wife, mother of three kids, and founder of *Pump It Up*, an inflatable party business that I successfully grew into a 70-million-dollar-a-year business with over 200 franchise locations by 2007. While that brief introduction and those numbers look impressive on paper, they came with many challenges, high prices and valuable lessons along the way.

I find business to be somewhat easy and invigorating but it has been the friendships and relationships that have posed challenges for me along the way. As a business woman, I was under constant scrutiny. It seemed to me that my character, spirituality and family life were under attack. Several friendships ended as my success and franchises grew. I became disillusioned—even with my fellow Christians.

In addition to the loss of friends, another high price to pay was my personal health. By 2007, I was experiencing painful migraines 15-20 times per month. It is no surprise now that the greater my success, the more frequent and intense my migraines became. Along with the physical pain, I was in emotional pain too. I was sad and hurt at losing what I once thought of as true friends and I was empty because my personal relationship with God had weakened.

Later that year, I decided to listen to my body and heed its warning, so I sold my business and moved with my family to Austin, Texas. We looked forward to a fresh start and new adventures. To my surprise and disappointment, my migraines did not subside. They grew even more frequent and intense. I became house-bound and bed-ridden.

It was during this painful and dark time in my life that I began to have horrible visions of abuse from my childhood. After five doctors and months of constant migraines, frequent panic attacks, insomnia and a 30-pound weight loss, I was finally diagnosed with post traumatic stress disorder (PTSD): My symptoms were related to undiagnosed and untreated traumatic events from my youth.

I believe that our soul waits until there is a safe time and place to introduce us to pains which need to be validated, processed and released. Physical symptoms, such as migraines, can serve to slow us down enough to take a look at the unthinkable pain with new perspective and to begin a healing journey.

I gained a great deal of knowledge and experience about business during the birth, growth and sale of *Pump It Up*. Now, I am gaining a great deal of knowledge and experience about myself, thanks to the health problems which led me to sell the business, to move, and to begin healing.

Our family has moved back home to Pleasanton, California. Together, we have opened a shop called Thriving Ink & Company—a custom-design, artist-collaborative t-shirt shop. My relationship with God is good and my relationship with my family is strong. I am growing and excited for the future once again.

As my soul heals, my migraines are also subsiding. I realize that in this next adventure, I will be working with a new-found spirit ready to apply lessons learned and to begin a different path. This is my new and improved success story.

Brenda Dronkers is the founder and former President of Pump It Up Inflatable Party Zone franchise system. Her most recent project is with her family called Thriving Ink & Company—a custom-design, artist-collaborative t-shirt shop launched in 2008. Brenda invites visitors to their website at www.thrivingink.com

Update from the author: Our family has moved back home to Pleasanton, California, and I am much happier where my roots are. My relationship with God is amazing and my relationship with my family is as strong as ever. I am developing new, healthier friendships. I am so excited for the future once again!

Crash

by Nancy G. Turner

~

"I was hit by a trash truck," was my reply to a young woman who recently inquired about how it is that I became a minister. I get asked this question quite often. Some people are simply curious. Others still find women clergy a novelty. For me, it was a quirky and twisted journey into ministry.

There are two important points to clarify before I tell the tale. First, no one was hurt in the trash truck encounter. My car was hit (and damaged) by one of those big orange trucks while I was driving. There was no damage to the trash truck. It was a simple, stupid accident but it was still a crash. There was also a citation and a visit to court that added up to a serious impact which altered my life.

The second point to clarify is that I have always been religious although not particularly spiritual. At least I think so, but some of my friends think otherwise. Usually, people say they are spiritual and not religious as a way to explain their non-association with an established faith community. I am Christian and grew up going to church. It was a great experience for me. The structures and traditions were well defined, yet flexible. I learned about God and Jesus. We served in the community and beyond. We sang beautiful music. I loved the people and they loved me. Church was a better home than home was lots of times.

At age 17, when most of my friends were leaving their parents' churches, I was drawn to ministry as a profession. So, I went to a meeting for youth interested in the ministry. It was me and a bunch of guys who were at the meeting. Not a surprise really–it was the mid-1970s and there were very few women ministers. I sensed that these guys would likely get ordained and later serve at various churches as pastors. I knew that no church would want me–a young woman as the leader of their church. At the time, women were just recently being accepted and ordained, but very few congregations were willing to call a woman their pastor.

I said no to God's call then but I continued to be religious. When I got married, my husband embraced being spiritual, so I drifted away from church for Sunday coffee and dog walks with my spouse. Like many young adults, it wasn't until we had children (almost a dozen years later) that we starting seriously searching out a faith community together.

Instead of professional ministry, I became a professional communicator. I earned a Bachelor's Degree with interests in printing, reading and biology. One day in my junior year, I remember asking God "if not ministry, then what do I do with a love of printing, biology and reading?" I had one of those Biblical encounters walking across campus as a voice from somewhere said "company publications." Next thing I know, I'm on a career path of writing and publication production for corporate and non-profit organizations. It was exactly where I needed to be at the time.

I came to love church again and being within my faith community. I also saw God's grace solidly apparent in the world beyond the church doors. In those years away from church, I grew up and matured enough to realize that life wasn't just about academics, work achievements and then happily ever after. Life often included job loss, illnesses, relationship discord, relocations and the kids leaving home. Sometimes, these twists and turns on life's journey caused great suffering for many people.

It became apparent to me that dealing with life's garbage in the context of faith offered hope—like compost as a rich fertilizer for new growth in life.

I found this to be true in my own life. There were illnesses, serious accidents, a job loss and other difficult changes in my family including multiple miscarriages prior to having our two sons. There was also the pain of suicides and a murder in our circle of loved ones. However, in addition to the challenges, there were wonderful changes and great joy as well. I saw a lot of life—both the good and the bad. I found that life could be better (even when there was suffering) when it included something spiritual and lasting.

I realized that I was facing a life transition as I was approaching 40-years-old. The publications career had lost its appeal. One day when I was reading the church bulletin board, I found some information about a special counseling program at a local seminary. Immediately, the divine calling into pastoral ministry struck me—far stronger than the gentle curiosity from my teen years.

A couple weeks later, the trash truck slammed into me.

~

I picked up my younger son from preschool that day. It was a lovely spring day—and it was trash day. We were driving to the market winding our way down a local street that's often an obstacle course of parked cars. When we got to the traffic light behind several other cars we noticed there was a trash truck directly across the street backed into an apartment building lot. It just finished emptying the dumpster into its gapping back end. "He's only looking one way," I thought. Then I realized the driver was guiding his truck across the street directly toward my car!

I was right. Within a split second, there was the crunch of metal. My car was up against the curb with a big orange truck looming next to us and directly behind my son. It was slow motion bumper cars only we were the target. My son was calmer than me through it all. Fortunately, the director of his preschool drove up seconds later and took my tot to the park while I dealt with the car, truck and police. At first, I was cited at fault but a witness came out of nowhere to explain that the driver did not look both ways. It was not my fault. I am grateful to the person who came to my rescue. Not many people would do that.

The driver contested the citation and I was called to court as a witness. I got to the courthouse that summer morning with editing work in hand. I took a seat in the back so I could work while waiting. I had some quiet time until a young woman sat down next to me. Clearly something was upsetting her as she fidgeted in her chair. I asked her if she was okay. She wasn't. She was there as witness for a domestic violence case and already testified before. She was very upset by what she saw and about testifying. Then my case came up and I asked her if she was going to be okay. She said yes and thanked me for asking about her.

It took all of three minutes for my case to be heard. The driver was charged and had to pay my insurance deductible. I was given a slip and told to go to the bail bond clerk to collect my witness fee–a whopping $7 to cover my parking.

As I stepped up to the clerk, there were two young employees heading outside for a break to smoke. The clerk proceeded to tell me about her father who was dying of lung cancer from smoking. "*Oh my, that must be hard,*" I said as the clerk talked more about it while she processed my fee.

When I got into the elevator a man started telling me about how his day was going without my asking him. I was in the county courthouse for 45 minutes that morning and three strangers confided in me about the suffering (*the garbage*) of their lives. As I left the courthouse it struck me and I whispered to myself, *"Okay, I get it, God. This ministry thing is the way to go."* Soon thereafter, upon exiting the parking lot, I saw a sign on a nearby wall: *"Go this way"* So I did. I realized then that the crash and all that led up to it and all that followed it signified a turning point for me to change my career path. I became an ordained minister.

It was the right way to go.

Nancy followed all the signs to pastoral ministry by attending seminary and becoming ordained in the United Methodist Church. She has a specialty ministry in pastoral care and has served in both city and suburban churches. Reverend Turner is now appointed to a community ministry that she developed called Art & Soul in which engages people of various faith backgrounds, levels of health, ages and abilities in transformational art experiences to promote healing and to increase community connectedness. She lives with her husband of 27 years, Dr. Mark G. Turner (a rocket scientist, yes, really), two teenaged sons, Luke and Graham, and a Lab/Newfie mutt named Mariner. You can read about Nancy's ministry at www.nancygturner.wordpress.com.

Reflection Points

I began to have an idea of my life, not as the slow shaping of achievements to fit my preconceived purposes, but as the gradual discovery and growth of a purpose which I did not know.
— Marion Milner (pseudonym Joanna Field)

From the authors in their own words

- *I grew up and matured enough to realize that life wasn't just about academics, work achievements and then happily ever after.*
- *I could lose myself in marriage and children, in a tract home, in decorating and redecorating it, in cooking too well and in excessive sleep.*
- *I knew then that I wanted and needed to be part of something that was much bigger than me.*
- *I realize in this next adventure, I will be working with a new found spirit ready to apply lessons learned and to begin on a different path.*
- *In a way, I had found my calling but still did not know it yet.*
- *There are decision points in every difficult situation.*

Questions to contemplate while standing at the threshold of discovering your life's work

- *Was there a decision point that radically changed the path to your life's work?*
- *Have you found your life's work? What is your calling in life?*
- *Where does your passion lie? What causes you to feel excited, challenged, inspired?*
- *What adds meaning and purpose to your life (what, not who)?*
- *What will be your legacy?*

Part Four

Facing Unexpected Crises, Challenges and Trauma

You gain strength, courage and confidence by every experience in which you really stop to look fear in the face. You are able to say to yourself, 'I lived through this horror. I can take the next step that comes along.' You must do the thing you think you cannot do.

– Eleanor Roosevelt

~

CHAPTER 7

Abuse and Other Traumas

"Never give up, for that is just the place and time that the tide will turn."
— Harriet Beecher Stowe

Chances are, you know someone who is (or has been) in an abusive relationship or who has experienced an abusive event such as a sexual assault, dating violence or stalking. Perhaps this kind of abuse has happened (or is happening) to you. Sadly, violence against women is not a rare occurrence. Most women in the world will experience some type of abuse, often at the hands of someone they know or trust. In many cases, their spouse is the abuser. The statistics for American women and girls (reported from reliable sources such as the FBI Uniform Crime Report, the Surgeon General's Office, the American Medical Association, the National Institute on Justice and many others) are startling. They include:

- 1 in 3 women will experience childhood sexual abuse or a sexual assault in their lifetime.
- 1 in 4 women will be sexually assaulted while in college.
- 1 in 5 female high school students are physically or sexually abused by a dating partner.
- 1 in 3 women report being physically or sexually abused by a husband or a boyfriend.
- Among all female murder victims in the U.S., nearly one third are slain by their husbands or boyfriends.

In addition, the Surgeon General reports that domestic violence is the leading cause of injury to women between the ages of 15 and 44, more common than automobile accidents, muggings, and cancer deaths combined. Violence against women touches all of our lives in some way.

It is not surprising that a significant number of the essays submitted were about abuse, domestic violence or sexual victimization. As one of our courageous authors reminds us, *"The sad fact is that far too many women can imagine this waking nightmare because they actually live it or have lived it, like I did."* Vicki Lyn Trusley and several other women bravely share with us their personal and painful stories of abuse. More importantly, they also share their stories of survival. We are grateful and indebted to them for helping us to better understand these issues in hopes that we might be able to help one of our sisters, friends or loved ones.

That is exactly what Paula Andresen chose to do with her life in the aftermath of the horrific death of her niece at the hands of an abusive spouse. Paula tells a heart-wrenching account of how domestic violence came into her family's life without any warning when they learned that their young niece was violently murdered. *"To survive this nightmare, I had to stay focused on the positive as much as I could."* Paula found a way to cope by speaking out on behalf of her niece and against domestic violence. In fact, Paula was instrumental in having an important law passed in her state to increase the safety net for abuse victims.

Vicki Lyn Trusley also found a way to survive years of abuse and control by her husband. After she escaped from her husband, Vicki was able to relocate and to begin a new life. In her fresh start, Vicki discovered, *"Instead of shutting the door on my past or turning my back on my experiences, I decided to do something to help others who are going through similar situations."* Both Paula and Vicki found ways to cope in the aftermath of the trauma by helping others. This is a common and healing response for many survivors and family members.

There can be numerous challenges before getting to the point of leaving an abusive situation. Most significantly, there are concerns about safety and wellbeing. Sometimes women feel trapped in a relationship and fear for their lives or for their children's lives. Leaving can seem impossible, but there are options and support. No one ever deserves to be abused.

In addition to concerns about safety and wellbeing, there are also the psychological and spiritual aspects of healing and moving on. It is not uncommon for victims of abuse or trauma to have doubts about their faith or changes in their views about the world. Some victims will question what happened or blame themselves. In "Remembering Mary" the author talks about questioning her beliefs, *"I struggled with my faith and belief system that, up until now, had carried me through so much in life. How could God have allowed this to happen?"* Other women may find that their faith is renewed and strengthened.

Many victims will also experience a profound loss of control and powerlessness. In "Black Rock" Nancy Smith reflects on her sexual victimization at age 14, *"I am unable to stop what is happening."* Smith describes the night an older (college) man took an interest in her after a night of heavy drinking. *"Writing his name forty years later still makes me feel edgy and unsettled."* Like many victims, Smith was able to go on with her life, but some of the residuals of that night remain years later.

For other victims, the abuse continues even after the women have taken steps to move on. *"When I signed the divorce agreement, I thought I would finally have peace in my life,"* noted Vicki Lyn Trusley in "Ending the Waking Nightmare." She took all the steps to get away from her abusive husband and took all of the precautions, but he still came back. Vicki noted that eight years after their divorce, her ex-husband continued to harass, threaten and stalk her.

Rape, sexual abuse, domestic violence, dating violence and stalking are experiences that no one should ever endure. It is important for women who are victims of abuse to find support. The path of coping with any type of trauma is one that should not be taken alone. When Paula Andresen realized *"I was not alone on this journey after all,"* it made all the difference in her healing. Paula knew that she needed support to get through this difficult journey and thankfully she found many others who had been with her all along. Non-judgmental support can help victims of violence to do what they need to do to take care of themselves and their children.

Remembering Mary

by

Paula Andresen

In loving memory of
Mary Lynn Anderson Babb
June 4, 1976 – January 9, 2007
Whose courage and strength gave me the will to fight
and survive my grief;
and whose love and friendship inspired me to work
to make some good come from our tragedy.

~

I have long believed in the old adage: *God will never give you more than you and He can handle together.* We had been through a lot together over the years and my faith grew stronger with each of life's difficulties. Never had my faith been tested however, as it was with Mary's murder. Violence of all kinds was completely foreign to my world, even to my realm of thinking. It was something I had read about or watched on the news but never did it occur to me that it would ever touch my world.

Mary was my niece and the daughter I never had. She was also my friend. From the time she was a baby her smile melted my heart. Mary gave me true joy her entire life. As Mary grew older, our love and our relationship continued to grow and evolved into a deep friendship. Things seemed to be good for Mary and Tom (her husband) for about five or six years. During that time we were blessed with the arrival of their son Sam. Mary was meant to be a mother. She adored her son and worked hard to do the right thing for him. He was her life. It was wonderful to see her so happy and so fulfilled.

Things were not going well with them, but she never told me she was being abused. I had no idea. I now understand that she didn't want me to worry. On August 23, 2006, she grabbed Sam in his diaper and literally

ESCAPED from Tom. She fled to the nearest police station. The whole story eventually came out. That night was the start of my living nightmare and it has not gone away.

Mary spent the next three and half months doing everything that she was supposed to do. She filed charges against Tom, filed for divorce and she obtained a protection order. Slowly, things started to come back together for her, but she was still terrified of Tom and what he would do next. She lived in constant fear and terror—always looking over her shoulder and watching her rear view mirror. Throughout this ordeal, Mary stayed strong and never complained but I could see the fear in her eyes and the stress was taking its toll.

On January 9, 2007 Tom waited in the parking lot where Mary worked. He waited for her to leave the building and then he rammed her car with his truck until it overturned. He walked over to her car and shot out the window. As she hung upside down and helpless (suspended by her seatbelt) he shot her. All of this happened in broad daylight and in front of witnesses. He told her that if she ever left him, he would kill her. She had, and so he did.

My world ended that afternoon with Mary's murder. All that I knew and all that I believed was shattered into a million pieces. I had always been a busy person, always doing something. Now I sat and did nothing, absolutely nothing. I found myself enveloped in an insulating fog that I didn't want to leave.

Along with our loss of Mary, we also had to deal with the fact that since Tom murdered her, Sam would no longer have either parent. I struggled with my faith and belief system that, up until now, had carried me through so much in life. How could God have allowed this to happen? Why wasn't Mary alive and Tom dead? Why did my prayers for her go unanswered?

The legal process was also totally foreign to me. In the beginning I said that I was not ready to face any of it. I simply could not do it. As things progressed, the prosecutor said they needed the family there. I decided that if they needed me to be there, then I would be there. I wasn't sure how, but I would do it.

This was also the start of a journey of personal growth that I could never have imagined. I have always been a very private person, a loner by nature, and my emotions have always ruled. I really wasn't sure that I would be able to do any of this.

My first challenge was the preliminary hearing. The thought of spending an entire day facing Tom, listening to the details of Mary's murder, and hearing the defense trying to excuse Tom's actions was more than I could bear. I reached back to my yoga and meditation days and focused on my breathing to calm myself. It was a long day but I got through it. It was exhausting and draining but not nearly as impossible as I had imagined. This was the first step for me to push myself to another level–a place where I was not comfortable or familiar, a place where I didn't want to go and where I didn't think I was able to go. I surprised myself and learned that I could. I could do what I needed to do.

Next came the three weeks of trial and my subpoena from the prosecution. The thought of listening to the defense trash Mary made me physically ill. When I considered the cross-examination by the defense, I worried I would either fall apart or fail miserably. Somehow, I had to get through my testimony. I had to do this for Mary.

I'm really not sure when the enveloping fog started to dissipate, but it must have been around this time. That was when I realized that my basic spiritual foundation was still there. It finally dawned on me that if God brought me to this, He would certainly see me through it. I still didn't want to do it, but I would. I knew that I could get through it. The trial was then postponed from June until October—typical legal game playing. Just before the October trial was to start, Tom pled "*No Contest*" to second degree murder (a plea he would later try to withdraw).

My next challenge was my Victim's Impact Statement. This is a chance to have your say to the judge before he pronounces his sentence. I have never been good at public speaking. It is another of those things that the thought of actually makes me ill. I knew I could put the words together; I just wasn't so sure about the delivery. I contacted my niece for backup, in case I fell apart. Once again, I faced my fears, I faced Tom and I did it in a room full of strangers with TV cameras rolling. I had my say. I did what I believed was right. Once again I was completely drained and exhausted, but at the same time I felt a sense of peace and satisfaction.

The original domestic violence charges were a part of the plea bargain package, so there really wasn't any point in making a statement at the hearing that followed a week later. It was basically just a formality. However, Tom's total lack of remorse convinced me that someone needed to speak on Mary's behalf—even if it wasn't going to make a difference legally. Someone needed to speak out about domestic violence and about Tom's actions.

I did it for Mary but I was slowly realizing that there was more to it. Mary's murder caught me completely unaware. I was totally ignorant about domestic violence. Someone needed to speak out and help inform people and to help them to heed the warning signs. With trembling hands and cracking voice, I once again got up to speak to the judge and once again, I got through it.

I agreed to do an interview with a television reporter who had also covered the murder sentencing, because I wanted to educate more people about domestic violence. We had the media's attention and now we wanted to get the word out to alert others to the warning signs that we had missed. Our interview evolved into an in-depth segment. One of Mary's friends from work and the director of the local women's shelter also participated. The reporter put together a wonderful piece on domestic violence awareness and it aired on January 9, 2008—the one year anniversary of Mary's murder.

Shortly after Mary's murder, Representative Bill Caul of Mt. Pleasant introduced legislation for Global Positioning System (GPS) tracking that could have prevented our tragedy. If this was a condition of Tom's bail, Mary would have known that Tom was waiting in her work parking lot that day. She could have called for help rather than walking blindly into his trap. Representative Caul asked the family for permission to call the bill, Mary's Law.

I was asked if I would testify at the House Judiciary Committee Hearings for Mary's Law. I agreed to do it. I was now on a mission. The day came for the hearings and once again I focused on my breathing, calming myself and silently chanting my mantra: *If God brings you to it, He will see you through it.* I had to remind myself to breathe a couple of times and I'm sure I must have gasped in the process but I continued.

The chairman and committee could not have been more kind, and they took their vote while we waited. It passed unanimously, as it did all the way through the House and Senate. Governor Granholm signed House Bill 4453 into law July 10, 2008. Mary's Law was now a reality. The 2-1/2 hour drive home was in silence with only my thoughts as my company. For me, it was as though I had just climbed Mt. Everest.

I always believed that you have choices in life and the most important choice you make is how you choose to perceive and then deal with what life sends your way. You can stay immersed in the past and the negative or you can struggle to find the positive and try to move forward. To survive this nightmare, I had to stay focused on the positive as much as I could. It certainly was not easy. I had a choice, though: I could dwell on my loss and devastation or I could stay focused on all of the joy and blessings that Mary gave me in her thirty years that we shared; I could give in to the devastation of my loss or fight to make some good from the love that we shared.

One of the things that helped me through this nightmare is a little project for Sam called *The Sammy Project*. I have collected over thirty years of photos and memories of Mary that I will share with Sam. Friends also saved newspaper articles of Mary's murder and Tom's subsequent legal proceedings. I want Sam to know how much his mother was loved and I want him to know, from an unbiased source, what his father did.

I also have my writing. I have been writing about surviving and making some sense of this totally senseless situation with the hope of healing and moving forward. I know that Sam will have his own battles to face. I want him to know that we can find ways to survive and to move forward.

My little project for Sammy is going a step further. It was opened up to everyone who loved Mary and struggled with her death. This has been another huge step in the process of my healing and moving forward. It helped me to realize the precious gift of Mary's friends. God brought them into my life to help fill the huge void left by her death—in my life and in my heart. I was not alone on this journey after all.

Mary's friends from work started fund-raising for Sam after Mary's murder. The outpouring of love and support from the community was tremendous and helped to restore my faith in humanity. I realize now that the good do outnumber the bad. Mary's friend Beth, the driving force behind so much of these efforts, took things to another level. With the help of her daughters and co-workers they started *Mary's Dream – Living Without Fear!* Mary's Dream is a non-profit organization dedicated to helping raise funds and awareness for the agencies that were there for Mary when she needed help.

The old adage, "*everything in its own time*" comes back to me time and time again. That first year really was a nightmare and it was a very slow and arduous process to try to emerge from my grief. The second year was a little easier, but rebuilding my life and my faith was not easy.

I had traveled life's journey as somewhat of a loner and my spiritual path led me inward with the help of some wonderful books and various spiritual leaders along the way. Paramahansa Yogananda, the Dalai Lama, and a very down to earth and caring Catholic priest kept crossing my path.

About halfway through the second year I sensed that I needed to move forward. I could finally take another step forward in the process and in the direction of my spiritual journey. After the second anniversary of Mary's murder, I can say that I am finally in a much better place right now. Life will never be the same as it was when Mary was alive. I am on a new road now and I am at peace with that. I still continue to give thanks and pray every day.

With Mary's murder, the road I was on took an abrupt turn and I lost my peace. This new road led me on a journey that enabled me to share my story and my pain in the hopes of enlightening others about domestic violence and the peace you can find when you connect with God. I have learned that God is there if you want Him to be there for you. My new favorite adage is:

God does not give us what we can handle, He helps us to handle what we are given. (author unknown)

Paula is 55 years old, happily married for over twenty years and a bookkeeper by trade. She is "still an old hippie at heart" trying to live life to the fullest and to find positive energy to hold on to. She has a strong connection with nature and usually finds her peace in nature and enjoying each day.

Update from the author: Since Mary's murder I have struggled to find my balance and peace again. I have re-evaluated every thing that I thought I knew and believed in. I learned a lot about myself in the process and have emerged a stronger person. I am now more comfortable with who I am—more than ever before. The voices and intuitions that guide me have led me to my current journey, which is to share our story to educate others and hopefully to spare someone else from this nightmare. I want to help people to be aware of the warning signs of domestic violence, to know that help and support are available and not to be ashamed or afraid to seek it. I believe that Mary is one of my guiding voices on this journey. I am doing this in her memory so that her death will not be in vain.

Ending the Waking Nightmare

by Vicki Lyn Trusley

~

Imagine waking up every day terrified and wondering if today is one of the days that you will be beaten up.

Imagine being afraid to fall asleep because you don't know what hell the night might bring.

Imagine trying simply to function—working and taking care of your family—on only two hours of sleep at night.

The sad fact is that far too many women can imagine this waking nightmare because they actually live it or have lived it, like I did.

I was married to an abusive man for fifteen years. We have two children together: a daughter and a son. The abuse began when my youngest child was born. My son had medical problems which required extra attention and time. I worked full time in addition to caring for him and our two-year-old daughter.

My husband became jealous when I did not have the time or energy for him. Instead of helping me with the responsibilities with the children or the household, he became more demanding of my time. When I didn't fulfill his demands, he would hurt me both physically and emotionally. He constantly told me I couldn't do anything right. He told me I was a lousy wife and a bad mother. He would say anything to tear down my self worth and my self esteem.

He also became extremely controlling of my actions and my schedule. I would do the grocery shopping with the children on Saturdays while he was at work. He demanded that I call him before we left the house (there were no cell phones back then) and call him again when we returned home. If he thought we were gone too long, he questioned me as to where else we went. If he wasn't satisfied with my answers, I would pay the consequences.

He was a security guard and he worked an erratic schedule. He expected me to have a full meal prepared for him when he came home from work even it if was midnight.

Every victim of domestic violence has her breaking point—the point where she knows she cannot take it anymore. My breaking point came the day my husband hit my son. I called the police and kicked my husband out of the house. I filed for divorce and obtained a restraining order. When I signed the divorce agreement, I thought that I would finally have peace in my life. I was completely wrong. After the marriage was legally over, I entered into a new, eight year nightmare when my ex-husband began stalking me.

He followed me to work and waited outside my house when I came home from work. He flattened my tires during the night. He called me constantly throughout the night and came into my house during the day when my children and I were gone, purposefully leaving signs that he had been there.

One night, I awoke with an uneasy feeling that someone was in my room. There in the darkness was my ex-husband. He did not say a word. He just stood there looking at me. He did not know that I had started sleeping with a baseball bat next to me in the bed. I raised the bat without saying a word. He turned around very slowly, went downstairs and out the front door. I jumped up and checked on my children who were, thankfully, fast asleep. I eventually sold my house because I did not feel safe there.

The stalking escalated until he was eventually arrested and put into prison. The final incident happened when he called me at 6:30 on a Sunday morning and left a message that he was going to kill me. He told me that I could choose the method—he could shoot me, stab me or burn my house down. He told me to call him back and let him know which method I preferred. The next day he was waiting for me at my workplace. The police were called and he was arrested. He served two years in prison for telephone harassment.

What I have written here represents just a small part of my ordeal with my abuser. This is what many women go through every day. My children and I were lucky: We survived. Many women do not live to tell their stories and many children lose their mothers to domestic violence at the hands of their fathers.

There are many reasons that postpone or prevent a woman from leaving an abusive situation including family and religious pressures and financial worries. In addition, many women believe (because their abuser has told them so) that if they leave they will face severe hardship and further retribution. Sadly, fear for the safety of her children and herself can cause a woman *not* to leave an abusive situation. Most deaths attributed to domestic violence occur *after* the victim leaves—or tries to leave.

Instead of shutting the door on my past or turning my back on my experiences, I decided to do something to help others who are going through similar situations. I am in the early stages of creating *NULIFE Residential Center, Inc.*, a nonprofit, long-term residential center for victims of domestic violence and their children. Victims of domestic violence need a safe place to stay and to learn independent living skills while putting their lives back together.

Vicki is the mother of two children and grandmother of one 2-year-old granddaughter. She volunteers as a Guardian ad Litem assisting others in the court system. In 2001, Vicki relocated to another city. She earned her Masters degree in Public Administration and later retired in 2006. Her ex-husband passed away in 2007.

Black Rock

by Nancy Smith

dedicated to Genie Zeiger

Reflections from Women Writing Contest Selection

In the car, my daughter Emma asks me, *"Will it always be this way? Will I always be so wild about boys?"* My twenty-year-old daughter and I are so alike, and I tell her this. I was crazy about boys too in my youth—seduced by the combination of testosterone mixing with pheromones making a juice of desire, with its absence of thought or logic and blindness to the consequences.

At fourteen, I found a boy to flirt with—outrageously. He was eighteen years old and home from college for the summer. His name was Jeff. Writing his name forty years later still makes me feel edgy and unsettled.

It was 1970 and a summer of parties. My family lived miles outside the center of our small village. On the weekends, my parents would drop me off at Sarah's house, my best friend and a "townie." They knew I would sleep over there. They assumed things would be safe since Sarah was so smart and her parents were well mannered and caring.

Come early evening, Sarah and I would set out on foot to the high school at the heart of town. Everyone met at the stone wall which lined the massive front lawn. We congregated there until the news of a party's location surfaced and spread. Our migration to the gathering was like grey smoke caught up in a breeze or, as on this night, like lambs to the slaughter. Once the meeting place was known, we would prepare for our arrival. We would hang out by Rizzo's Liquor Store. It was easy to approach slightly older kids and ask them to "buy" for us since the drinking age in New York was still eighteen. We would get cheap vodka, Boone's Farm Apple wine, Mateus Rosé— whatever the night called for.

This night it was a fifth of Smirnoff's and a can of Sunkist frozen orange juice. We went into the woods with our stash, ripped off the top of the juice container, took a lick of its frozen concentration, a swig of vodka—and voila! We had a backwoods screwdriver! We did this until we were ripe for partying, then we buoyantly swayed our way back to the road to hitch a ride to Oak Ridge Lane. Everyone hitched in those days. There were no perverts out there waiting to kidnap you or do terrible things to you.

We arrived at the party with our wheels already greased. Then I caught sight of Jeff. I'd seen him at other parties that summer: Tall, lean, blond, blue-eyed, a college man of confidence and sophistication, dressed in a cream T-shirt, cut off jeans and flip flops; the feathering of light hair on his muscular calves was an immediate turn on. He was talking with a group of people, some I knew, some I didn't. It was a big party and there were overflowing coolers of beer behind the house—Schlitz, Miller and Budweiser.

Eventually I found my way to a lounge chair near Jeff. I teased, I smiled, I laughed. I made no secret of my interest. However, being fourteen, I did not fully understand what consequences my actions might set into motion. I knew I was exuding sexuality. I wanted to let desire out, to meet it and to discover it. As the evening wore down, the pairings began. Jeff chose me and Peter chose Sarah. Jeff had a car, so the four of us went to Black Rock, a local swimming area on a stretch of river that ran though a remote wooded part of town.

At Black Rock, the night is as black as the swimming hole's name. We decide to go skinny dipping, me, Jeff, Sarah and Peter. I am swimming, oblivious to the others leaping from rocks, and thrilled with the feeling of water on my naked body. As I climb out of the river to jump from yet another rock, I feel something sharp and painful on my right big toe: I cut my toe on broken glass and it's bleeding. Jeff comes over, attentive and concerned, to examine the gash. We see that it will heal quickly.

Then I realize that Sarah and Peter are no longer with us. The beach is empty. Jeff kisses me. I'm drunk and I have never been completely naked with a boy. When our skin touches, it's electric. We kiss, we caress, his erection is fascinating, frightening.

Suddenly I realize that I am in a place I did not intend. I am in over my head and I don't know what to do. I feel Jeff firmly take my hand and lead me over to the left side of the beach where there are less river stones and more soft sand. He kneels down and lays his shirt and cut-offs on the beach as a makeshift blanket. I silently watch and then understand that this is where he wants me to lie.

He beckons me to this "bed" with a gesture, a few light pats on his flattened shorts, leaving my mouth dry. I obey and take my place on the clothing, prone, like a corpse. I leave my body. I am unable to stop what is happening. I am so vacant and limp that it is Jeff who arranges my legs so that he can be on top of me. I comply, empty, abruptly sober and mute. He tries to penetrate me, but I am a virgin— tight, dry and no longer open and available. After a few painful thrusts, Jeff roles off me frustrated, disgusted. We dress in silence.

The sky is black and starless. As we are about to walk down the wooded, quarter mile trail to the car, I meekly ask, *"Will I get pregnant?"* My naiveté exasperates him and he responds with a dismissive expulsion of air from his lips. I don't know what this means but I don't ask either. We continue to make our way wordlessly, hastily, back to the car with me trailing a few steps behind him. Sarah is there with Peter. She confided to me later that she was able to say no to Peter and they waited there awkwardly for our return.

We climb into the brown Valiant and Jeff drives us to Sarah's house. I don't recall any conversation on the way back. What I do remember is a feeling of shock and a closing down of something that had been so open, so fun, so innocent and so basic to my nature.

I wait for weeks for my period. It does not come. With the help of my friend Patty, we make phone calls to find out about abortions. Luckily the shame of the night was punishment enough: I finally got my period. I realized later that I was so overcome with anxiety, partly due to my lack of understanding the basics of sex, that I had scared myself right out of my period. In later years, I learned from a doctor that extreme stress can affect a woman's body in this way.

It's been many years since that night. I find myself watching over my daughter, observing how she enjoys her body and all the breathtaking sensations it brings her. I have tried to support her delight in the discovery of her body as well as the appropriate giving of her body, but I have also tried to gently rein in that sexual energy. I share with Emma some of the conversations I had with my friends about our sexual experiences. I am hopeful that I might guide her to make better decisions than I did in adolescence.

Eventually, I did share the happenings at Black Rock with my own mother. Three years after that regrettable and confusing night, I was prompted in my 11th grade English class to write an essay on a significant event in my life. For some reason, I chose to reveal the details of that summer evening. I had a teacher I loved and trusted, so I aired my humiliation through the written word. A few nights later, while my mother was getting ready for bed, I joined her in her bathroom. Pale green tiles lined the walls, and the window by the sink was slightly cracked, letting in the evening air. As she washed her face, I sat on the toilet and calmly read my essay to her. When I was done, she turned to me with red, glistening eyes, her face absent of color, her fingers spread over both of her blanched cheeks as she whispered, *"I wanted to be there for you when it happened."* I did not answer her. I knew I couldn't have let anyone be there for me that night, not even myself.

The only time I saw Jeff again was at the Grand Union, a small, local grocery store in our town. It was now my turn to be home visiting from college. My mother gave me a grocery list for the upcoming week's stay. I was maneuvering my half full cart around a corner when I saw Jeff. I froze. He was standing sideways to me about halfway down the aisle talking to a woman. I don't recall what he was wearing. I don't know who the woman was. I don't remember what I was looking for because the present abruptly vanished. Instantly I was back at the river, my emotions swirling like dark, fetid water. My knees buckled and gave way beneath me. Had I not been holding the cart, I would have dropped to the ground like a heavy stone in a night river. I felt bile rising in my throat.

Then hurriedly, using panic's strength and leverage, I pivoted the cart and rushed back around the corner, careening down the cereal aisle heading toward the checkout counter. It didn't matter that I had not finished shopping. I needed to get out of that store immediately and invisibly.

As I drove back to my childhood home, trying to calm the pounding in my chest, I kept asking myself—as I continue to do to this day—does the inability to say *"no"* discount the actuality of being raped?

Nancy Smith lives in the hills of Western Massachusetts. Formerly a teacher of young children with special needs, Nancy's new passion is writing. She participates in two weekly writing workshops, has had a few short essays published and when time allows, pinches pots to classical music in her clay studio. Nancy has three grown children, two fat Labradors and one wonderful husband.

Update from the author: Writing this piece, almost forty years after the fact, helped me to understand what actually took place that night. The event had been a dark, multi-layered burden in the center of my chest. By giving it voice, I have been able to begin healing an old wound.

Reflection Points

The period of greatest gain in knowledge and experience
is the most difficult period in one's life. ...
Through a difficult period, you can learn,
you can develop inner strength,
determination, and courage to face the problem.
— The Dalai Lama

From the authors in their own words

- *I learned that I could. I could do what I needed to do...Once again, I faced my fears.*
- *By giving it voice, I have been able to begin healing an old wound.*
- *We can find ways to survive and to move forward.*
- *I always believed that you have choices in life and the most important choice you make is how you choose to perceive and then deal with what life sends your way.*

Questions to contemplate while standing at the threshold of an abusive relationship or other abusive events

- *What is a happy and healthy partnership/marriage/relationship to you? Is the relationship that you are in right now both happy and healthy?*
- *What are your instincts telling you about this situation?*
- *What is your breaking point (as Vicki referenced in her essay)?*
- *Who do you turn to for non-judgmental support? If you do not have anyone in your life right now that you can talk to about the abuse, find a counselor or call a crisis line. You do not have to deal with this alone.*

~

CHAPTER 8

Addiction and Loss

I've learned that no matter what happens, or how bad it seems today, life does go on, and it will be better tomorrow.
— Maya Angelou

If you love someone with an addiction (or you personally have an addiction) you know just how painful and destructive it can be for all involved. This is a difficult journey no matter where it begins.

Addictions can present themselves in many ways: alcohol, illegal drugs, prescription medications, gambling, sex and even food can be the culprit for some individuals. There are other sources as well, including pornography and the Internet. It is becoming more widespread in our culture and women are not immune to these illnesses.

In this chapter, two women wrote openly about their own experiences with addiction and loss. They offer two different sides to this devastating problem: one from a mother whose son had a history of drug abuse and dependency; the other from a woman who faced her own demons with alcoholism. Both experienced significant suffering. Both offer us some important lessons about moving forward, no matter how fearful the struggle or formidable the emotional pain.

Mary Martha Christianson shares the heartbreaking story of her son's addiction and his difficult life journey in the essay, "David and Mom." She reflected, *"He lived between the heaven of his hopes and the hell of his addiction...He did not understand that happiness is not having what you want, but wanting what you have."* But Mary remained hopeful that David would pull through. She saw him through many attempts at treatment and she saw him the week before he had an overdose. Mary's story reminds us of how drug addiction can permeate any family and how incredibly difficult it is to conquer an addiction or to stand by when a loved one is hurting in this way.

Maryellen Grady tells us about the pain of her own addiction in the essay, "Transformation." Maryellen speaks out honestly about her struggles with alcoholism. *"I could see now that I didn't have much longer if I remained on the self-destructive path that I was on."* For Maryellen, it took a crisis and a tragedy for her to have a wake-up call to sobriety. Maryellen's life was turned upside down, but events that followed allowed her to realize, *"Finally, I wanted to be clean and sober for me...I surprised myself by proving that I was worthy of self-love."*

Mary Martha Christianson learned something similar about her son before his untimely death. She recalls, *"He was a handsome little boy and even more handsome as a man. He was talented, athletic and creative. But David never felt confident about himself."* Like many others who become addicted, both David and Maryellen were unsure about themselves in some way. When Maryellen discovered that she was worthy and deserving, she was able to find the confidence to fight her addiction by loving herself first. As David's mom recalled, *"He always expected too much of himself and of others."*

There are many paths that lead into addiction. For some individuals it might be rooted in feelings of inadequacy or uncertainty, or of fear, ambivalence, anxiety or depression. For others, it's a matter of biology or family history. These essays provide us with some insight about addiction and a glimpse into the lives of these two women and their personal experiences. Their stories could be anyone's story. If we look closely we'll discover that addiction is another one of those common ground issues—it touches all families, in one way or another. We thank these two women for their courage in sharing their journey with us.

David and Mom

by Mary Martha Christianson

I would like to dedicate this to David:
Friend, Brother, Son, Lover, Designer, Dude

~

I got the call on a Friday afternoon from a Washington D.C. detective, telling me in a very gentle way that David's body had been found. I did not want to believe what the detective was telling me. David had just called me the day before; not for money or for any kind of help, but just to say *"hi."* A week earlier he'd taken me out to dinner for my birthday. He was doing better.

That was the last time I ever saw him.

It can't be David! I still find it hard, knowing that he was alone at the time.

~

David was in a kind of limbo. His anger at not being able to overcome his addiction, like his anger at not being able to "just have a beer like normal people," kept getting in his way. He lived between the heaven of his hopes and the hell of his addiction. I know that now; I did not want to believe it then.

David was my middle child with an older brother and a younger sister. He was a handsome little boy and even more handsome as a man. He was talented, athletic and creative. He loved the outdoors. But David never felt confident about himself. I was also shy as a young girl, so I thought I understood how David saw the world.

David's life was that of a normal child his age until he was in junior high school. He had a best friend, played sports and teased his sister. Then, he was suspended from school when marijuana was found in his locker.

At the time, I was involved in a divorce and in graduate school. I took him with me to my school for ten days. We talked a lot. He was upset about our family and what was happening to it. I was not very stable myself during that time period. David and his sister moved with me while their brother went to boarding school. I didn't realize what was happening to David. He spent more and more of his time with friends that I didn't know. I am sure that he lied to me often.

Then, I had a chance to move to Alaska. David loved this new world. He still drank and got drunk but it didn't seem to be due to depression or frustration. I would help him out when he got into fights or got a DUI. I knew, even then, that I should not have done so, but I felt so guilty. I felt like it was my fault. I wanted to show him that I cared.

As the years went by, David got his Masters degree in Fine Arts and worked in his chosen field of Set Design. He was also a sailor and salmon fisherman. He became an associate professor and got married. But there were more and more incidents of drug and alcohol abuse. He would call me asking for money. He told me he would pay me back. He began to lose jobs, but he always found others. I would receive letters from him telling me that he loved me. His wife told him that she would leave him if he did not clean up his act, and eventually she did.

David began to go in and out of rehab programs. Usually, after two months, he would leave because he was certain that he was cured. I always wanted to believe that. In between programs, David stayed with me or with his father. He finally found a rehab he could stick with, and he stayed in that city to work and to live with a new girlfriend. After a year, I felt that maybe, just maybe, good things were going to get better. David also felt that way.

I know that David wanted desperately to be happy, but he did not understand that happiness is not having what you want, but rather wanting what you have. He was a perfectionist. He always expected too much of himself and of others. He also hated knowing how much the people who loved him wanted him to change. So he would lie to us, telling us he was ok. He wanted us to believe him and to deny the truth. I did tell him once that he was killing himself. He said he knew, but he couldn't stop himself.

It has been seven years since David died. I am finally able to not feel so much guilt. I used to go through all the "what ifs" almost daily. "*What should I have done differently?*" I probably should have used what is called "tough love" more often. But he was a prodigal son. I always welcomed him and helped him out. I must admit that after his death it was a relief not to get the phone calls asking for more money or telling me he was in some kind of trouble.

We had a memorial service for David in the mountains that he loved. All of his family and friends were there. There was a beauty of remembrance in the air. There is still. My grandchildren talk about their Uncle David. His brother named their new little son for David. His ashes are strewn in all the places that he loved. I think David would have been very happy.

I throw him a kiss as I pass his picture on the wall, but…

I miss my David.

Mary Martha Christianson was born and raised in St. Louis Missouri. She has lived in Seattle, England, Alaska and various other places. Most of her career has been with non-profit agencies in the field of human services and family therapy. She presently lives on Folly Creek on the Eastern Shore of Virginia with her husband, cats, dog and visiting children and grandchildren,

Update from the author: David died in 2002. Until I wrote this essay, I found it was very difficult for me to speak of him. Writing about him has made it easier to talk about him.

Transformation

by Maryellen Grady

I dedicate this life story to the memory of George M. Hunt who made it possible. George, I love you forever and will never forget you. And to my children, Sonja and Eric Bugvilionis whom I love more than life.

I sat waiting in my Fort Lauderdale apartment. It was hard not to get up and pace. I was waiting for George to return from Toledo after three months. He'd gone to take a contractual job in his field of psychology. Now he was coming back to get me and we would finally be married. I was excited and I was scared.

Could we really cut it? I wondered. He hated my drinking. Even as I waited for him to come home, I wasn't able to keep from drinking. I had a bottle of mouthwash handy so I could get to it quickly when I heard his wheels hit the driveway. *Didn't he know how bad my drinking really was?* After all, alcoholism was his area of expertise in psychology. *Did he just love me too much to see it clearly?*

It was getting late. I thought he said he would be home before now. *What was keeping him?* I re-lit some of the candles I had set out for a little romantic ambiance.

I went to look in the mirror again to be sure I looked okay. I was 28 years old and starting to look haggard around the edges. Then I had a few sips from the bottle that I was hiding in the bathroom.

By 11:00 p.m., I wondered why he hadn't called. Now I was starting to pace. There was a queasy feeling in my stomach and I couldn't relax. Something was wrong. I just knew something was wrong.

I hated to do it but I went over to the neighbor's house to see if he'd heard anything. He was a good friend of George's and sometimes he had lines of communication that I wasn't privy to. He didn't much like me, so I wasn't looking forward to going over there.

Fortunately, Stan was still up. *"I just wondered if you had heard anything from George,"* I started.

"His sister called me a couple of hours ago. He and Noel went boating on a lake there in Jackson, a storm came up and now they're missing."

I wanted to ask why he didn't come over to tell me but it was obvious that it was because he couldn't stand me. He was a recovering alcoholic and he knew how much I was drinking while George was away. Stan felt I wasn't good enough for George, pure and simple.

"I want to go up there, Stan," I said after a long period of silence.

"I'm waiting to talk to Earl. Maybe we'll be going up tomorrow." Earl was another good friend of George's. There was no invitation to ride along with them.

"Well I sure would appreciate a ride if you go," I begged.

He wouldn't look at me. *"We'll see."*

I left and went straight to the convenience store. I would need more beer to get through this night. It was a shame and a pity, but it was just the way it was.

I got out a rosary that a lady at work had given me when she discovered what a lost soul I was. She told me it was blessed by the pope. I didn't try to say the prayers since I had forgotten them, so I just hung on to the rosary all night for comfort.

The next morning Earl surprised me by knocking on my door to invite me to go to Jackson, Mississippi with him and Stan. I was very grateful and told him so. Earl was also a recovering alcoholic, but he had more sober time than Stan and didn't seem to judge me quite as harshly.

I threw a few things in a suitcase and walked over to Stan's house. I sat in the back seat and tried to make myself inconspicuous. I didn't want to fall apart in front of them. I didn't deserve their sympathy or even their empathy. I had let George down these past few years. *"Please God, let me have a chance to make it up to him,"* I prayed.

When we got to Jackson, there were other friends there along with George's parents and the rest of his family. They claimed they loved me, but I always felt that they could see through me and saw me for what I really was: a drunk, a loser, and not worthy of their son.

George's father was a Methodist minister. He was heartbroken, but remained calm and soothing to the others. His beautiful mother showed concern for me. *Why did they have to be such wonderful people?* I was so ashamed to have them see me that way.

One of George's friends put out a bottle of whiskey and I didn't wait for an invitation. After a few rounds, we decided to go out to the woods surrounding the lake to look for the boys. I called George's name until I was hoarse. My mind wouldn't let me think that I was wasting my energy. It had been 24 hours.

We went back to the house and drank some more. His parents and sisters were busy praying. The next day it was the same thing. The day after that when I called out his name I sensed the futility of my actions. He was gone and I knew it. On the afternoon of the third day, they finally found their two bodies.

That's when I broke down and sobbed. I called my mother so I would have someone to comfort me. I couldn't expect these wounded people to have anything to give me when they were so hurt themselves.

Someone put out the whiskey bottle again, but for the first time that I could remember I didn't want to drink. I wanted to prove to George that I was worthy of his love, that he didn't just waste years of his life loving me. I asked God for help; I knew I couldn't do it alone. I knew it would take me some time to do this, but all I had left was time.

I wanted to straighten up and fly right to prove to George that I had been worth the trouble. Alternatively, I thought that I could just go wander off and let death have its way with me. I could see now that I didn't have much longer if I remained on my self-destructive path. I prayed, "*God, help me stay clean and sober. God help me prove that I was worth loving.*"

The morning of the memorial service dawned bright and clear. I felt brand new. The mother of the other man who drowned came up to me and said, "*Girl, what has happened to you? I almost didn't recognize you. You're not the same person you were when you first got here a few days ago.*"

I said, "*I know I'm not. God has worked a miracle in my life.*"

I felt good that my change was already showing on the outside.

After the memorial service, I went toward the parking lot to wait for the others. As I stood there in the parking lot alone, I swear I saw the George and his friend walking happily over a hill, looking like they didn't have a care in the world. They were smiling and laughing. They seemed not to see me and I didn't call to them. They were on the other side. As they faded away, a yellow butterfly flew in very close to me. It hovered near me for the longest time.

It reminded me of a book I'd read which said that the Chinese believe that the soul reincarnates as a butterfly. For the next few years, it seemed that whenever the pain of missing George would come over me, a yellow butterfly would appear. It renewed my faith every time.

I didn't know it then, but I was on my way to a long sober life. One day at a time, I continued to show George I was worthy of his love. Then, I surprised myself by proving that I was worthy of self-love. Finally, I wanted to be clean and sober for me.

Update from the author: I have continued to live a life that I can be proud of (and George would be proud of too). I eventually married and today I have a daughter, 23, and a son, 19. They are the joys of my life. I am a successful freelance writer and feel so blessed to work at something that is my bliss.

Reflection Points

Even the strongest have their moments of fatigue.
— Frederick Nietzsche

<u>From the authors in their words</u>

- *He was killing himself. He said he knew, but he couldn't stop himself.*
- *I used to go through all the "what ifs" almost daily. "What should I have done differently?"*
- *I thought that I could just go wander off and let death have its way with me.*
- *I asked God for help; I knew I couldn't do it alone.*

<u>Questions to contemplate at the threshold of addiction and loss</u>

- *What insights do you take with you from either of these women's stories?*
- *If you take an honest look into your life, are you facing an addiction or loving someone with an addiction?*
- *How has addiction affected you and your life? What losses have you already experienced because of addiction? What are the losses ahead if the addiction continues?*
- *What can you do to take one step forward toward your own healing?*

Part Five

Coping with Illness, Healing and Loss

(It is)...an "in-between" zone,
a state in which we are neither who we used to be,
nor who we are becoming.
It's like standing in a doorway, or being in a passageway,
or even in a long, dark tunnel, between two phases of our lives.
–Jean Shinoda Bolan

CHAPTER 9

Facing the Diagnosis and Treatment

Yesterday is gone.
Tomorrow has not yet come.
We have only today. Let us begin.
— Mother Teresa

"I have become more acutely aware of what we all face–tomorrow is not a promise," author Katie Ford Hall reflects on her unexpected diagnosis of breast cancer. *"At age 41 and without any family history of breast cancer, I never saw this coming."* At the time she was diagnosed, Katie's children were 6 and 8 years old and she was at a happy point in her life. She was about to face a challenge that she had never anticipated.

Receiving an unexpected, serious medical diagnosis is often a significant turning point in women's lives. If you receive such a diagnosis, a new chapter of your life will quickly begin as you learn to accept the illness which has come uninvited into your body. Along with the diagnosis many questions will surely follow:

Why me? How can I get through this? What is the best treatment? Can I afford it? What can I do to change the course of this illness? Should I get a second opinion? How will my family cope with this news?

Likewise, there are a wide range of feelings that come with an unexpected diagnosis or chronic illness: denial, shock, fear, frustration, anger, despair, determination, hope and much more. These are all very normal reactions to the uncertainty and they are all normal reactions to a situation that has turned your world upside down.

The women in this chapter share their journeys of receiving and facing a significant medical diagnosis. In the first essay, "This Story has a Happy Ending" author Carol Kabakoff takes us on the path of her breast cancer diagnosis. Carol uses her humor to cope as she describes some of the horrendous and challenging procedures that women endure just to get a diagnosis. Beneath her humor, however, are fear and uncertainty: *"As I wait for the results, I can't help but speculate about what the news will be and how I will react."* The process from the initial mammography to diagnosis is rife with ample time to speculate. Many women will relate to Carol's story and appreciate her good-humored approach to a very stressful situation.

The ways in which women respond to their diagnoses are diverse but not so different from each other. Women often have an intuition or a sense that something is not right in their bodies. Initial reactions for some women include ignoring or minimizing their concerns. *Maybe it will go away. If I just wait awhile, I'm sure I'll be fine.* In this initial awareness, women may delay getting a medical opinion. When a physician is consulted, the diagnostic process that follows can often be frustrating and anxiety-producing.

Once the diagnosis is confirmed, it can also be a challenging and confusing time with many questions and uncertainties. *"Deep down inside this wasn't making sense to me,"* noted Janice Moszynski in her essay "Journey into Light." She went on, *"The doctor's prognosis was not good and their recommendations for treatment were few."* Janice was told she had lung cancer at age 50. *"I felt like I was just beginning to fully live my life."* Janice knew she had to find a way to accept her diagnosis and face it head on with all the energy she could muster.

Katie Ford Hall was also confronted with a diagnosis of breast cancer and initially struggled with how to move forward. *"Cancer patients are under an immense amount of pressure to live each day to the fullest."* In her essay "Resurfacing," she learned that *"It was time to listen to my own voice."* Katie found a healing path to peace through her connection with others and her writing. Other women indicated that writing was a powerful and important part of their healing journeys as well, whether it was a personal journal, a blog, a website, poems or an essay for this book! Writing is a way to accept what is in front of us and to process the uncertain journey with others.

In "Taming the Monster," Linda Tefend writes about her healing process after learning that she has a chronic and painful illness. *"I felt ungrounded and was plagued with an irresistible impulse to do something about it."* Linda became actively engaged in her treatment, researching, reading, consulting and writing about her experiences. She also made several changes in her lifestyle and diet to accommodate her illness and to minimize the symptoms.

When initially diagnosed, Linda was angry about her illness: *"I really, really resented the fact that my body – or what I thought it was – betrayed me."* In time Linda found her way to acceptance, realizing that her illness was helping her to grow in ways she had never expected. Linda concluded, *"I wouldn't sacrifice where I am now for anything in the world."*

We can learn a great deal from these women and how they moved beyond the threshold of a serious disease. At a time when their lives and their routines were unexpectedly disrupted, they faced their diagnoses, their illnesses and their treatment with courage, determination and positive outlooks. That is what all of these women have in common—they realized that they had some choices in how they responded to these unexpected and unwelcome illnesses, and with the support of their friends and loved ones, they found ways to cope and to go on.

This Story has a Happy Ending

by Carol Kabakoff

Mammograms are something I schedule, have about once a year, and then forget about. I don't worry about it before or after the event. However, the past few years there always seemed to be a new slant to the procedure. I remember that 2002 was the year of including all the tissue in the armpit into the mammogram. In 2003, it was apparently the year of neck tissue inclusion. I could feel my eardrum changing from round to oval as the monster machine compressed, pulled on every bit of skin from my naval to my eyebrows, and then the technician told me to hold my breath and not move. Next time I'll pay the extra five bucks for that little 50 cent comfort cushion that they offer.

Then the results came in the mail a few weeks later. I always hate the results. Not because I ever think for a minute that there will be anything wrong, but because they always chew me out. *"The breast tissue is VERY dense and hard to read." What are you thinking, lady? Didn't we tell you that last year??? Why did you bring THESE breasts back in here?? PLEASE, next time bring in some different breasts!!* The letter indicated that, in addition to my outrageously dense breasts, now I had some abnormalities. Perhaps what you see in the X-ray is the earwax that was stretched down into my neck tissue and compressed by your sadistic machine? Instructions were given to schedule a time for an additional mammogram. Why not? I have nothing else to do.

This time the volunteer did not even offer me the mammography comfort cushion, not for any amount of money. They took the necessary pictures, with enlargements. Anyone who has seen my breasts know there is no good reason for enlarging, for heaven's sake. I was told that the radiologist would look at the images after each set, just to make sure she had all the right shots. So there I was, gown on/gown off, gown on/gown off, with waits of increasing length between each x-ray. Then, unexpectedly, I am extended an invitation to consult with the radiologist in person ...right then!! Wow! Isn't this special?

Here is where my surreal *mind-out-of-body* experience begins. I am led down a long hall into a dark kaleidoscope, with black and white pictures in all of the panels at the end of the tunnel. Whew!! What a relief. I have seen these pictures before—just last-night at the informational meeting about the proposed highway bypass. They are aerial photographs of our County. I can see the wetlands, the agricultura1 areas and here is the commercial zoning area. This is nothing to be concerned about. Then the voice begins to talk to me and point at the aerial photographs. She's talking about tissue, needles and incisions.

It is a very kind voice and the words are not coming out too fast, but for some reason, I have just lost 50 IQ points and I can't follow a thing she is saying. I catch up and hear that she wants even more pictures. Okay, I will have some time to compose myself and to clear my brain. You're not talking to just anybody here, you know. I read books and articles, listen to NPR and watch 20/20. I know what I am supposed to do now. This is when I am supposed to ask to see your Board Certification and inquire as to how many of these procedures you do each year and to ask about your success rate. I don't hear that voice at all. Instead, the other voice gently explains to me that I can take all of the information and get a second opinion, or just let everything sink in for a few days—or, I can do the biopsy tomorrow. *"Do it tomorrow,"* I hear my voice say, *"I go back to work in August."* I'm thinking that I need to wrap this thing up as soon as possible, put it on my *"To Do"* list for July 17th: Get gas, work with Justin, get my haircut and find out if I have cancer.

I decided that I should not tell anybody about the procedure at this point. After all, I would have real information to share soon enough. Why tell people something just to cause them worry, unless you want to annoy them or take pleasure in a little pay-back from the times your own children worried you to death? This whole plan failed under another IQ lapse. I must have forgotten where I was living. The volunteer at the Woman's Health Center in our small-town, rural hospital was an old family friend. It was not her regular day to be there.

She couldn't find the paper work so she quite apologetically sent me back to the building receptionist to try to retrieve the missing papers—more opportunities to run into acquaintances and bring attention to myself.

What next, an announcement over the public announcement system? *"Carol Kabakoff, date of birth 1/1/49, we have found your paperwork for your breast biopsy. Come on back to the Woman's Health Center. Bring your younger husband with you."*

Then I heard even more kind voices explaining to me what was going to happen that afternoon.

Using a syringe as big as a car muffler and a needle the size of a drinking straw, we will pull tissue from both the dark spot (the black hole) and the calcifications (the constellations) that lie in the deepest interior tissue of your breast.

Lay down here on this padded lead blanket and make yourself comfortable, as long as your breast is hanging through the hole, your right arm is bent at an awkward angle against your side, and your left arm is clutching the side of the table, out of the way of the breast compression machine.

We have given you (us) plenty of time for this procedure. You are my challenge for the day. This is going to be very difficult because of where the tissue is. Have I mentioned that your breasts are very dense? But we'll work at it!

Then came the flesh-crushing X-rays followed by extensive studying of the X-rays, with a lot of head cocking and comparing the old with the new, and an occasional inquiry as to where my head would be if it were in this picture. There was quiet whispering behind the curtain and more sighs and puzzled expressions. More rearranging of the essential body part: smashing, folding, turning, twisting.

Okay, let's go. *"You will feel a little pinch, then some burning."* It was kind of like the shot you get for a filling at the dentist: Easy enough to deal with. Then things changed. Minutes passed with sharp prodding and pulling. My face began to reflect the discomfort. *"Oh gee, does that hurt? You need to tell us if it hurts."*

"IT HURTS." I calmly state. Then a stab, a jump reflex, tears down my cheeks and an apology. I wasn't supposed to move and my worst fear was that I screwed up the whole thing. *"I'm sorry, I am so sorry,"* I said.

"Well it isn't supposed to hurt, why didn't you tell us? We could do something about it." Well, we have all read the hospital brochures that describe childbirth as a slight pressure in the lower abdomen. I had no reason to believe that the brochures describing a huge needle being jammed into your breast as *a slight discomfort* weren't written by the same man. Silly you, they can give you more local anesthesia. Well, look at my birth date ladies! I went to school in the sixties and have no fear of drugs. Plus, look

at the size of the mass you are dealing with here. This is no padded B cup you're dealing with! Bring it on! Finally, the first sample was placed in a jar and labeled. I was permitted to turn my head and move my arms but only momentarily.

Then they started the whole procedure all over again, including the whispering behind the curtain, the look of bewilderment as they examined the old and the new X-rays, and the arranging and rearranging.

This probe was for the calcifications that were near my chest cavity. It was the most challenging positioning of the two. *"We'll give you extra Novocain this time."* Thank you, thank you! There was the pinch, the burning and the pressure. Period.

"You can't be doing the same thing you were doing before." I said, hoping the answer would be that they were indeed—and it was. Okay, this could work out for me. *"Hey, while you are sucking things out of there, I would love to go down two cup sizes. What do you think? I'll get the other breast matched up somehow at a later date—my problem, not yours."* Another sample, another jar, another label and it was done.

"Now just put these ice packs (the size of a dime) on the incisions (in the warmest part of your body) to prevent excessive bruising and bleeding. Change them every ten minutes. Here is an extra set for the waitress to put in the freezer for you if you eat out tonight. Call on Monday afternoon to see if you have cancer. Have a nice weekend!"

∾

My story continues in a *choose-your-own-adventure* format, like the kind of books my boys used to read when they were little. As I wait for the results, I can't help but speculate about what the news will be and how I will react.

Choice number 1:

"Hello, Mrs. Kabakoff. The tissue is totally benign, without a doubt. We tested every tissue sample that needed to be tested. There is not a chance in hell that we missed anything. Your only problem now is that your right breast will be setting off the airport security alarm because of the small metal clips we inserted where we did the biopsy. See you next year."

I will scream *"YES"* and vow to take better care of myself, starting with a membership to the recreation center with a personal trainer. This will be the problem that never was, and a miss that was as good as a mile.

Choice number 2:

"Mrs. Kabakoff. There is atypical tissue in the samples we extracted. We are referring you back to your doctor. He will go over all of the information with you and discuss treatment options. I hope you can get in before October."

Now is time for all the clichés: I will appreciate my life, my family, my friends and nature so much more. This is an early detection and the world is cluttered with breast cancer survivors. They can do so much more now, so many new advancements. I will review my lifestyle and my routine. First on the list is a good exercise program that will reduce my weight and increase my physical endurance. I think I will get a membership to the recreation center with a physical trainer for starters.

See, I win either way!

Update from the author: I am happy to report that my five year survivor anniversary is in the rear view mirror. As life's transitions integrated aspects of the past, present and future, I took an early retirement from a career in education in order to appreciate the joy of flexible time spent with aging parents and adult sons. Oh Yes, there is always the ongoing exercise routine, diet monitoring, and wellness programs, some years more vigilantly than others. I am grateful for the opportunity to share this experience in the hope that my reflections help those who are faced with similar circumstances.

Resurfacing

by Katie Ford Hall

~

After putting the kids on the bus I slipped away from the kitchen table, away from my husband and my visiting in-laws. I had been dreading this day since I scheduled the surgery six weeks before, and I wanted to be alone. In order to take a badly needed shower, I had to remove the surgical dressings and face my new reflection in the mirror. Showering has become an almost holy ritual for me, the only place I can safely indulge my anger, sadness and fear.

One of my main goals during treatment was to keep my children's lives as unaffected as possible. I became keenly aware that people took their cues from me, so I consciously kept up the appearance of a positive attitude. The upside of acting "as if" was that I was often convincing myself, too. I found that when I spoke with such upbeat authority, I was really persuasive. On the other hand, I set myself up to confront my own tornado of emotions alone. In the shower, I could cry, sob even, let it go and wash it all away in a few, tidy, efficient, watery minutes.

I peeled off the gauze quickly and took it in slowly. The incisions were still raw, and bruises had started to form. My chest was swollen in some areas and sunken in others. *"Hideous,"* was all I could think. Tears welled up; I needed the shower. With shaky hands, I opened the shower door and noticed the nozzle had been turned to face the wall. With those angry stitches and the sensitive surgical drains, I could not reach up and adjust the shower head.

I had to ask for help—something I am historically loath to do. I called for my husband and wrapped a towel around myself. When he came upstairs, I could only choke out "Sorry, I can't move the showerhead." I fixed my burning eyes on the floor, too vulnerable to face his reaction to my newly mutilated body.

~

Six months before this moment, I began walking this dark path during what was a happy point in my occasionally turbulent life. My children, ages six and eight, were settling in to school. I loved my job. Our family was comfortable. The detour started with a standard mammogram and wound through the bleak bramble of two misdiagnoses. Finally, it led to an incredible surgeon who didn't mince words. She helped me put the pieces back together and regain my strength by facing this reality head on.

At age 41 and without any family history of breast cancer, I never saw this coming. A diagnosis with a disease that takes the lives of 40,000 American women every year tears your world apart. I had been aware of cancer, but only in the margins of my life. I was vaguely aware of a distant aunt who died of cancer when I was a child. In those days the word cancer was whispered and the word breast was never mentioned. As an adult, I'd noticed the outbreak of pink ribbons every October. A few years ago I heard of an acquaintance that developed breast cancer. Like most everything else in my life, I never really understood breast cancer until I experienced it myself.

Without a doubt, the worst part of having breast cancer is the waiting. Once I assembled my team, I clung to my treatment plan like a life preserver. However, the times between the first mammogram callback, the test results, the diagnosis and the treatment plan were excruciating. It was two and a half months between my original mammogram and my first chemotherapy. My fear created scenarios far worse than the reality turned out to be. My life had come to a grinding halt. I spent days in bed crying, imagining morbid scenarios of my children growing up without a mother and my husband growing old alone.

I couldn't even bring myself to tell anyone. The words "I have cancer" didn't feel like they belonged to me. I think that somewhere inside me I believed that their utterance would bring something horrible to life. I was in shock.

Fortunately, my husband thinks clearly in times of crisis and he wisely advised me not to tell anyone until I had a firm diagnosis. Even after we decided to share the news, I couldn't face the idea of calling a list of people and telling the story over and over. A funny thing happens when you tell people you have cancer: They are *almost* as overwhelmed as you. You end up having to comfort them and to assure them that everything will turn out alright. I was still unsure myself, so I couldn't assure anyone else. I took the somewhat cowardly route of sending out a group email explaining the situation. Then I asked people to respect my wishes to be left alone for a little while.

I had to do something to avoid getting stuck in this place, so I turned to the best self-therapy I knew—writing. I wrote my morbid scenarios out in my journal. When I reread them, I ripped them out and threw them away, fearing the laws of manifestation and frankly feeling a bit silly about the melodrama.

I found myself resurfacing tentatively. Before beginning chemotherapy, I created a blog to communicate information to others and to process my own feelings and thoughts. It became a life-affirming process as I laid out some very personal information and received positive feedback and encouragement from readers. As time went on, those dark places and my tumor got smaller. I began to feel more connected and supported than ever, even before the cancer. Before long, I found myself laughing again and able to talk about something other than breast cancer. I realized that, mercifully, I had outgrown the gloom and doom. I started to live again.

Of course, there were important issues to tackle in my writing. I spent a great deal of time wondering why I got cancer. If I knew the answer, I could probably win the Nobel Prize. I envisioned all of the junk that I carried as being trapped inside my tumor. I put all of my wounds and resentments in there—all of those tightly held memories of betrayals and transgressions alongside my treasure trove of secret shame and regret. I knew for some time that my anger and my grudges weren't serving me well, but I guess I hung on to them because the familiar monster is preferable to the one you've never met. More accurately, I tried to avoid going face-to-face with any monster at all.

But, there's nothing like a gun to your head to entice you to change your ways. I armed myself with information, realizing that the only chance I had was to look breast cancer right in the eye. As I write this, I have completed four months of chemotherapy. I am recovering from a double mastectomy and I am getting ready to undergo radiation therapy. My odds are pretty good.

I have become more acutely aware of what we all face—tomorrow is not a promise. When I start to regret all of my wasted time, I remind myself that every step I have taken was essential to arriving at this moment, even, or maybe especially, the steps I would sooner forget. Sometimes I find myself returning to my old, worn-out, negative, self-deprecating narrative. In those moments, I close my eyes, focus on a few breaths to break the cycle, and remind myself that today is actually quite remarkable.

Cancer patients are under an immense amount of pressure to "live each day to the fullest." At first I felt guilty when I didn't feel the delirious joy of every sunrise or find intense pleasure in refereeing my children's arguments. I started examining my "I should" thoughts and realized that they were nothing more than the chatter of the so-called experts that I internalized my whole life. It was time to listen to my own voice, to gently accept that I will have grumpy moments and that sometimes I want nothing more out of my day than to sit around in my pajamas and watch television. Most of the time, it seems like I am walking on the edge of indulging myself and pulling myself up by my bootstraps. I believe that will always be a battle for me, but I am grateful for the chance to live consciously instead of coasting through my days on autopilot.

Through the entire process I have continued writing. I have discovered that the more I write the more that the unhealthy parts of my life reveal themselves. Most of these things I already knew, but I recognize this as a time when I am ready to accept the possibility of new paradigms. As I type out my life, its bleak darkness and intense light, I release the tortured memories from the prison of my own limited and suspicious perceptions. Like a fog lifting on a warm fall morning, the love and beauty that surrounds me became brilliantly clear. They continue to reveal themselves to me as long as I am willing to pause long enough to notice.

My story is neither a fairy tale nor a tragedy. The medical community has come to see cancer as a chronic condition rather than a death sentence. Healthy diligence will likely remain my companion. My journey with cancer has been one of letting go—of grudges, of body image, of mistrust, of isolation and of stubborn self-reliance, to name just a few. So far, every time I step out of the door, life is there to greet me. I have learned that accepting meals from other people doesn't bring about the end of the world. Neither does releasing bottled up feelings nor letting my husband adjust the shower head. The world's a little tougher than that. As it turns out, so am I.

Katie Ford Hall is the mother of two and the Assistant Director of Women Writing for (a) Change in Cincinnati, Ohio. She was scheduled to complete her breast cancer treatments in September of 2009. Katie will likely spend the rest of her very long life redefining the word "normal." Her blog (katie's little c) helped to keep her a little bit more sane during her treatment and has provided a great source of authentic records for this and future writing projects. You can read more of Katie's writing and reach her at www.katiewriter.com.

~

Journey into Light

by Janice Moszynski

~

To journey into light one must know the darkness. Only by crossing the threshold of consciousness can that which is conceived in darkness that which lay mostly unseen below the surface— be brought to light.

At the age of 50, I found myself at the entrance to one of life's inescapable turning points—facing a life-threatening diagnosis. I was at the crossroads of despair, forced to go deeper within. I needed to pay attention to my unconscious mind in order to summon the will and the courage to find my way back from this diagnosis. I was so close to losing everything that I finally became aware of my conscious living. I was about to find out that it was time for me to emerge.

~

On my way to the health club one morning, I got a call from my doctor. She sounded panicky. She spoke as if she could hardly get the words out fast enough, like they were suffocating her. *"I'm sorry, but you have lung cancer."*

"What?" I said at least three times.

She offered apologies again. At that moment time stopped. I felt I was in an altered state or another dimension. I felt separated from my body as my unconscious mind took over and handled the responsibility of driving me home while my conscious mind went off somewhere far removed. I tried to find a way to process my searing fear from the deafening diagnosis. When I arrived home, I was disconnected and numb for hours. I paced the kitchen floor and didn't call anyone, not even my husband.

How could this be? My mind raced to come to an understanding of how this was happening to me. I felt like I was just beginning to fully live my life. At 50, I was coming into my own skin like never before. It fit so well now and I looked forward to my future. I knew clearly what I wanted my future to look like—and it did not include lung cancer. My creativity was blossoming and I was ready to move forward with a fresh maturity. I was going to enter the middle passage to my autumn years with strength and zest for life; with all that life blessed me with and taught me along the way. Now I had to deal with lung cancer.

As the days wore on, I contemplated what this would mean (other than what I feared most). Deep down inside it wasn't making sense to me. I felt I could survive, but I wasn't sure how I would be able to do it. The doctor's prognosis was not good and their recommendations for treatment were few. I desperately needed to make sense of the muddied waters of my mind. I had to find a way to direct myself away from my fear and to reconnect to a healing light within. I needed to become re-acquainted with my thoughts, my feelings and my inner voice. I needed to find my way back to health and wholeness.

As I made my way through the internal crisis I started to unlock the door to my heart and my emotions. I began a daily journal. To hear my heart's longings, my mind had to be still and quiet. This had a restorative effect. It was something I could do immediately. Journaling is like excavating the true self from your heart's center. I was ready for anything that might flow out of that process.

What I discovered was that I wasn't in the flow of my life at all. I was often caught up in the whirlwind of events and my to-do lists. I spent little time being present without doing something—or multiple things at the same time. Although I was putting forth the effort, I was off course and not reaching my destination.

At times I felt I couldn't breathe. I was suffocating my own life force. I didn't know how to slow down. Fatigue and confusion met me as I tried to paddle upstream. I was living out of my head—justifying and analyzing—not from my heart center. It was as though I was a spinning top with no roots grounded in the earth.

At a conscious level I realized that I was trying to move forward but my circumstances were holding me back. At a deeper level I didn't really believe I was moving forward at all. I felt stuck. I was just going through the motions. My conscious desires were in conflict with my unconscious desires. My true self was buried under expectations and a life on auto-pilot. In order to find my way back to health, I needed to learn how I was sabotaging myself. How was I depleting my physical and spiritual nourishment? The light and joy within me were blocked and turned into the darkness of disease.

I learned to sit quietly with the pain and ask, *"What can I do to help you?"* Instead of imagining that I could not deal with it, I began to listen. Like a parent to a child, I wanted to give my body the love, attention, time and patience it needed to heal. I had to sit with it awhile to understand and to acknowledge it. I learned that it is a process that takes time. If the pain did not leave, I tried to find wisdom in the suffering. Before my diagnosis, I did not honor myself with the love and self care necessary to manifest health and happiness. I gave away my power for so many years. Now, I was paying a dear price for it.

Illness has a way of stopping the madness and the overwhelming expectations we place on ourselves; at least it did for me. Illness has a way of stopping the madness and the overwhelming expectations we place on ourselves, to accept what is. There I was with no more expectations to impose upon myself. I was given a freedom pass to seek, to re-emerge whole and to choose once and for all my own health and well-being. I was forced to live in the moment and reevaluate everything I knew to be true. It's a fine balance to go from darkness to light. It takes all the courage, faith and resources you can find to get you there.

It was through my faith and the power of family and friends that I needed to rely upon during this time. They allowed me to learn to ask for and to accept help in my time of need. Cancer is too big of a journey to take alone. There are many supports available: Doctors, family, friends, faith in God's healing and guidance, spiritual healers, meditation and prayer. There is much to draw upon for strength and healing during this journey.

I no longer deplete myself of physical and spiritual nourishment. I learned that unmet expectations can tie you up in knots and carry you away. I also learned to forgive myself and to forgive others for not doing the things I wanted them to do. I realized that we are all on our own life path. Everyone has a purpose and their own life's journey.

The most important part of my healing was to believe in myself. I learned to be my own advocate for my health and well-being. I challenged and sought out the best medical treatments that I could find. I had faith in my own intuition and faith that I could heal despite my prognosis. To move forward, I found the place inside of my heart that affirms my life and my healing. I am choosing to focus on wellness. I practice this through sitting and walking mindfulness meditations. I now attract still clear waters that have replaced the muddy mind of hurriedness and the darkness of disease.

I've also found my breath again. The tightness in my chest from living in fear is subsiding. I found this calm through taking care of myself. I know that I need laughter, sun, rest, rain, compassion and nurturing. I am also reconnecting to my passions. There's a balance now between the dark and light, the temporary and permanent.

Now I honor my time of renewal. I create my own rituals of rejuvenation and I am reminded of God's great love. Through all of this I have received the gifts of freedom and observation. I have made a commitment to claim my dignity, my voice and my connection to the truth because I want to live. For me, healing was about remembering who I am and reclaiming my health and my life.

~

Janice is a writer and photographer. She is also passionate about lung cancer advocacy. As a survivor, she attended the first and second annual lung cancer advocacy summits presented by the Lung Cancer Partnership to acquire tools to spread awareness and increase funding for lung cancer research. She also is a member of the Lung Cancer Alliance. Both are leading organizations working tirelessly in the fight against lung cancer. She has traveled extensively and lived in Spain for four years. She is now enjoying her hometown of Plymouth, Michigan with her husband Gary. Janice also maintains a blog at www.enteringthelight.wordpress.com to help inspire those facing serious illness.

Update from the author: Since I wrote my essay, I am free of disease and filled with gratitude for the opportunity to share my journey of healing and to enjoy the blessings of health.

~

Taming the Monster

by Linda Tefend

A monster is living inside of me. She has probably been rambling around in there for decades, sending out the fear signals that threaten to tarnish even the most joyful of my life's transitions. Until a few summers ago, however, we had never been properly introduced.

In June of 2006, I was diagnosed with Interstitial Cystitis (IC), a chronic inflammation of the bladder for which there is neither a known cause nor a known cure. Although individual symptoms vary, the most common characteristics are the constant sensation of a pack of lit cigarettes being extinguished in the vagina and the need to pee urgently most of the time. IC attacks predominately women, and it attacks indiscriminately.

I still can't shake the question of how or why this happened to me. What I can admit, embarrassingly, is that my journey from shock to acceptance has not been pretty. Yes, I have blessings to count for this *involuntary personal growth experience*. But to say that the trek has been grace-filled is, at best, sidestepping the truth, and at worst, insulting the sensibilities of other chronic disease sufferers who are moving their way to physical and emotional health.

For anyone who is facing a similar hurdle, it may be reassuring to know that acceptance after a loss does come, but only after facing some of the villains that live in our souls, the ones that appear only during the dark and challenging times.

I'll confess that during the first year post-diagnosis, although I could see the light at the end of the spiritual tunnel, my progress was impeded by my own internal monster—a teeth-clenching she-devil who despises change and fears pain. As it turns out, she also has some redeeming qualities. After all, if it were not for her, I wouldn't have had the opportunity to gain strength from facing this opponent. Although I haven't made friends with her, she and I have worked out, let's say, an amicable roommate agreement.

Looking back I can pinpoint three ways this gremlin initially gained some temporary ground following my diagnosis.

Phase I: This cannot be happening to me.

I really, really resented the fact that my body—or what I thought it was—had betrayed me. In my previous life, I considered physical illness a sign of weakness. My impeccable health regimen was secured by a thick layer of prejudice toward the smokers, McDonalds' patrons and non-exercisers of the world. I thought that they were the people who attracted diseases. In other words, I was the perfect candidate for this journey.

A tortoise moves faster than it took me to accept the fact that I was living with a chronic illness. My monster apparently has a teensy little stubborn streak. I felt ungrounded and was plagued with an irresistible impulse to do something about it.

So I wrote. I talked it out. I got involved with a local support group. I wrote some more. All of which served as solid practice to help reality soak in. Through the blessings of supportive, patient friends and professionals, I was gradually able to accept this new identity without being defined by it. In the words of Joan Borysenko, author and speaker on the mind and body connection, *I learned to be responsible to my illness as opposed to being responsible for it.* This was exceptional progress for a proverbial *Guilt Queen* like me.

Phase II: How will I ever live a normal life?

The chronic discomfort (oh ok, pain) felt confounding and hopeless. To my mind, there was no way I could continue in my roles as a mom, wife and professional and endure the constant burning and urgency of IC. The order felt too tall. Not a day went by when I didn't long for a pain-free day. I was furious at the universe and I was angry at myself for not appreciating what I had before the IC appeared in my life.

So I did what I always do when faced with a hurdle—I learned. I researched, listened and dug my way through as much information as I could find on IC and how people live with it. It became clear to me that no "magic pill" existed. There were many remedies and varying strategies to deal with this illness.

Eventually, I generated what I call my "four-pronged approach" to coping with a chronic illness: medication, nutrition, exercise and mental health. The magic of this combination lies in the relationship between all four prongs. By itself, one is infinitely less effective. But, together, miracles can happen. By balancing and respecting all four components, I was able to mitigate a significant percentage of the pain, allowing me to live a relatively "normal" life. That is, if you consider being an over-achieving perfectionist "normal."

Phase III: You have got to be kidding.

The IC diet was, by far, my most formidable hurdle. Up to that point, the notion of a "diet" was as foreign to me as Saturday sunrises are to teenagers. I never denied myself any particular food. I never restricted myself. This diet, however, is not about getting into a smaller swimsuit size. It is one of the several recommended holistic approaches for managing the symptoms of IC.

The *Interstitial Cystitis Diet* comes complete with an attractive colorful brochure, compliments of the Interstitial Cystitis Association. The gist of The Diet is that I can eat and drink everything except: coffee, alcohol (and, yes, that includes red wine), chocolate, aged cheese, citrus fruit, carbonated beverages, condiments, artificial colorings, flavorings, additives and preservatives. Oh, and perhaps yeast.

I discovered when my foods read: Ghirardelli, Cabernet, Starbucks, and Parmesan Reggiano and were taken away from me, my monster resurfaced and got ugly. Fast. It wasn't that I was resistant to The Diet. It was that I despised it. Picture a foot-stomping toddler and we're getting closer to the truth of how I felt about this diet.

This was a news flash for me—food and drink, in reality, isn't about food and drink. It's about ritual, delight and comfort. It's about wrapping my hands around a mug of steaming Italian Roast in the morning or sharing a glass of Pinot Noir at the end of the day with my husband. It's about savoring chocolate ANYTHING. It's about socializing. As in, *"Let's get a cup of coffee sometime!"* Or, *"Why don't you meet us for a glass of wine next Friday night?"*

The DNA in my family of origin is programmed to drink wine with dinner. This is a biological fact. The sound of a popping cork, and the aroma of an earthy red being poured into a stemmed glass is, to me, synonymous with evening. At the first family gathering following my diagnosis, I half-expected my siblings and parents to forego wine with dinner. You know, as a familial show of solidarity. Clearly, this was the misguided princess in me, dreaming of eternal empathy.

That was one of my first indications that I had a long way to go on this journey.

At subsequent gatherings, family and otherwise, as I drank my spring water—from a pretty glass, of course—the sense of personal denial was palpable. Invariably, someone would look at me with that scrunchy-eyed, *oh-I'm-sorry-I-forgot-you-can't-drink-anymore* look, take a mouth-bursting sip of merlot, change the subject, and inch away so she wouldn't have to face me.

Was I resentful because I couldn't drink and that others could? That others would drink around me when they knew I couldn't drink? Or, was it the isolation that arose from the collision of all those realities? The requirement that I be a really good sport while I watched other people indulge in what was forbidden to me felt too stiff. The proverbial insult to injury was that I not only had to deny myself these earthly pleasures, but that I had to work doubly hard to make others feel comfortable around me while they indulged in them. I felt a strange kinship with recovering alcoholics, as they grapple with this elephant-in-the-room in their quest to socially re-align themselves back into an alcohol-based culture.

My therapist—and ultimately my savior—told me that this would continue to be excruciating for me until I looked at my dietary restrictions as a choice I was making, not something that was imposed on me. *"Making choices,"* she said, *"is empowering."*

Envisioning these restrictions as a "choice" felt like driving a bulldozer up a muddy hill in the rain. The picture I created in my mind usually involved some over-the-top scenario of sainthood, to which I could never aspire: I attend, with glee and delight, a party with trays of elegant cuisine and bottles of private collection wine. *"No thanks,"* I respond sweetly to the hostess. *"I'll just have water,"* in a pretty glass. I am the picture of grace and composure. I socialize deftly, asking clever open-ended questions to the attractive party-goers who are growing more loose-lipped by the hour. I do not crave the substances that tempt lesser mortals. I am on a redefined and infinitely more peaceful plane. The only thing I am missing is a halo. And, of course, a wine charm.

Three years later, real-life social events now elicit sensations that fall somewhere between blatant suffering and canonization. I've learned to put aside my all-or-nothing thinking and practice potentially frustrating situations in terms of duality. I must accept and believe that two seemingly paradoxical states can actually coexist. By simply replacing my but's with and's in my mental self-talk, I become more present to reality and better able to accept what is. For instance, it is difficult to watch others sipping wine and I'm deeply grateful that I'm among friends. I do crave chocolate cake and cheddar cheese and I'm empowered to be in control of my health. I wish I could drink something besides water and I'm feeling blessedly pain-free at the moment. I love being a mother and I find some of my teenage daughter's behavior to be enormously frustrating. (Oh, how did that last one sneak in there?)

Every day, I am clear that I make choices that will either decay or strengthen my sense of rightness with the world. Each morning I am privileged to open my eyes, to prepare and enjoy food that will sustain me and the ones I love, to touch others' lives through the course of my work, to hug a friend, to drive a car pool, and to close my eyes at night to the satisfaction of another day well-lived. I do not have a halo, but there are days during which I think I've legitimately earned one.

One evening recently, a friend posed this question as we were driving home from the bookstore, *"If God gave you a choice to erase your IC experience or keep it, what would you choose?"*

I won't lie. I had to ponder this a bit. Although there have been times when I've wished the disease would go away, I never thought about the totality of my experience up to that point, and what it would mean if it were erased from my life. The streetlamps started to blur as it occurred to me that the personal growth I experienced as a result of IC did, in fact, far outweigh the inconveniences. I was lucky to recognize and to make peace with my own personal monster, and that's a blessing not everyone gets to experience. Keeping both hands on the steering wheel, I glanced her way and smiled, *"I wouldn't sacrifice where I am now for anything in the world."*

~

Linda is a wife to her husband of 22 years, mother to two teenage daughters and Career Coach to individuals experiencing work and life transitions. She writes for fun and sanity. She and her family live in Ohio.

Several months following the submission of her essay "Taming the Monster" Linda experienced a sudden and intense flair of her IC symptoms. She is now re-acquainting herself with her earlier wisdom, thankful that the learning cycle is briefer this time around.

~

Reflection Points

That is what learning is.
You suddenly understand something
you've understood all your life,
but in a new way.
— Doris Lessing

From the authors in their own words

- *Cancer is too big a journey to take alone.*
- *It takes all the courage, faith and resources you can find to get you there.*
- *I began to feel more connected and supported than ever, even before the cancer.*
- *In those moments, I close my eyes, focus on a few breaths to break the cycle and remind myself that today is actually quite remarkable.*
- *I will appreciate my life, my family, my friends and nature so much more... See, I win either way!*

Questions to contemplate while facing the threshold of your own diagnosis or illness

- *When you have faced difficult times in the past, what helped you through?*
- *What do you need in order to face this difficult journey? How can you get what you need?*
- *Would a second medical opinion ease some of your uncertainty or offer other considerations?*
- *What is one thing you can do to have some control over your situation?*
- *How can family or loved ones help? Will you be able to ask them?*

CHAPTER 10

Illness and a Loved One

I understood how a man who has nothing left
in this world may still know bliss,
be it only for a brief moment,
in the contemplation of his beloved.
— Victor E. Frankl in "Man's Search for Meaning"

Each of us will face a time in our lives when someone we love is coping with a serious illness. *"This is the impermanence of life and all that is living,"* I note in my essay, "On Living with Dying." Given that it is inevitable, the question then becomes, how do we respond when this difficult challenge confronts us in our own lives?

"I don't believe anyone knows how he or she will react to a situation like this until it actually happens," wrote Lana Swearingen after she was told that her husband had a rare brain tumor. I echoed a similar message following the terminal illnesses of both of my parents, *"I wondered how I would be able to deal with what was ahead."* As it turns out, we do find ways to cope with these unwelcome and painful experiences because they are a part of life.

When your loved one has a chronic or terminal illness, you will not escape being affected. It might even seem as though a part of you has become ill too but in a different way, of course. You might feel it deep in the pit of your stomach, or your heart actually aches, or your mind becomes preoccupied with your loved one or with their illness. You feel emotional and sometimes even physical pain as you bear witness to your loved one's suffering.

Lana Swearingen tells a beautiful love story in her essay, "Don," describing how she and her husband faced his illness together. When she first learned of his diagnosis she recalled, *"...my heart broke. I pulled myself together only because I had to do so for Don...I learned how to deal with doctors, hospital staff, insurance companies and scheduling. As time went on, I also learned how to get by on little sleep."* This was affirmed over and again throughout Don's illness as she discovered, *"I knew that I could not give in to my own despair."* Lana found a way to cope with one of the most painful experiences of her life to that point. She and her husband walked the journey together with the support of their family.

Author Misty Kiwak Jacobs shares a moving and loving story of her father's illness and death in three poignant poems. The trilogy, selected as one of the top ten recipients in the Reflections From Women writing contest, is included in this chapter. In "Negotiating with the Unwell," Misty reflects on a visit to her father's hospital room while he is connected to a respirator. As she sits at her father's side, she chants, *"Mantras of wellness blow over my lips, rest and heal and breathe."* She reminds us of the hope that is often intertwined with a deep sadness when a loved one is suffering.

In her poem "Omission," Misty comments on the difficulty of acceptance, no matter the person's age or history, *"How unbecoming was infirmity- how unlike you, swift decline."* This was a common element among all of the essays on this topic—the initial disbelief at the unsettling news that a loved one is gravely ill. Disbelief, denial or emotional shock is often the gateway to the grieving process. This is the threshold where most of us begin once we learn the diagnosis.

Grieving is a natural response when a loved one has a serious illness, whether or not the illness is considered terminal. Chronic illnesses and disabilities also bring feelings of loss for what was or what might have been. The process of coming to terms with a loved one's significant diagnosis can include a range of feelings and reactions. After the initial shock or disbelief, there may be anger, depression, despair, hope, sadness and finally (hopefully) acceptance. The contributors who wrote about their loved one's illnesses and deaths all shared a common bond: they eventually found acceptance. Their journeys to acceptance were personal paths that they had to discover for themselves. Some found peace with the help of family, friends or counselors and others realized acceptance with the help of their dying loved one.

In the poem "Visiting," Misty Kiwak Jacobs recalls one of her last visits with her father: *"I offer memories which you accept politely: a lifetime unraveling..."* Sharing the memories of a lifetime when at death's door can be comforting to both the living and the dying. We, too, recalled the events and people who were a part of my dad's life. Even in the hour before his death we reflected, we smiled, we cried. *"It is that uncertain time when everyone knows that death is coming—we just don't know when"* I wrote in my essay *"On Living with Dying."*

The time in-between disbelief, anger, sadness, hope and acceptance is actually a gift. If we are fortunate to have some time between diagnosis and death, we can appreciate the minutes that we have together. We can be grateful even for those moments which challenge us in ways that we wonder if we can survive. But we do survive. We find a way to move on because life demands that we do so. This is the nature of life and all that is living.

Trilogy

by Misty Kiwak Jacobs

Reflections from Women Writing Contest Selection

Dedicated to the memory of my beloved father, E. David Kiwak whose love prepared my heart for things eternal.

~

Negotiating with the Unwell

Entering the house
I find his leather gloves on the counter,
the collapsed form of my father's hands.

I'm taking these, I say to the brother I love,
his head bowed over the documents
of illness.

I walk to the back of the house,
through the museum of a man
who has suddenly stopped moving, hide
proof of his living in my bag.

In the hospital, over his bed,
my body loses itself in grave negotiations:
my forehead upon his forehead, gray hair
curling through the insistent mothering

of my fingers, pale feet alert
under the sheets, urgent kisses falling
like hammer blows to break open sleep.

Mantras of wellness blow over my lips,
rest and heal and breathe. I breathe
with the respirator. I breathe
against it.

Wood chisels arrive in the mail,
remain propped against the side door.
My brother relights the water heater.
I warily drink the last of the juice.

Visiting

Loss falls over the swing-line
of the door. Passing room
after occupied room,
I come to kiss a starry vastness
in your receding cheek.

I offer memories
which you accept politely:
a lifetime unraveling
as I gather stray threads
at your bedside.

This is the distillation of regret.

You ask for your roan horse,
sold thirty years ago.
You ask for my coffee,
and I explain again
that you can't swallow,
that you would choke.
You ask again.

Death sifts through the spaces
in the room.

Pointing to the cartoon
my daughter is watching
you whisper, You have to negotiate
with that little black duck
for your coffee,

and I,
missing the metaphor,
disagree with you.

Omission

It occurred to me that I did not pray
for a miracle, unacquainted as I was
with finality.

You were all about repair:
the tight-trimmed hedge, the glossy baseboard,
an impassible red brick house, its roof trussed
at each end by a trinity of fur trees.

A proper English saddle shop, crisp bills
in a glinting money clip, Saratoga cigarettes,
a tidy meal of shredded ham on white bread.

How unbecoming was infirmity- how unlike you,
swift decline. And how presumptuous
of me: No reassuring presence, no illumined clarity.
Just loss. Like water in water.

You are shattered glass.
I am irreparable.

~

Misty Kiwak Jacobs was born in Scottsdale Arizona. She is a graduate of Sarah Lawrence College in New York, and has studied at The Russian School, Norwich University, The Summer Institute of Linguistics, University of North Dakota and the Maurice Thorez Institute of Foreign Languages, Moscow, Russia. She has studied poetry under Norman Dubie at Arizona State University. In addition to many local publications, Misty's work has been published in The Sarah Lawrence Review and The Red Rock Review. Pulitzer winner Gary Snyder placed one of her poems among the top three in the Tucson Poetry Festival Statewide Contest, 2002. Currently, Ms. Kiwak Jacobs classically home schools her two children in her native town. She is an aspirant of the Order of Carmelites Discalced Secular.

Update from the author: "One White Towel" and the trilogy of poems about my father share the themes vulnerability and loss. Turning away from contemplative life, I lost myself in the minutiae of motherhood, housewifery and materialism for many years. The death of my father in 2003 began my return to prayer. The loss of my father, with whom I was very close, left me psychologically crippled. It was a great blow to my image of self as a daughter loved by a protective and caring father. Thus began the slow and painful stripping away of my "idols", those things of this world that I put before God. By His grace my first vocation that of prayerful surrender has been restored, although I do it quite badly.

~

Don

by Lana Swearingen

Reflections from Women Writing Contest Selection

To my children, Jerry, Debby and Dee Dee, for being there.

It started with a loss of fine motor skills in his left hand. Being left-handed, he found it difficult to hold a pen and sign his name. We were sure that it was a pinched nerve, maybe in his neck or shoulder. Our primary care physician, while not outright disagreeing about a pinched nerve, suggested my husband see a specialist.

The next day, we made the 20-mile trip to the nearest big town, to meet with a neurosurgeon. He, too, did not discount a pinched nerve, but he directed us to go to the hospital immediately for admittance and further testing. The battery of tests included an MRI of the head and neck.

When the doctor told us the results of the MRI, we didn't really comprehend what he said: *A small spot on the brain.* What does that mean? *A glioma?* We'd never heard of it. He quietly explained that a glioma was a primary brain tumor that grew in stages and was usually inoperable.

Even now, looking back, I cannot adequately describe the feeling of abject despair that ran coldly through me. I was suspended between that moment of not knowing and sudden awareness. When I looked at the horror and disbelief on my husband's face, I knew that I could not give in to my own despair. Don choked back a sob and it took everything in my power not to cradle him in my arms and release a torrent of tears. Instead, I morphed into the take-charge, we're-going-to-beat-this-thing person, which gave Don some time to gain his composure.

And so, we knew. We knew that this type of tumor could be treated with chemotherapy and radiation. We knew that if it was in an early stage the prognosis would be more encouraging. We knew that the tumor is what would eventually kill my husband.

The world outside the hospital looked different, almost surreal. Everything became a hazy backdrop against which I looked at the vivid image of the man I shared my life with. I kept thinking that this is not real. Talking to our family, one by one, I could no longer fool myself.

Then, my heart broke. I felt it give way and I was lost in an emotional blitz that I thought would never end. I pulled myself together only because I had to do so for Don. I don't believe anyone knows how he or she will react to a situation like this until it actually happens.

I learned how to deal with doctors, hospital staff, insurance companies and scheduling. As time went on, I also learned how to get by on little sleep.

The neurosurgeon wanted to make sure Don didn't have a stroke, because it can show up similarly on the medical tests. So, for three weeks we were hopeful that it was just a stroke and that Don might show some signs of improvement. Instead of improving, Don was not able to hold a pen or a fork any longer. He started to train himself to eat with his right hand, and I signed everything for him. Soon thereafter, a biopsy of the tumor revealed that it was indeed a Stage 3 astrocytoma—the worst being a Stage 4 glioblastoma. We still hoped that chemotherapy and radiation would get rid of it. His prognosis ranged from one year to six years. Of course, we were pushing for six.

The treatment seemed to work and the next CT scan showed that the tumor had shrunk considerably. We were hysterical with happiness. No more holding on to each other for dear life, crying and crying. No more anger that this had happened to us. We would have time: Time to plant the garden, and we did; Time to renovate the bathroom, and we did. We started acting normal again. Whew, what a relief.

Don's 66th birthday approached and his three daughters and two grandchildren came for a big celebration. We blew up 66 balloons and hung them from the upstairs railing, had a huge cake and all the trimmings of a great party. The only detraction was the fact that Don had started limping. He was having a hard time directing his left foot to lift up and move. After the party, he quietly told me that he had just seen his last birthday. I got mad at him for even thinking that.

One morning at breakfast, Don complained about difficulty with swallowing. It became progressively worse, so we went back to the oncologist. The doctor said that the tumor, which was in the right parietal lobe of the brain, was affecting the left side of his body. He immediately admitted Don to the hospital where another scan showed that the tumor had spread again. They placed a feeding tube in Don's stomach and taught me how to feed him through it. The thought that he couldn't eat again devastated Don. He wasn't ready to give up his favorite foods and I just couldn't deny him that pleasure. So very carefully, he started eating again – things like pizza, chocolate and all the goodies he loved. He would often start coughing and choking but I pounded him on the back until it passed. I knew it was risky, but I couldn't say no.

Shortly after that episode, Don's leg wouldn't support him anymore so he wound up in a wheelchair. We talked about it being just temporary, but we were starting to realize that things were not good at all. My life was soon consumed with taking care of my once strong but quietly accepting husband. As the disease progressed, his left side became paralyzed. He could not stand, sit or change positions without my help. Then he started going in altered states of mind.

He could still follow some of the stock reports on TV, but he would abruptly start talking about clipping the ears off the teddy bear he held in his right hand while stroking its soft fur. Or he would think I was someone else or tell me to take his sock off because he had to go to the bathroom. While I attended to the clinical aspects of his care, when these things happened, I often had to leave the room and just cry. He was so tender with me. One day while I was brushing his teeth and shaving him, I asked if I could have a hug. He took a while to formulate the word, and then simply said, *"Always."*

Our family really rallied together during this time. I had help from all six adult kids, mine and his. They put their lives on hold and came from all parts of the country to be with Don and do whatever it took to make life easier.

I have talked about the progression of the disease but not too much about the feelings associated with it all. Maybe that's because it is so very hard to explain. It's hard to put into words what it was like to hold each other and talk about a shared memory, or to discuss whether he was afraid to die. *"No, I just don't want to"* he would say. We prayed too. We prayed for a miracle, knowing it wasn't coming.

We laughed a lot too, over things that no one would ever imagine could be funny. We laughed when he would try to manipulate his wheelchair and end up banging into the walls. We laughed when he would try to put as many M&M's in his mouth as he possibly could. We just enjoyed being together. When we would go outside to the garden, I would pick the ripe tomatoes and place them in the basket in his lap. How can I possibly explain how much that garden meant to us or how happy we were in our retirement house overlooking the lake? We finally made it to the place where we both found such peace and contentment. How can I explain how it felt to watch my husband slowly leave me?

During the last two weeks of his life, my children and I camped out in his hospital room. His three girls came to take care of his mother, who also lived with us. They came to the hospital every day. Each day the doctor would tell us it would be his last. He was still doing things on his own time.

On the morning of November 13th, the day before my birthday, I asked everyone to leave the room so the nurse could bathe Don and make him as comfortable as possible. I had a feeling that he needed to be alone. Even though he had not been conscious for days and the tumor had taken over the entire side of his brain, I still knew my husband. He didn't like a lot of people fussing over him. When everyone stepped back into his room, he looked fresh and peaceful. As I sat next to him, he took a breath, let it out with a sigh, and then he was gone.

When walked into the house without him, we saw his birthday balloons from four months ago—still full of air. We took our small boat out on the lake that Don so loved and released the balloons as a final farewell.

I miss him and always will. I have discovered that life does go on, but it goes on with all of my memories to keep him close to my heart. I believe he is still doing things to let me know he is with me, like that day my son and I went to the funeral home to make the arrangements. We walked out of the funeral home with a big butter cream cake. As it turned out, the local bakery supplied the funeral home with cakes to give to the families. It was my birthday that day. Don always made sure I had a cake—including that day.

I will always remember what he said to me as we held each other, gazing out on the lake at the sunset when we knew that he wouldn't be here much longer: *"Wherever I'm going, I'll be looking for you."*

After retiring from a career with the federal government, Lana is a writer, a vocational archaeologist and volunteer at a nature preserve. Shortly after the death of her husband, she relocated to Arizona to be close to her three children and four grandchildren. Her time is now spent enjoying her family and pursuing her many interests. In retrospect, it is only now that I can talk about this with some objectivity. The final 18 months of Don's life were the most incredible, sad, funny, happy, angry, miserable, fearful and hopeful times of our lives.

On Living with Dying

by Terri Spahr Nelson

To my husband for standing with me every step of this journey and holding me up when I needed you.

Spring, 2007

I knew it was going to happen eventually.

I have reached an age where my parents have become old and developed ill health. It was inevitable. This is the impermanence of life and all that is living.

My mom died about four years ago. To this day, I have a hard time remembering the year. I can recall some of the most insignificant details about all kinds of things, but for some reason, the year of my mom's death escapes me. I don't know why. I just know that no matter how much time passes, I still miss her.

So, here I am now at the age of 46, with one parent deceased and the other dying. No, he is *living*—but we are very much living with his dying. If you have ever been in this situation you know exactly what I am talking about.

It is that uncertain time when everyone knows that death is coming—we just don't know when.

My father was diagnosed with cancer in the Fall of 2006 at the age of 84. With courage and grace, he declared that there was no reason *"at his age and health"* to go through chemotherapy and put everyone else through it. (He knew the chemotherapy would make him feel sicker because he watched my mom cope with her cancer treatments for three years until her death.) He said he wanted to live the rest of his life as naturally and as fully as possible. It was his decision and no one tried to talk him out of it. We knew that when he made up his mind that's how it was going to be. I was grateful and in awe at the same time of his courage and his faith.

So, we try to make the most of these final weeks, days, hours and minutes together even though this waiting time is so uneasy. It's as though life is on hold, but it's not. I feel compelled to speed things up (to do, say and be all that we can for each other in the remaining time—to try not to forget anything) but on some days I am filled with such exhaustion, it's all I can do to get dinner made. He has moved in with us and we are fortunate enough to be a part of his life every day, but that also means caring for him and being a witness to his suffering.

I try to comfort him (and myself) in small ways that seem to make a difference. *"Sure, dad, I would love to watch that John Wayne movie with you"* (even though the laundry is piling up, I'm falling behind on my job and the bank account is running low.) I have to remind myself that these tasks will still be there tomorrow, but he may not.

It's uncomfortable because we all *know* his time here is short. He is dying. Hospice is involved. He's taking morphine for his pain and it's getting harder for him to walk, eat, drink and breathe. He's dying, but he is still very much alive.

It is spring now and the flowers are starting to appear. The birds are gathering around the feeder and singing their mating songs. The warmer weather is calling us to come outdoors. It's challenging because some days I don't even want to go outside. It seems as if life is continuing in the world outside, but it is on hold here inside this household. I feel like I'm holding on so tight because if I don't, he'll be gone before I'm ready to let go of him.

Plans for summer are tentative. Time with friends is limited. Work projects are taken on with an eye on the deadline. Our focus is on being with him and encouraging him to do what he needs or wants to do in these last weeks, days and hours.

Life goes on, but it's different. This is indeed a transition and one that is challenging me in ways that I never imagined. I only hope that I will find a way to face this threshold when the time comes. Until then, we are living with the reality of dying–with death waiting somewhere in the distance—and we're trying to make the best of each precious day we have together.

Fall, 2008

It's been two years since my dad came to live with us. And, it's been just over one year since he died here at our home in the beautiful, bright yellow room he called his own. It was in the summer of 2007 when he took his last breath, with the sun shining, the birds gathering around the bird feeder outside his window and his children and grandchildren nearby.

He was exactly 85 years and 3 months old on July 18, 2007 as I told him that morning when we had our last conversation. I reminded him again of how much we all loved him and that we were grateful he was with us. I told him he was the best dad ever (as I often did) and I said that he and mom did a great job of raising all of their children. I mentioned that he would be joining the love of his life, his wife of 62 years, as well as his own parents and siblings. He nodded and whispered he loved me. It was the last time we spoke. I think we both knew that his time here was coming to an end. Minutes later, his last surviving sister arrived at his bedside to say goodbye. She blessed him with holy water and he took his last breath in peace surrounded with so much love.

As I sat there with him only moments earlier at the threshold of his death, I knew the time had come to let him go. I wondered how I would be able to deal with what was ahead for me—how would life be with both of my parents gone?

It's been nearly six years since my mom died and one year since my dad died. I still miss them both so much but I am comforted in knowing that their love for me lives on. I am reminded of a message from the Buddhist teacher, Thich Nhat Hanh:

> *"If you look deeply into the palm of your hand, you will see your parents and all generations of your ancestors. All of them are alive in this moment. Each is present in your body. You are the continuation of each of these people."*

I was able to face these difficult transitions when death arrived for both of my parents because I knew my dad and mom would always be with me. They live on in me, in my son and all of their other children and grandchildren as well as the countless lives they have touched.

I witnessed my parents face their illnesses and the end of their lives with such courage, faith and love. They both taught me how to live and how to die. I have confidence now that I will be able to face that transition when my time arrives. I only hope that I can face my own death with the grace and dignity as they did.

Thanks mom and dad. Once again, you were there for me and saw me through another difficult time.

Terri Spahr Nelson is the editor of this anthology and author of several other works. She has been married to the love of her life (and business partner) for nearly three decades–and counting. She is also the proud mother of a 27-year-old son whose writing and wit outmatches her own (check it out: www.EnviroKnow.com). They all share a common desire to make the world a bit better for others. In addition, Terri has a private practice in psychotherapy and provides trainings and retreats to professionals and women on a wide range of topics. She found her passion in the helping profession many years ago and her path to writing has been a natural sequence to that niche.

Update: I will always be grateful that I had the opportunity for my dad to live with us during the last year of his life and to die peacefully at our home. It was a life-changing gift that he shared with all of us.

Reflection Points

"Although the world is full of suffering, it is full also of the overcoming of it."
— Helen Keller

From the authors in their words

- *We finally made it to the place where we both found such peace and contentment.*
- *It occurred to me that I did not pray for a miracle, unacquainted as I was with finality.*
- *I have discovered that life does go on, but it goes on with all my memories to keep him close in my heart.*
- *I was able to face these difficult transitions when death arrived for both of my parents because I knew my dad and mom would always be with me.*

Questions to contemplate while standing at the threshold of a loved one's illness

- *If you are caring for a loved one during their illness, how do you take care of yourself?*
- *What does your loved one need from you at this time? If you do not know, ask them.*
- *Are you able to let your loved one choose their own path in this journey even if you disagree with some of their decisions? How do you deal with these differences?*
- *If you were the one who was ill, what would you want from your loved ones?*
- *What will help you to overcome this suffering and to find peace, whatever the outcome?*

CHAPTER 11

Death and Loss

"There's this place in me where your fingerprints still rest,
your kisses still linger, and your whispers softly echo.
It's the place where a part of you will forever be a part of me."
— Gretchen Kemp

Each of us will experience the loss of loved ones. Death as a turning point in women's lives is the focus of several essays in this book. Although it is a universal issue, there are many paths to and through this difficult threshold in life. This chapter highlights five women's experiences as they faced the deaths of their loved ones. They include: a best friend and college student who died at age 19 from cystic fibrosis; a sister-in-law who died at age 49 from a sudden blood clot; a husband of six years who died in his 50s from a heart condition; a dear friend and mother of three young children who died at age 30 from cancer; and a baby girl who died in her mother's womb before she was delivered.

The essays and poems in this chapter are heartrending accounts of how death and the circumstances leading to it affect women in very different ways. Some of the women were faced with sudden and unexpected deaths of their loved ones; others had time to prepare, but found that it was still incredibly painful to accept.

In the several months preceding her husband's death, MaryKay Mulligan discovered that coping with the complications of his illness became a series of ups and downs. In her essay, "The Day the Sun Shined Again" MaryKay noted, *"Problems cropped up one at a time and we dealt with them as they came."* However, she soon discovered that her husband's primary heart condition created many other health problems, some of which were also life-threatening. MaryKay was devastated when, after several setbacks followed by returns to equilibrium, her husband passed away just a few weeks after their anniversary. She found it difficult to go on, *"Routines comforted me but I wasn't capable of much at that time. I just put one foot in front of the other."* Although her husband was ill for some time, she spiraled into deep despair for a period following his death.

Likewise, being present at the ending of a life can be particularly difficult. *"I can't do this. I can't, but I have to do this,"* says Alice Coggin Bagley as she reflects on being at the bedside of her dying best friend, Kelly. In her essay, *"I'm Here,"* Alice tells about her ambivalence while witnessing her friend's final moments at a hospice facility. Her dear friend was dying from cancer and Alice did not know how she was going to be able to be there with Kelly at the end. *"I don't want her to die...I don't want her to give up."* When Alice did find the strength to be in Kelly's room, she realized *"(I was) paralyzed in my spot at the end of her bed."* Alice continues, *"And then I feel arms go around me. 'I'm here.' Mama... She is holding me tight and my tears—buckets of them—come at her selfless sacrifice."* Alice was able to be with her friend at the end, along with her own mother and Kelly's family and children.

Saying goodbye is an important part of letting go, whether it is days, hours, or minutes before a loved one's death—or even after their death. Cassandra Walker's poem "Gone" is a tribute to her best friend Devon and is one of her ways of saying goodbye to him. Cassandra was aware that Devon was seriously ill with cystic fibrosis but his final hospitalization and death affected her in unexpected ways. In her loving poem, Cassandra writes, *"I had no idea I wouldn't be able to talk to you again...I came to see you while you were still here, but you probably didn't know...I can't get over seeing your end."* His death came too soon and too suddenly.

Sudden loss can trigger shock and horror, as described in the poem "Cheri" by Jeannie Martinelli. Remembering her 49-year-old sister in-law who died abruptly from a blood clot, Jeannie writes, *"She went to work on Friday, was admitted to the hospital on Saturday and died on Sunday."* The poem speaks to the family's anguish at the unexpected and untimely death of their loved one.

"There are no words," write Alice Coggin Bagley as she tries to find a way to comfort a dear friend whose young wife has just died. Indeed, no words that can truly express the pain, loss and suffering that comes from the death of a loved one.

The pain is almost unbearable for Joy Brubaker, writing about the tragic loss of her dearly loved baby girl while the infant was still in her womb. In her essay, "When the Baby Died," Joy describes her reaction upon learning that her baby was no longer alive, "*I didn't cry. I didn't have questions. I was in shock... I could hardly grasp the reality.*" Joy was told that she would have to continue the pregnancy until the baby delivered naturally. When her baby girl was finally delivered, Joy recalls being wheeled past the nursery at the hospital, "*I stared straight ahead...summoning all the courage I had to avoid wailing.*"

Truly, words cannot adequately describe this kind of emotional pain nor fully express sympathy for someone who experiences such a tragic loss. Yet, we try our best to comfort each other when a loved one dies. We try to find a way to ease the pain and to keep them in our thoughts and in our hearts.

Reflecting on the final moments of her best friend's life, Alice Coggin Bagley remembers, "*She is literally surrounded with love.*" At such difficult, almost unbearable times, this may be the best we can do: surround them with love.

Cheri

by Jeannie Martinelli

Reflections from Women Writing Contest Selection

~

CHERI
12/12/04
YOU DIED
AND
WE CLAMPED OUR HANDS
OVER
OUR GAPING MOUTHS
AND
SENT UP A CHORUS
OF
SILENT SCREAMS

OUR ANGUISH IS UNQUENCHABLE
WE ARE SORE FROM INTERNALIZING
OUR MOURNFUL CRIES
AND
WEAK FROM SWALLOWING
THE PAINFUL TRUTH
-YOU'RE DEAD-

Jeannie Martinelli has been married for 25 years to Larry. They are the proud parents of a 12-year-old daughter, Lisa Katherine. Jeannie is also a Montessori teacher.

Update from the author: I would like to honor the memory of my husband's sister Cheri who died suddenly at age 49 from a blood clot. This poem describes our shock and horror when the doctor told the family that Cheri would not live through the night. She went to work on Friday, was admitted to the hospital on Saturday and died on Sunday.

I'm Here

by Alice Coggin Bagley

In loving memory of Kelly Hinesley who continues to be the best teacher I know.

I remember my phone ringing but I don't remember who I spoke with first. I remember the words: *"Alice, it's time."*

After the first call, they all started calling. I was trying to get my stuff together to leave work. My co-workers were coming from various corners of the office.

"Alice, they called."

"Alice, it's time."

I know. I know, but I'm not ready.

I feel hands touch me gently. I hear prayers whispered.

"We're here. We're here. Just call us later."

I can't do this. I can't, but I have to do this. I know. So I get in my car. I'm on auto-pilot. I'm calling her mother, calling my mother, calling the school to let the counselors know.

Just function, Alice. Just do this now.

I text message my friends: *We're here. Let us know what we can do*

I pulled up in the parking lot. It's so quiet. As I walked in the doors, I feel every eye in the place on me. They know. Today I have to watch her die. I cannot do this.

An elderly woman wraps me in her arms and puts a small gold cross in my hands. *"We prayed over this at my church,"* she whispers. *"Today will be hard, hold on to this cross."* It is a tangible symbol of intangible faith. I do not put it down all day.

I walk to her room and as I get closer I feel like I can't breathe. I can't catch my breath. I don't want to go in. I don't want to see her.

I'm scared.

I take a deep breath as I open the door. I see Eddie sitting with his pastor, his head bowed. He looks up at me and I go around and kneel in front of him. There are no words. He hugs me and cries with complete abandon. He is in agony and I can't do anything to make it better. I try to absorb his pain through our hug, but I realize that there aren't hugs that strong. Our grief over Kelly has been the tie that binds us for the past two years and now that tie is stronger than ever. I don't want this anymore. I don't want to sit and watch a man watch his wife die.

"I'm here, Kel."

Her breathing is ragged. This is awful. It is nothing like I imagined. Her body is shutting down and it is not an easy process. It is ugly and gruesome. It is excruciating to watch. She swore she would fight to the end. It is heart-wrenching to know that no matter how hard she fights, she's still going to die today.

I stare at her. I know this is it. It is time for my really-final goodbye. We've had several already. It feels like we've had millions. But today there will be no reprieve. I don't know what to say. Should I touch her? Should I say something out loud or just in my head? Should I cry? I should cry, but I can't. Where are the tears? What kind of friend am I? Oh my God, it doesn't even look like her. Even though I've watched this steady decline over time, it does not seem like her lying there. It's not Kelly. It's not my Kelly. They keep telling me it's time to say good-bye to her.

I want her to open her eyes. Even if she can't talk I want her to open her eyes and to see me and know that I'm here. I want her to absorb the image of me to take along with her. *Please open your eyes, Kelly. Please.* I feel that if I concentrate hard enough I can make her look at me one last time. That is all I want. She does not open her eyes. I will not get the meaningful look that I need—but today is not about me.

The hospice social worker takes me out of the room. The kids need to be here. I'm not sure why she's telling me this. Kelly's mom runs past me into the room and I hear her saying, *"I'm here, baby, Mama's here"* and I hear Eddie sobbing. I realize the social worker is telling me because today I have to be the grown up. They have been my kids for the past two years. This is my last act as their guardian—to bring them to watch their mother die—before I turn them back over to Eddie. He won't even get a break. He will have to go from caring for his dying wife to caring for his grieving children. It's not fair.

I call the school. I feel the lump in my throat. They all know, of course. *"It's time,"* I whisper. It's all I can say. She understands. I'll have the kids ready for you.

Then my mom calls my cell phone. *"Alice, I'm on my way."*

"Why?"

"Because I can't let you do this alone."

She says she will get the kids, so all I can do is wait. The air conditioning is broken at hospice. It is August and people in this building are dying. It is almost unbearable.

On the day that your loved one is dying at hospice, the family and loved ones are the guests of honor. The place revolves around you and your needs. Water, tea and cold towels are constantly offered. More family arrives and we all sit in the waiting room. It is almost like waiting for a baby to be born—except it is the exact opposite—and we are quiet. Then we talk and even make some jokes. I wonder what I am doing joking when she's dying.

When the kids arrive, I entertain them to keep me distracted. I'm here for them I keep telling myself. Kelly and I have already had our goodbye. I had told her when she first started talking about dying that I would hold her hand if she needed me. She was afraid her mom and Eddie wouldn't be able to do it and she didn't want to die alone. But they are troopers. They don't leave her side except for when the nurses come in to check on her. They touch her, talk with her, soothe her. I can't. Even though I promised, I can't bring myself to go in there and touch her. I am grateful that her mom and Eddie can be there for her in that way. I stand in the doorway and stare. Then I have to leave.

I call everyone that Eddie needs me to call. I call people for her mom. I keep in touch with the people who can't make it in time. I am their lifeline to Kelly's dying.

It is 4:20 on an August afternoon and something changes. I am dispatched to get Kelly's step-dad and to find Grant. I usher them into Kelly's room and stand in the back. I already said I wasn't going to be in there when she died. I felt that it was for family. They are calling me to be there. Of course, I am family, now. *"Alice, come on. Alice, it's time."*

My mom nudges me and tells me to go. "I'll be right here."

I. Cannot. Do. This.

Please, God, don't make me watch her die.

I can't.

I can't.

I can't.

When I look into her room, I see Grant standing at the foot of her bed by himself. He looks so small. I can't let him do this alone. He is her child. He is her child and she entrusted him to me. In that moment of clarity I realize that she is leaving me the very best part of her in triplicate: Tyler, Grant and Katelyn. So I slide into the room behind Grant and wrap my arms around him.

Kelly's mom is holding her left hand, Eddie is holding her right. Tyler is beside Eddie rubbing her leg. Kelly's sister, brother-in-law, Eddie's cousin and the pastor are all in the room with us too. We form a circle around the bed. She is literally surrounded with love. Everyone is crying except for me and Grant: He is silent. I tightly hold the gold cross in my hand, searching for strength.

The room is quiet except for Kelly's gasping for air and everyone else's muffled sobs. This is awful. I want this to be over already. Shouldn't we be praying now? Should I start praying? There's a preacher here, she knows better than me. What should we do? How can we just stand here? How can we watch her die like this?

Oh, God, please make this stop.

Oh, God, please help her.

Oh, God.

Please.

Please.

Please.

She is dying. God, SHE IS DYING! I find myself holding my breath as she struggles for the next one. I am trying to breathe for her. Or suffer with her. I'm not sure.

I want this to be over.

I don't want her to die.

I want her to stop struggling because it physically pains me to watch.

I don't want her to give up.

I want somebody to do something. Help her!

I am paralyzed in my spot at the end of her bed.

And then I feel arms go around me. *"I'm here."*

Mama. She couldn't even go to see Kelly in the end because she couldn't bear to see how bad she had gotten, but she will not make me do this alone. She is holding me tight and my tears—buckets of them—come at her selfless sacrifice.

And then, a final breath.

Her mother, who has laid her head on Kelly's chest, whispers, *"She's gone."*

Silence.

It is 4:28 on an August afternoon and my best friend is dead. It took her eight minutes to die. She is 30 years old.

Grant starts keening in this animal sound I have never heard. It is the first time he has cried since Kelly was diagnosed. I don't know how to comfort him, so I hold him until the others can wrap him up in their arms and in their grief. I realized that I didn't hold her hand while she died. Instead I held her heart. I held her little boy. The poignancy almost breaks me.

When everyone leaves to make funeral arrangements, I tell Eddie I can stay. He doesn't want her to be alone. He promised. I still can't bear to go into the room, so I sit in the waiting room. My step-father shows up to sit with us. I didn't expect it but I am extremely touched. I am able to joke with my mom again. We talk about Kelly giving God an earful and it makes me feel better. I still can't believe it. She was so real to me, so alive, even in her illness.

How can she be dead? How could I have watched her die? I am still in shock over sharing this incredibly intimate and final detail of her life. It's like watching someone give birth to a child: It binds you for life.

And I hear a voice—her voice.

"I'm here."

She is letting me know that she is there. I realize, in those final eight minutes, that Kelly wasn't suffering. In those final eight minutes, she was finding her peace.

I have finally found mine.

I'm here.

~

Alice Coggin Bagley is a public relations professional who handles PR for a faith-based children's home in Georgia which serves hundreds of children each year who are victims of abuse, abandonment and neglect. She and her husband Ervin recently had their first son, Austin. He was also welcomed by big sister, Erin.

Update from the author: Kelly died in August 2006. I wrote this essay on the one year anniversary of her death. Unbeknownst to me, Ervin visited my mom and dad on August 10, 2007 (unaware of the significance of the date) and asked my parents for my hand in marriage. My mom later said she felt like it was Kelly's way of giving her approval for the marriage. We were married on 06-07-08 and

Kelly's daughter, Katelyn, stood in her memory as my maid of honor. On July 4, 2009, I gave birth to my son, Austin, who was born exactly 5 years to the day (and in the exact same hospital) where Kelly received her initial cancer diagnosis. Proof again that I have a guardian angel watching over me and letting me know she is still with me.

When the Baby Died

by Joy Brubaker

To my two sons, Josh and Ben, who are my raison d'être.

I got pregnant with my eldest child the first month that we didn't use protection. It was so easy. In the fall of my husband's last year in law school I told him that I wanted to get pregnant. We had been married four and a half years. He would be graduating soon and have a job. I was teaching at a small rural school to support us until he became a lawyer. Now I was ready to let him be the breadwinner while I stayed home and raised children.

Not long after my announcement, as I lay in bed one morning, I had a sharp, quick pain in my womb. I wondered at the pain, which quickly passed. Somehow I knew that at that moment the little embryo had attached itself to my uterine wall. Soon I missed my period and started having flu-like symptoms which a friend said was probably a sign I was pregnant.

Three pregnancy tests at my gynecologist's office showed no pregnancy. Finally I went to my hometown family physician. She did a physical exam and said, *"I don't care what the urine test says. Your uterus is enlarged—you're pregnant."*

I was ecstatic. However, my enthusiasm was dampened by my nausea—acute morning sickness that lasted all day, every day, for weeks. Nevertheless, I worked through it and as the baby grew and my abdomen expanded, I was truly content. On sunny days during the summer months, I would flip the bottom of my maternity top up, roll my elastic front pants down, and sit on the fenced-in patio of our tiny little apartment, exposing my watermelon belly to the sun.

"Here, little one. Enjoy the sun," I would say, imagining the golden glow of my skin filtering the sun's rays as they made their way to my inner sanctum. Rubbing my belly and talking to my baby, I imagined him or her swimming in a warm golden glow of love.

I thought it was a girl. My mom wanted it to be a girl. She bought pink trimmed sleepers and coats. Jim's dad kept saying, *"Well, when SHE arrives . . ."* Jim's mother already had two grandsons and (although she didn't say so) I think that she, too, secretly hoped for a girl.

My due date was in late July but my brother teased and said I would just have to wait until his birthday on August 8. The due date came and went. On the night before my son was born, the eve of my brother's birthday, I couldn't eat. Not sick and not in pain—it was just an odd feeling that precluded eating.

At 1:00 a.m., I got up to go to the bathroom. When I slipped back into bed my water broke with a pop. The bed was immediately soaked. I woke my husband and he drove me to the hospital. After 13 long hours of erratic, difficult labor, our son was born—on my brother's birthday!

The moment they placed my son in my arms, I felt a rush of love unlike anything I had ever felt before, like I had fallen through a trap door and into a river whose powerful current carried me far out to sea. I was lost. I was found. I was enthralled and a slave to this little being who already had me wrapped around his unimaginably tiny finger. His every movement brought me an endless universe of wonder and recognition.

This was good stuff and I knew I would want another of these little gods. After two years, I started trying again. I wanted a little girl so badly that I did research and found a book on increasing the chances of selecting the sex of the baby at conception. I used vinegar douches and the positions the book recommended for girls with my hips elevated. No luck. I couldn't get pregnant.

What had been so easy the first time turned out to be extremely difficult the second time. After more than a year of trying, I finally went to the clinic at the Air Force base where my husband was stationed. The gynecologist had my husband's sperm count tested and found out that it was fine. Our next step would be a more extensive examination of my uncooperative body.

But soon I missed a period and felt as if I had the flu. Even without a test, I knew that I was pregnant.

With this pregnancy, I was much more nauseated and spent long, draining days trying to care for our three-year-old son. Some days, just walking into the kitchen and smelling the odors coming from my apparently clean kitchen sink made me run to the bathroom to throw up. I was miserable for nearly five months. I even went to the emergency room once because I had so much pain, nausea, and vomiting. I was worried about the baby.

Then I started feeling better. One evening around my sixth month, I felt the baby turning while we were lying in bed. As it turned, its head or butt caused my belly to become a huge mountain on one side. I grabbed my husband's hand and placed it on the mound, saying, *"our baby"* as we lay there side-by-side enjoying the moment.

The next change was subtle at first and difficult to notice—the absence of something. Was it my imagination or had it been a while since the baby had turned? Maybe he or she was just resting. Didn't my belly seem a little smaller? Not possible. The baby must have just settled lower. This went on for days, even weeks, as I pushed away my doubts and suspicions that something was terribly wrong. Then one Sunday I started spotting dark blood. I mentioned it to my husband, who was reading in bed. He barely looked up from his book. I persisted, noting with some alarm that I was not yet in my seventh month and that if the baby was coming now, it probably wouldn't survive. He turned a page, suggesting that if I was worried I should go into the clinic the next day. Since I wasn't in any physical pain, he was sure that I wasn't in labor.

When my husband went to work the next day, I went to the clinic. It was Memorial Day and the person in charge was a no-nonsense nurse practitioner. I told her about my spotting and she asked about the baby's activity level. Then she said, *"I'll need to do a physical exam."* So I exchanged my maternity clothes for a hospital gown and climbed onto the cold examining table. She couldn't find a heartbeat. She slipped on her rubber gloves, inserted a speculum and started poking around. I don't remember much else about the exam except her asking, *"Where is your husband? We need to call him. We'll need to run a few tests."* As I stood, I saw that the examining table was covered with dark brown blood, old blood, on the white paper-covered table.

Soon my husband arrived and we were ushered into a small room where they said they would do a new test called a sonogram. I was told that I would have to drink a lot of water and hold it so that the technician could get a clear image of the baby. I drank more than a quart of water and waited. The technician squirted a cold gel onto my abdomen and scooted the probe over my belly. He tried to find a heartbeat and to get a clearer picture. I was in agony with a bladder that was bursting, and I kept begging the tech to let me go to the bathroom. He finally agreed, but cautioned me to avoid fully emptying my bladder. Going a little was worse than not going at all—and the tech then made me drink more water to replenish what I had voided.

Finally the tech said he needed to do an x-ray. I knew that it was unusual to x-ray a pregnant woman, so this was not a good sign. After the x-ray we were taken into a small office. By then there was an obstetrician on duty. He had come in to deliver a baby. He was not my regular doctor. In fact, I had never seen this man before. I had passed my regular doctor, my obstetrician, in the hallway earlier, so I knew he was there. For some reason this stranger was taking charge. In my pain, I imagined that people in the hospital hallway were turning away and whispering about me as we walked into his office.

The doctor said, *"The baby is dead."* He was 99 percent sure of this diagnosis. The x-ray had shown that the little skull had collapsed. However, the doctor indicated that I might have to carry the fetus to term. He insisted that there was no danger to me. It would simply be a waiting game until my body decided to let go of the baby on its own.

With this pronouncement, he sent us home. I didn't cry. I didn't have questions. I was in shock. I was carrying a corpse. I could hardly grasp the reality. I looked pregnant. I was pregnant, and yet not pregnant.

A few days later, my husband wanted to make love—I suppose in an effort to feel connected with me. I just couldn't. I felt like my body was a crypt, and the path to the crypt was littered with bloody bits of my child. The idea of having intercourse was a grotesque reminder of how the life had begun. It was shocking to even think about.

Days passed. I refused to leave the house or to face people as they might ask me when the baby was due or try to pat my tummy. My husband went back to work. When his boss found out what had happened, he sent him home, saying that I needed him there.

My husband called my mom and his parents. We all played the waiting game. How long could this go on, I wondered? Sometimes I self-medicated by drinking alcohol before I went to bed. But waking up to another endless day was the worst. Would I survive this agony?

Mom flew out by the end of the week. She bustled about taking care of my husband, my son, the house and the meals. I scarcely talked. What was there to say? Sometimes I would go outside before daybreak, sit on my son's swing set and wait for the sun to rise, since sleep was not an option.

A week after the clinic visit, I got a phone call; or rather, my husband did, since I wasn't answering the phone. It was the Air Force base OB/GYN clinic. The staff had consulted with University Hospital about my case. The University Hospital doctors were adamant that there was a very real risk to me of infection or injury. They wanted to see me immediately. So the next day I went into University Hospital and had another painful sonogram, another painful probing. The doctors decided that labor needed to be induced. I was scheduled for the abortion/induction for the next day.

I went into labor that night on my own, probably because of all the probing. My labor was relatively short, only six or seven hours as compared to thirteen with my first pregnancy. The hospital chaplain, a member of my church, stopped by and told me that this was the worst moment of my life. I thought angrily, *"What do you know about my life?"* When delivery was imminent, I was wheeled into a sterile room. I was given no drugs, no painkillers—nothing. Did the staff think that because my pregnancy wasn't full term that labor and delivery wouldn't be painful or difficult? They were wrong.

As I pushed out the little dead body, I closed my eyes. I didn't want to see something that was already decaying and distorted in death. I didn't want to have that image stuck in my head for the rest of my life. After the delivery, the nurse cleaned me up and put me in a wheelchair. The only way out of the maternity floor was past the nursery window. So I was wheeled past rows of cute little blue and pink bundles. I stared straight ahead, gritting my teeth, summoning all the courage I had to avoid wailing. I was a living coffin; relieved of my corpse, but still a coffin. The cradle within me had been turned into a death bed. My whole body ached for the baby that was gone.

At my six-week checkup the doctor told me that there had been an umbilical cord accident: the finger of the baby, the longed-for daughter, had been stuck in the amniotic sac. As the baby had turned, the cord wrapped around her hand and pinched, cutting off her lifeline. Without a shred of doubt, I now know that the moment weeks before when I had placed our hands over the little mound in my belly, thinking that we were saying hello, our little girl was saying goodbye.

~

Joy Brubaker is a writer, artist and former teacher who splits her time between Yellow Springs and Wilmington Ohio. She has two sons, Josh and Ben. Joy may be contacted at mbrubaker1@aol.com.

~

Gone.

by Cassandra Walker

This poem is dedicated to all who suffer from Cystic Fibrosis, and especially to Devon Conley, my best friend. Rest in peace.

Gone.
The one day I needed you by my side you were gone.
Gone from me, and gone from everyone else.

They thought I was the leader–the one to pull everyone through.
I couldn't be one for them.
I wanted to be a follower for once.
I just wanted to see you one more time to say, *"I love you."*

I took a lock of your hair.
It was the best thing I could do since you were gone.
I wanted to have a piece of you, friend.
You took a part of me, too.

I tried to have the strength to move forward,
but I wasn't ready.
I was in denial.
If I hadn't been, things may have been different

We never really talked about you being gone
even though I thought about it while you were still here.
I should have spoken up.
It could have made a difference.

I had no idea I wouldn't be able to talk to you again.
No chance to tell you my true feelings,
to say *I love you and goodbye.*

I came to see you while you were still here,
but you probably didn't know.
Your mind and soul were gone,
but your heart was still going strong until the end.

You didn't look like yourself.
The stories your parents told were too hard to fathom.
I lost control.

The tubes...the struggle for life.
The tears, the yells, the ultimate fight.

The sad part is
after all this time
I can't get over seeing your end.

And you're still gone.

Cassandra Walker is a 19- year- old college student who intends to graduate from Purdue University in West Lafayette, Indiana. She is interested in women's studies, journalism and photography. In 2005, Cassandra joined her high school's newspaper as a freshman and by her junior year she was the Editor-in-Chief of the newspaper.

Update from the author: On August 5, 2007, I watched as a genetic disease called Cystic Fibrosis took the life of my best friend Devon Conley. I was with him and his family when he took his final breath. Seeing him pass away in the manner he did still haunts me to this day. I find comfort knowing he's not suffering anymore. If you want to know more about Devon Conley, you can visit his memorial page at www.myspace.com/devonconley_8_5_07_ilovu. You can also learn more about cystic fibrosis from their website at www.cff.org.

The Day the Sun Shined Again

by MaryKay Mulligan

In loving memory of Gordon Herbster and joyous celebration of Orest Pelech

When you get married at 46, you can wear whatever you want to wear. I wanted beads and sequins and black chiffon. No matter that the wedding was at one o'clock in the afternoon. I wanted sequins and I wore sequins. It snowed every weekend in New Jersey that January. Parking lots were covered in grey, frozen slush, but on January 20th the sun was out. It was clear and the sky was blue. It was an omen and a perfect day for sequins.

I met Gordon seventeen years earlier. I hated him. Who was that big, rude, loud, misogynistic lout lounging in my office telling off-color stories? As a favor to a friend, I hired him to teach an English course and to serve as an advisor for adult students at the college where I was the dean. What was I thinking? Well, he grew on me and I guess I grew on him too. I am a complete sucker for an unusual turn of phrase.

The bombastic, off-color Gordon was a product of years as an Army military policeman. One day he roared into my office, apoplectic about a bureaucratic bungle with a student's record. *"How mad are you?"* I asked, sweetly. *"I wouldn't piss on her hair if she were on fire!"* he replied. In time, I got to know the kind, sweet Gordon, the political Gordon, the sports fanatic Gordon, the gourmet Gordon, the passionate Gordon and a host of others. As I said, he grew on me.

For seventeen years, we were buddies, lovers, good friends, colleagues and playmates, but not an engaged couple. Gordon never married. He was looking for the *Perfect Magic Princess*. He would know her because she would be, in a word, perfect. He would be love-sodden, blown away in a mystical trance, etc., etc. He'd gone through a series of *Perfect Magic Princesses*. I was not his *Perfect Magic Princess* because he'd known me for far too long. He liked me, perhaps even loved me, but the bloom was off the rose.

He moved to Virginia, but we continued to see one another. He came back to New Jersey and we continued to see one another. Then, I moved to Virginia, in part because my relationship with him was going nowhere. We continued to see one another. Whatever we did, we came back together. After all of those years of hemming and hawing, he decided that perhaps I was his *Magic Princess*. He finally decided that perfect does not actually occur in nature.

By the time Gordon recognized my magic princess qualities, he was in his early 50's with cardiomyopathy, a heart condition that could be managed but not fixed. He finally decided to retire from his job in New Jersey and move south to Virginia. I found the perfect sequined top, and we were married.

Life was good. I continued to work and Gordon enjoyed volunteering with the hospital, the historical society and the local Lions Club. We traveled to places that we had dreamed of visiting: Paris, Northern Italy, Ireland and Scotland. We visited friends and family. We had parties for our friends. We spent a lot of time laughing. It was a happy time for both of us.

Gordon's illness was the monster in the closet. When we met with his cardiologist, I asked how long the heart drugs would keep Gordon healthy. The answer was chilling: *"We don't know. These drugs will work for a while and then they won't. There's no telling how many years they will work."* We put that monster back into the closet but it was never far from my mind.

Problems cropped up one at a time and we dealt with them as they came. Each crisis was followed by a new equilibrium. Diabetes required a change in diet and another drug. Gout required a change in diet and another drug. Liver problems required a change in diet and another drug. Coping with these and other issues one at a time was okay. However, the accumulation of problems left us with a very complicated drug schedule and an amazingly restrictive diet of low protein for the gout and liver, low carbohydrates for the diabetes and low salt and fat for the heart. There were days I thought we would end up eating twigs and berries. I developed a balanced diet that did not set off any health alarms. We were able to adjust to the changes as long as we could still laugh.

We were married for five and a half years when the monster became too big for the closet. Gordon took a strong diuretic to help his kidneys rid his body of fluid. One hot day in late August, his kidneys went on strike.

We went to the cardiologist's office where the doctor injected a heavy dose of the diuretic to convince his kidneys to work, but they refused. Gordon moved into the local intensive care unit. He was there on 9/11/01. I remember watching the second plane hitting the tower and realizing that between Gordon and work, I had no spare energy to worry or to grieve.

Later that week, Gordon, the monster and I moved to a bigger hospital with a better heart unit. The doctors implanted a brand new device in his heart. He was the 17th person in the country to get this new pacemaker. It worked beautifully for the first 48 hours. We could walk the halls of the hospital without Gordon getting short of breath. We visited a friend who was in an adjacent wing awaiting a heart transplant. His wife was living in the guest wing of the hospital in the room next to mine. We were all elated that Gordon was responding to the pacemaker. I started to stuff the monster back into the suitcase, hoping to put him back into the closet for a few years. Then Gordon's heart weakened again and he needed intravenous drugs to strengthen his heartbeat. We went home with a permanent IV. I learned how to flush the lines, change the IV bag, and keep the batteries in his pump charged. The monster stayed in the closet, whistling in the dark, for a while.

January brought another intensive care admission, this time for liver failure. It broke my heart to see him confused and weak. One doctor told me that Gordon's organs were failing, but I did not want to believe him. Another medicine brought Gordon back to his mind, if not his strength. Then, in February, Gordon got appendicitis. That was one complication we were not expecting.

We stayed all day in the emergency room. Since he was on blood thinners, it was nine in the evening before they could risk surgery. He survived; and the next day, he was cracking jokes and talking basketball with his cardiologist.

The recovery did not last. Each day he grew weaker. I found him talking to people from his past who were no longer living When his kidneys failed, his doctor called me into a small lounge. *"Gordon has a living will. What does that mean to you?"* I told him that if he could not bring Gordon back to the comfort level that he had before the appendicitis, we had to let him go. No dialysis, no heroic measures. He was so tired of dying slowly. The poor guy had had enough, and I knew he was ready to go. Gordon died February 11, 2002.

There was a burial in Pennsylvania and a memorial in Virginia. There was a mountain of paperwork, thank you notes to write and people to call. I know now that my friends, family and coworkers could not have been kinder or more generous. I was too numb then to know much. When the intensity of the funeral activities faded, the house was so quiet and I felt so idle. The quiet settled around me like soft fog that kept the sharp edges of emotion from cutting me to ribbons. Routines comforted me but I wasn't capable of much at that time. I just put one foot in front of the other.

Every morning I drove to work down a country road. There was an enormous tree off to the right side of the road with a sturdy brown trunk and a tangle of branches. It looked wise, as if it had seen a lot through the years. My fog eventually faded and the jagged edges of loneliness and grief began to hit me. I kept looking at that tree. One turn of the steering wheel and I could leave the road, hit the tree and find dark, black, velvet peace. I wondered if I would have the courage to do it: Would some innate will to live make me veer off at the last moment? It became a dark game I played with myself.

One morning that summer, I looked at my tree. The sun was shining on its leaves. The wind was making the upper branches dance. How could I have harbored such dark thoughts? That tree was so full of life. I knew then that my life still had surprises in store for me, wonderful surprises. It took some time, but I realize now that I was right that day—and wonderfully surprised.

~

MaryKay Mulligan is a retired college dean and sociologist. She is a reader, a knitter, and a wannabe weaver. In 2003, she reconnected with a graduate school buddy. After he proposed in 2004, he was diagnosed with a cancer that only one in ten survives. They decided that someone had to be the one in ten. Now with her husband, Orest, she seeks out exotic groceries and cooks astounding meals for friends and family. MaryKay and Orest have been joyously married for five years, but that's another story.

~

Reflection Points

Unable are the loved to die. For love is immortality.
— Emily Dickinson

<u>From the authors in their words</u>

- *Our anguish is unquenchable.*

- *No chance to say I love you and goodbye.*

- *I now know that the moment weeks before when I had placed our hands over the little mound in my belly, thinking that we were saying hello, our little girl was saying goodbye.*

- *I took a lock of your hair...I wanted to have a piece of you, friend. You took a part of me, too.*

- *And I hear a voice—her voice...She is letting me know that she is there.*

- *I knew then that my life still had surprises in store for me, wonderful surprises.*

<u>Questions to contemplate at the threshold of the loss of a loved one</u>

- *"If you have the opportunity in the days, weeks or months preceding the death of your loved one, what do you want to do or say before she or he dies?*

- *After your loved one has died, listen deeply within for their voice. What are they telling you? How are they helping to guide you through this time?*

- *What memories of your loved one bring you joy or a smile to your face? How can you keep these memories close to your heart and readily available?*

Part Six

Moving Forward and Beyond the Threshold

Far away there in the sunshine are my highest aspirations.
I may not reach them, but I can look up and see their beauty,
believe in them, and try to follow where they lead.
–Louisa May Alcott

CHAPTER 12

Faith Found (and Lost)

May today there be peace within.
May you trust God that you are exactly where you are meant to be.
May you not forget the infinite possibilities that are born of faith.
May you use those gifts that you have received, and
pass on the love that has been given to you.
May you be content knowing you are a child of God.
Let this presence settle into your bones, and allow
your soul the freedom to sing, dance, praise and love.
— Saint Theresa's Prayer

There are many perspectives and deeply held beliefs about faith, spirituality and religion. As with the other turning points addressed in this book, the experiences and views on this topic are as diverse as the persons who describe them. Finding and sometimes losing faith was a profound and significant turning point in the lives of several women who contributed essays for the book.

As with the other chapters, this one is not intended to support one perspective over another, but simply to offer reflections from women about their different experiences. We learn more when we seek information, listen to other perspectives, contemplate the viewpoints and then make our decisions. The following essays will provide you with an opportunity to learn more about this topic from four women with different faiths, spiritual beliefs and practices. Two of the women write about their belief in God, one woman writes about her experiences as shamanic healer addressing spirituality based in nature, and the other woman reflects on her lack of a belief in God and her practice of spirituality founded on Buddhist principles. The complexity and uncertainty that often accompanies faith is where we will begin.

"Death seems so much easier for those who have faith," admits Rene Brannen in her essay, "Losing My Religion." Like many women, Rene was raised with a strong religious upbringing but started to question her faith as an adult. In her essay, Rene is facing a considerable turning point in her life as her mother (a devout, lifelong Catholic) is dying from a terminal cancer. For Rene, this raises concerns about faith, religion, and her belief in God. Rene's story is not unlike many other women who question the faith they were taught during their childhood. Then, later in life, they find themselves trying to make some sense of their separation from those beliefs. In her biography, Rene refers to a quote from Buddhist leader, The Dalai Lama, *"Kindness is my religion."* This, she says, is the foundation of her spiritual practice.

Questioning or doubting one's faith is something that numerous women experience regardless of their religion or spiritual practices. In the essay, "Misery Optional," Anne Richardson recounts how her faith was challenged after she was sexually abused as a child. Anne would pray to God for the abuse and pain to stop. *"But when it seemed that God continued to ignore me night after night, week after week, I started to blame Him...For over a decade, I did not speak to God and even sought to ridicule Him when the opportunity arose."*

Andrea MacEachern also questioned her faith when she faced a sorrowful turning point in her life. *"I found myself trying to make peace with God for taking away my beloved grandfather on the most peaceful day of the year"* she notes in her essay, "Christmas Heartache." In times of great suffering, tragedy and conflict, it is not uncommon to question one's faith. Some will often ask, *"If there is a God, how could He let this happen?"* This can be a normal response in the aftermath of a trauma or personal crisis.

Dr. Alicia Powers also explored this in her essay, "The Way of the Wounded Healer." In her work as a shamanic healer with persons who are ill or suffering, she believes that "*wounds mark the places where a person's spirit has been damaged or a piece of their true identity has been lost."* She has also discovered in her personal and professional healing work that *"sometimes in life, unattended wounds demand complete attention."* The avoidance of pain or trauma can sometimes make matters more complicated or create more distancing from one's faith. As Anne Richardson discovered, her ten year efforts to avoid her trauma and discount her faith led to further suffering in her life.

Both Anne and Andrea describe how their faith was re-affirmed despite a period of doubt and questioning. In Anne's situation, it took many years and great effort for her to realize, *"I have learned that professional therapy and talking with others can be very helpful, but for me, God is the only true healer... Despite what the world throws at me, I now rest comfortably in the confidence of a faith I fought hard to regain."* For Andrea, after only a day of grieving her grandfather's untimely death at Christmas, her faith was reaffirmed. Andrea writes, *"I knew this was a sign from my grandfather,"* and then she felt at peace.

Wherever or however women find their spirituality or faith, whether it is within themselves, in their daily practice or with a spiritual being such as God, Allah, or Buddha, it seems clear that a connection to a faith or a spiritual practice is common and important among women. As Alicia Powers reminded us in her essay, *"The way of the wounded healer is within each of us."* This message is comparable to one passed along in many faith communities, that 'God is within you." And then there is the simple, but profound message from Rene's mother, a devout Catholic, to her agnostic daughter, *"You don't have to go to church to be a good person."* Rene reflects, *"It was her way of accepting my decision to leave the Catholic Church even though it was very dear to her heart."* Like many women, Rene, Alicia, Anne and Andrea all faced a turning point in their faith, and they all found peace, although on very different paths.

Christmas Heartache

by Andrea MacEachern

~

The most peaceful time of year for me has always been Christmas. There were always so many people around our home during the holidays and with them came many traditions. On Christmas Eve, my parents, sisters, grandparents and I would pile into our family mini-van for a long evening drive to look at the Christmas lights. We were in church by 12:00 AM for Midnight Mass. When we arrived home we were allowed to open one gift. Then it was off to bed to get rested for the next day and another round of holiday visits, meals and presents.

The Christmas tradition in my family was like this every year until the year 2000. That was the first year we spent Christmas without my grandparents. My grandmother had passed away suddenly the previous summer. After the shock of losing her, my grandfather's health began to fail and he was admitted to the hospital in October.

A few days before the holiday, we decided that we would surprise my grandfather ("Papa") by taking him out for a few days so he could enjoy Christmas with his family. Everything was going as planned. The day before Christmas Eve, he was in high spirits when we told him he would be at home with us the next day. Dinner was already in mid-preparation and we had a room ready for Papa at our house.

The next morning, when my dad went the hospital to get our grandfather, something wasn't right. Papa was quiet and withdrawn as he stared straight ahead. My dad must have sensed that Papa wouldn't be leaving that hospital so he stayed there with him. Papa turned around to look out the window one last time and then he quietly passed away.

Christmas in my family would never be the same again without my grandparents. I spent the day in my room grieving the loss of my grandfather. I found myself trying to make peace with God for taking away my beloved grandfather on the most peaceful day of the year.

I must have cried myself to sleep that night, I don't remember, but I do remember waking up to a sound that I had not heard in a long time. It was familiar, but I wasn't sure what it was. When I discovered the sound, chills went down my spine. It was coming from an alarm clock that my grandfather gave to me years before. That clock had not worked in five or six years. The time was set to 11:30 PM. Immediately, I knew this was a sign from my grandfather because every year at 11:30 we all were on our way to Midnight Mass. I believe he wanted us to carry on like we normally would every Christmas.

As I walked in the newly fallen snow to the small church on the hill, I knew everything was going to be alright. I knew my Grandfather was there with me, and suddenly, I felt at peace.

Andrea MacEachern is freelance writer living in St. John's, Newfoundland. She has degrees in Business and Media Communications. She is currently working at a call center where she does market research, editing, and monitoring. Some of her writing credentials include co-writing a script for a 30-minute film which was screened at an international film festival and writing a number of short articles and non-fiction pieces published in various magazines and anthologies. She is also working on a feature length movie script.

Since writing "Christmas Heartache" Andrea has been working on a blog entitled "Another Day for Grace" She has also been steadily writing articles both online and offline.

Losing My Religion

by Rene Brannen

~

My mother is in the last stage of her life and it scares me to death. Maybe it would be more correct to say, death scares me. You see I'm not convinced there is an after life, a heaven or a hell, or reincarnation, for that matter. I've been thinking that maybe this is what we have, right here, right now, whether we like it or not.

Sometimes, I wish I could be someone who believes there is a life after death, or that we will all meet again someday. Death seems so much easier for those who have faith. They talk about it as a *'coming home, joining Jesus and their loved ones, or having an everlasting peace.'* Heaven is said to be a magical space and time where there is no evil, no harm and no pain. Everything is supposed to be beautiful, loving and forgiving. Dying is simply the transition to a better life or the next life–whatever that may be.

I'm just not there, but my mom is. She believes with a deep conviction that there is a Heaven and that she will be with her own mother and father again one day. She has some peace in her heart knowing that when she leaves her life here on earth, when she takes her last breath, she will be just fine. She has faced her imminent death and it only seems to make her stronger.

It was nearly two years ago when she was diagnosed with *'end stage cancer'* in her bone marrow. The doctor would not talk in weeks or months, so neither did we. She did what she needed to do with the chemotherapy (every week), the blood transfusions (every three weeks) and the daily medication regimen (morning, noon, evening and bedtime.)

Today, she is visibly weaker, thinner, and paler, but she's stronger in so many other ways. For two years, I have been a witness to how her body has changed and how her thoughts have become more confused. The look in her eyes is more distant, as though she's already left us in some ways. I wonder what she's thinking during those times. Is she thinking? Is she scared? Is she at peace?

I cannot imagine being at peace, knowing with certainty that my years, my days, my hours are limited. Knowing that this might be the last birthday or family gathering, or that I may never get to visit all the places I still want to experience, or that I may not meet or get to know my grandchildren. I can't imagine leaving my husband behind, wondering if this will be the last kiss or the last embrace we have for each other. I can't imagine saying goodbye to my son, not knowing if it will be the last time I get to look into his eyes or the last time we speak. How could I say goodbye knowing there is so much more to say? There is so much more I have to do.

Yes, it would be much easier to believe in Heaven or in an after life, a place and time where we will live together forever. I just don't. Not now—maybe not ever.

In the meantime, I believe that every day has to count. I have to live in such a way so that I won't leave with any regrets. My friends will know how much I value them. My family will know how much I love them. Maybe in some small ways, I will have made a difference in this world while I was here. It won't be easy to leave but I can't imagine it any other way.

Post script: One year later

My mom died Thanksgiving weekend. Some days I miss her presence here so much it feels as if we are worlds apart. Other days, it seems like she has never left my side.

Before she died, she gave me a very loving and precious gift. She told me (knowing that I did not go to church, did not pray the rosary, and did not practice Catholicism any more) *"You don't have to go to church to be a good person."* It was her way of accepting my decision to leave the Catholic Church even though it was very dear to her heart. It was also her way of telling me that she saw me as a good person even though I did not go to church nor believe in the teachings of Catholicism. Her acceptance of me as I am means more to me than she will ever realize.

I still don't know if I will ever see her again but I truly hope she found the Heaven she dreamed of while she was here on earth. I believe her faith helped her to live and to face her illness. It also helped her to have the courage to leave when it was her time. I don't know if she found a Heaven, but I know she found peace, and finally she was not in pain any more.

P.S. Mom, if you're listening, please send me a sign. I miss you.

Rene Brannen was born and raised Catholic. When she was a young adult, she began exploring other religions and faith communities. Ultimately, she left the Catholic Church after her family's priest of several years refused to marry her and her husband in the church since they already said their vows in a civil ceremony with a Justice of the Peace.

She has since found great acceptance and compassion with Buddhist principles as a way of life. Her favorite quote on the topic is from the Dalai Lama who once said, "My religion is kindness." Rene tries to live her life and treat others with that thought in mind. While she respects others' beliefs, she does not believe in an 'after life' but does believe in life everlasting.

Misery Optional

by Anne Richardson

This story is dedicated to Jesus Christ, my Lord and Savior, and to His many faithful disciples, who have influenced and transformed my life for the better.

~

Sitting on a psychologist's couch every week for the better part of a year was not how I envisioned my life. Even though I had a degree in psychology, I never thought of therapy as something that was for me. At best, it was a resource for depressed people who had no one else in their lives to talk to. At worst, it was a fad the wealthy engaged in to justify their insecurities. Either way, I didn't fit the bill. Besides, there wasn't anything wrong with me. I was an even-keeled, well-adjusted, working adult woman. I should be able to deal with this on my own.

Despite my resistance, I found myself in therapy, slumped into that soft leather sofa week after week, recounting the horrid nuances of a single afternoon from my youth. At first, it wasn't so bad. I was able to recite the facts perfectly as though I were reading from a newspaper article: *"Girl, 12, raped by neighbor."*

Eventually though it began to sink in that this sad story was not about some unfortunate girl two towns over. It was about me. Having buried the experience long ago, I suddenly found myself in the mindset of my younger days: horribly confused, scared half-to-death, and heartbroken. I lost countless nights of sleep and nearly twenty pounds in the slow-motion fog of rehashed trauma. Why was this so hard? I was torturing myself over something that had happened years ago. The psychologist had diagnosed me with mild post traumatic stress disorder. What was wrong with me?

Eight months later, I figured out what was wrong and it was not something any psychologist, doctor, or pill in the world could fix. Talking about the rape was definitely valuable and I had no regrets about it. Yet, the emptiness in the pit of my stomach was still there, like a bullet permanently lodged beneath my ribs. Curiously missing was my ability to breathe deeply and joyfully in an otherwise ordinary life. I resigned myself to the fact that I was never going to be fully well unless I faced the root cause of my misery: my fractured faith.

~

My journey with God began in earnest with the death of my grandmother. My mom told me one night that Grandma was very sick due to a blood disorder and there was nothing the doctors could do for her. She was going to die. At nine years of age, I understood what that meant. I also believed in a loving God and so I resolved to pray all that night for God to save Grandma's life. The next morning, I was deeply dismayed to learn that she passed away during the night. Perhaps if my prayers had been better or if I hadn't fallen asleep she would still be alive. Before I could confess my disastrous failure, Mom told me that Grandma's death was actually a blessing. She had been suffering greatly so God was quite merciful by taking her to Heaven. I was stunned by the wisdom and graciousness of God and thus my faith deepened.

Three years later, I was in the midst of the agony that brought me to the psychologist's couch. This time, I found my faith being attacked along with my body. In the pain and terror of the rape, I cried out twice to God. The first time, my attacker said, *"God can't hear you."* The second time, he said, *"Don't you get it? God isn't there."* It was tempting to believe him under the circumstances, but I knew he was wrong. God was there even if for the moment I lacked the ability to reconcile His presence with such a horrific experience.

I suffered deeply following the rape and I prayed often for relief. *Please God, just allow me to die in my sleep. This hurts so much and I'm never going to get better. You stopped Grandma from hurting. Please do the same for me. Thank you, Amen.*

Despite this nightly prayer, I awoke to a painful life each morning. At first, I thought my prayers weren't clear or ardent enough. But when it seemed that God continued to ignore me night after night, week after week, I started to blame Him: *I guess you can't hear me. Or maybe you don't want to hear me. Or maybe you don't care about me. You let this happen to me, and now you won't make it better. I'm done with you.*

For over a decade, I did not speak to God and even sought to ridicule Him when the opportunity arose. I attended church with friends on occasion, but I hated being there. It disgusted me to hear people talk about their love of God. I buried God with the rape and moved on with life.

I enjoyed school, friends, and activities like any teenager. But deep in the tender recesses of my soul, the pesky realization of God's presence would not leave me. Whether I wanted to believe it or not, I simply felt that God did exist. He must have been very upset with me. How dare I tell God off and then make fun of Him? I pictured God sitting on a regal throne with a disapproving expression on His face, tapping a heavy wooden paddle in His hand. I could almost hear Him say, *"I'll teach you to speak about me that way!"* I became convinced that God was going to punish me by giving me the one thing I had repeatedly asked for—death. But I didn't want to die anymore. I grew intensely afraid of God such that I actually expected to die nearly every day. It was a miserable existence for a young person. After a while, it occurred to me that God probably had better things to do than taunt me with the possibility of death and besides, I grew tired of worrying about it.

I still could not bring myself to talk to God. The divide between us was just too big. Not only had I shamefully insulted God but I also assumed that He hated me enough to want to kill me. I no longer felt afraid of God, but what I did feel was crushing guilt. I believed in Him but I believed the words of my rapist more. I learned that Jesus died so that my sins could be forgiven, but did that really apply to me? I felt that I did not deserve to have a relationship with God and for years I simply gave up trying.

~

So there I was with the therapy behind me and the rest of my life ahead of me. I definitely felt more comfortable in my skin as a survivor of rape, but I mistakenly expected that therapy would cure everything that ailed me. I still lacked the inner spark of life and, worse yet, I lacked the motivation to seek it. I felt defeated and believed that being happy and communing with God would not ever be possible for me. Knowing that the problem was my broken faith, I faced a decision: I could continue to avoid God and live under the weight of quiet and persistent misery; or, I could face my pain before God Himself and allow Him to heal me. It was the most important decision of my life.

My father in-law was involved in a program through his church called Stephen Ministry. Stephen Ministers are ordinary people who are trained to serve as lay spiritual counselors for individuals who are dealing with questions and crises of faith. I knew from my father in-law's experience as a Stephen Minister that it was a good program and my best hope. I called the church and a few days later, I met with the Stephen Minister who had been assigned to me. Her name was Liz. She was a short, petite, bubbly woman in her late 40s. Liz was everything I was not: outgoing, charming, joyful, energetic and confident in her faith. I worried that someone so different from me wouldn't be able to understand how I had fallen so far from God.

Through the hot and humid weeks of summer, Liz and I met at a local park to walk and talk. From our first walk, I was firmly convinced that I did the right thing by calling the church. Despite my initial concerns, Liz was ideal for me and helped me to know that God was very much a part of the process. I felt completely at ease and able to share everything with her. At the end of each walk, Liz invited me to say a prayer, but I could not muster the courage or the strength to do so. For many weeks, her beautiful words spoke to God with the emotions my heart longed to express.

God's love eventually reached me through Liz's leading and example. I finally found the courage to speak to Him. At first my prayers were saturated with pain and guilt. *I can't take this anymore...I don't want to live like this...I know you must think I'm horrible....* Raw emotion quickly melted away to the simultaneous realizations that I was in desperate need of God and that God was ready and willing to take me in. The questions of *"why me?"* and *"how could you let this happen?"* seemed to answer themselves. After years of running from and fearing God, I finally experienced the quiet, constant and tangible presence of a loving God that made me whole. The bullet that was once beneath my ribs rapidly dissolved.

~

Today, I am experiencing a new restlessness in the form of an unquenchable thirst for God. Whereas before I avoided Him at all costs, now I seek Him in everything. I have discovered a calling in helping others who are suffering. Although I don't get the opportunity often enough, I long to share with these sufferers the truths I have learned about God and His ability to heal us. Liz and I now enjoy a close friendship and she is the godmother of my daughter. She continues to inspire me in my daily walk with God.

I would be lying if I portrayed my life today as utterly perfect. Life doesn't work that way. Sometimes, I am still haunted by memories of the rape and the needless suffering I endured. Sometimes, witnessing the suffering of others shakes me to my core. Often I find myself in a fog of seriousness, such that having fun and feeling light-hearted is difficult. And sometimes I don't take the time to pray as often as I should.

Despite what the world throws at me, I now rest comfortably in the confidence of a faith I fought hard to regain. I have learned that professional therapy and talking with others can be very helpful, but for me, God is the only true healer. I have learned that we all experience pain and loss in our lives and that each such experience presents us with an opportunity: Learn from the pain and use it for the good of God. I have learned that God is always there. Trust me on that one.

Recently, I drove past a small, rural church with a sign by the road. It read, *"Suffering is inevitable. Misery is optional."* I couldn't help but smile when I saw it. *Amen.*

Anne is currently an administrator for a victim services program and has been working in the non-profit sector for the past eight years. She lives with her husband and daughter in the Midwest and enjoys reading, writing and photography. Following the events depicted in her story, Anne began volunteering to support other survivors, which led her to a career in victim services. Today, she also volunteers as a bereavement counselor for a hospice program. She is interested in someday pursuing pastoral counseling or ministry. Her ultimate desire is to share God's healing love with those who suffer from life's difficulties. She and Liz remain close friends and attend church and Bible studies together.

The Way of the Wounded Healer

by Dr. Alicia Powers

It is one of my core beliefs that no matter the person or circumstance, it is nature that calls each one of us to strive to become whole.

Wounds mark the places where a person's spirit has been damaged or a piece of their true identity has been lost. Sometimes in life, unattended wounds demand complete attention with utter disregard to what may seem important at the time. Life must be rearranged because the pain will not allow you to move forward. The more you try to conceal the wound, the larger it seems to grow. Love and care are necessary. We cannot put a band-aid on a wound that requires so much more to heal.

A while back, an astrologer called me a *wounded healer.* The words hung in the air for a few seconds. She told me that the work that I had done to heal my own wounds helped to make me a gifted healer to others. Her words provoked an emotional response in me. At that time, I thought of wounds as weaknesses.

As an adult, much of my life's energy had been devoted to tending to my wounds, assessing the damage and attempting to heal. I learned, from one day to the next, that there are many paths to wholeness and so many speeds at which to get there. The more I thought about the astrologist's words, the more I recognized that taking care of my own wounds motivated me to search for and to discover powerful ways to heal.

One path that has been very helpful to me is remembrance. Reflecting on a pure and simple memory of a time before the wound—before the missing piece and sometimes before my incarnation—brings me peace and healing. I find solace in knowing that in our truest form we are all whole. Each day, I become more adept at remembering and knowing this to be true.

Now, I am a healer. I am a feisty, stubborn, and sometimes reluctant healer who has answered the call to share my gifts with others. I integrate many forms of intuitive healing including tarot, Reiki energy work and Shamanic practices. I have used these paths to heal myself.

The astrologer's reading came at a time in my life when I was just starting to share my gifts with others in need. It was new, foreign and sometimes uncomfortable to release these gifts that I had previously only practiced in solitude. I learned to trust that what I had to offer would benefit others as well.

Since then, I have been blessed to assist many people as they travel on their path toward healing. It gives me great comfort to know that when it comes to the search for healing and wholeness, we all have wisdom to share. The way of the wounded healer is within each of us.

Dr. Alicia Powers is a Modern Shaman and Reiki Master who has studied with spiritual teachers from around the world. She helps others to discover their path and realize their wholeness. She invites you to visit her website at www.aliciapowers.com.

Update from the author: Since I initially wrote this piece, I have continued to help others find their path to knowing wholeness. I work with clients across the country and around the world. I feel blessed to have the opportunity to do what I do.

Reflection Points

Everything in life that we really accept undergoes a change.
— Katherine Mansfield

From the authors in their words

- *I have learned that we all experience pain and loss in our lives and that each such experience presents us with an opportunity...*
- *I have to live in such a way so that I won't leave with any regrets.*
- *Life must be rearranged because the pain will not allow you to move forward.*
- *I knew my Grandfather was there with me, and suddenly, I felt at peace.*
- *I have learned that God is always there.*

Questions to contemplate at the threshold of faith and religion

- *In what way, if any, are your beliefs about faith or spirituality different from your parents' beliefs? If you have children, what have you taught them?*
- *What do you believe?*
- *Has there ever been a time in your life when you questioned your faith, and if so, how did you come to terms with your doubts or questions?*
- *Knowing that there are so many different beliefs and viewpoints about faith and spirituality in the world, how do you reconcile these differences in a way that is consistent with the teachings of your faith?*

CHAPTER 13

Starting Over

You decide to do something, perform one small action,
and suddenly it's a tide, the momentum is going,
and there's no possibility of turning back.
Somehow, even though you thought you foresaw
all that would happen,
you didn't know the pace would pick up so."
—Amanda Cross

Starting over can be an intimidating and overwhelming undertaking for anyone, especially if it requires leaving your old life behind. For some women, it means going to a new country with a different language, different laws, a different culture and a different lifestyle. The three women in this chapter started over for three very distinctive reasons and from three very dissimilar parts of the world. Minerva left a hard life and an abusive partner in Mexico in order to be safe in America, where her parents lived. Va left Laos in the 1970s as a young child with her family to escape the dangers in her homeland and to find sanctuary in America. Doreen left behind the pain of a recent divorce and the betrayal of her friend and ex-boyfriend to go to Ireland to be on her own for the first time in her life and to do something for herself. All three of these women needed a fresh start on their lives.

Their journeys were vastly different and across the globe, but they each ended up getting to their destination and finding peace. The trip was grueling and life-threatening for Minerva and her two young boys as they fled Mexico. In her essay, "The Most Important Turning Point in My Life," Minerva tells about the night that changed her life. She and her sons left behind years of abuse and an unsafe household in the middle of the night. On their journey, they faced torrential rains, closed roads and detours. Midway through the trip, when Minerva was told the roads were closed and transportation was not available but she vowed, *"Nothing was going to stop me now."* In her determination to save her children and herself from further abuse, they took a treacherous walk in the dark of night, over a railroad bridge with rising waters below and a downpour of rain from above. When they made it to the other side and finally reached her parent's home in America, Minerva was relieved, *"Finally, I had escaped."* She did what she needed to do for herself and for her children to start over and to be free from abuse.

Va Vang and her family left a violent, war-torn and politically-charged homeland to find safety. Their situation was very different, however. It was 1975 when Va and her family were forced with thousands of others to leave Laos. In her essay, "A New Challenge," Va recalls the hardships with the many moves until they reached their new home in America, *"Many times we wanted to give up but something told us that if we did not try, we would not survive."* Va tells how she and her family persevered despite the obstacles and uncertainties in this foreign land. *"We faced new challenges everyday and learned how to survive each time we moved."* Her family had to adapt to a new culture, educational system and laws in order to make this country their home. *"We wanted to see what the world had to offer,"* Va concludes with a deep sense of pride and honor to be settled in America with her family.

A very different story about starting over is told by Doreen J. Garrigan in her essay, "The Roundabout Way to Becoming Me." Doreen also found herself in the midst of a life-changing crisis which led to her a turning point decision. Doreen knew she had to find a way to move forward after her recent divorce and a painful betrayal by a friend and ex-boyfriend. So, for the first time in her life, she decided to take some time on her own to heal and to care for herself. Doreen's turning point began on a trip to Ireland—a country where she knew no one and would be on her own. Doreen discovered how this decision made her feel stronger and more independent, *"I realized for the first time I was doing something completely new and exciting without a man by my side."* In her essay, Doreen tells about her adventures in another country which led to finding some peace within and as well some experiences that offered her further insights about love, loss and life. Her journey was transformative: *"The roundabout path led me to find out who I truly am and that quite frankly is priceless."*

Starting over can lead to a new life for many women. As Minerva concluded, *"Making that decision was the most important turning point in my life."* As these three women learned when the doors to the past closed behind them, starting over opened doors of hope and possibility for a new life.

The Most Important Turning Point in My Life

by Minerva

The bus stopped in Camargo, a little city in the state of Chihuahua, Mexico. The driver told us he could not continue. It seemed that due to severe storms, it was not possible to pass to Chihuahua City. The bad news was that the road was destroyed by the flow of the heavy rains.

We were told we would have to wait until the next day to know the damage the rain had done to the highway. I decided to go to my best friend Velia's house since she lives in Camargo. She is the wife of the manager of the bus line. I was sure that her husband Octavio would help me because he knew the kind of life I had. And yes, they did. They offered us their home for the time that we needed it.

Later, the news informed us that the rain would continue for several more days. I could not take a chance that *he* would catch us, so, I decided to cross the river through the only way available: the railroad. My friend Velia was crying as she pleaded with me not to leave until the next day but I answered, *"No, absolutely not. Nothing was going to stop me now."* It was imperative that we continued since we were half way to being safe.

It was about midnight and only 30 minutes since we had left my dearest friend's house. We realized that the news was true. The whole state was flooded from several days of rain and the highway was destroyed. The only way we could cross the river was to walk over the railroad bridge. My friend was terrified, but we had to go.

We could see thousands of gallons of water roaring under our feet. The rain continued coming down like an open faucet which allowed for no relief in the ferocity of the current of the river. The turbulent flow was dragging animals, trees, trash and parts of houses downstream. Just glancing at this scene was terrifying for me and, of course, for my two little boys who were also petrified. They were only ten and nine years old at the time.

My 10-year-old son Marcello was helping me to carry some of our possessions that I was able to grab during our escape. These were things we would need for our new life. The rest of our belongings were carried by two soldiers who were helping us. I carried Miguel, my youngest son, on my back because he suffered from a spider bite on one foot. He was crying and trembling as he listened to the sounds of the torrential rain and watched the devastation that the river was causing below us.

He told me that he was scared and he wanted to go home. Poor boy, he did not realize that we no longer had a home. Several times, I told him not to look down but he did so anyway. At one point, he was trembling so severely that I lost my balance and we almost fell into the river. I needed to shake him and slap his face to make him to stop. Throughout the tribulation of it all the bridge seemed to be ten miles long. Finally, we reached the other side of the bridge.

Exhausted from the terrifying experience, we then waited in a long line of people for our turn to get seats on the bus.

Later, when we arrived at my parents' house, they could not believe it. They knew the roads and bridges were destroyed by the torrential rain, but somehow we made it. Finally, I had escaped. From there, I would start a new and different battle: to overcome all the abuse I suffered for nearly twenty years.

I understood that my children did not deserve that life. I also understood that he would never change. I put together the love for my sons and the courage that I needed to leave him. Discovering those facts and making that decision was the most important turning point in my life.

~

Update from the author: I was able to follow my dream of going to college! I started studying ESL (English as a Second Language) at the same time I was giving my best effort to get my GED. I did it! I was rewarded as the "Student of the Year" among 35,000 students from the whole state. Next, I was ready to continue with my college goal. I enrolled in the New Mexico State University. First, I earned an Associate's degree in Microcomputer Technology. Then, I got two Bachelor's degrees—one in Sociology and the second in Languages and Linguistics, both at New Mexico State University.

~

A New Challenge

by Va Vang

~

No one really knows what life might throw at us. One day, we think that life will be the same and we will be doing the same thing all our lives. Then, change strikes without warning. My family had to unexpectedly move from Laos in 1975 to Thailand and then to America. We faced new challenges everyday and learned how to survive each time we moved. We experienced what many other minorities have to go through in a new culture including learning the language, the economy and so much more.

We had to move from Laos to any country that would take us in. The Hmong people were scattered all over to other countries when moved from Laos. Some moved to Vietnam, Thailand, Cambodia and some stayed in Laos. We first moved to Thailand and stayed there for five years; then we came to America in 1980.

We arrived in Union, Oregon. The United States of American became our new home; it is beautiful. We knew that we would face challenges but that it would be all right. We would learn to adapt to our new home, new neighbors and new community. Our Mom and Dad did not speak any English, so we had to leave everything to our sponsor, Robert Miller. He took us to the stores, doctors appointments, and he enrolled us in school.

We had to learn our new language, English, to be in school. My siblings had to be in their own class rooms. We could not stay in one class together like in Thailand where everyone attended the same class for the first year. I was in fifth grade, my younger sister in fourth, my two youngest brothers in first and second grade and my big brothers were in high school. We were so scared of what was going to happen to us. We were afraid that if we did not know what to do our teachers would punish us like in Thailand. Teachers in Thailand used a stick if we did not learn what was taught; we had to put our hand out and let the teacher hit our hands if we had trouble learning. Or, for even more disgrace, the student that did better in class would be the one to hit us, that way, according to the Thai theory, we would learn better and faster if we were embarrassed. Before school started, my brothers said we had to be strong and we should not let our weakness show. He did not want us to embarrass him.

My two older brothers and I had the privilege of learning English in Thailand but we only knew half of the alphabet and could only count one through ten. We could not communicate with anyone just yet. We started to learn the alphabet. During the school hours our sponsor Mr. Miller spent at least two hours with each of us learning English words by using visual aids and audio tapes. He also studied with us at home after school. Mr. Miller was an *English as a Second Language* (ESL) teacher so he was very patient with us. Before long, we knew our English alphabet and some new words. We started to talk in sentences but we did not have the confidence to do so. It took us a long time to learn English. My parents also attended ESL classes but it was too hard for them to learn and to hear the words. They lost hope after a while.

After six months in Union, Oregon, we moved away from Mr. Miller and to Portland, Oregon. My parents and grandma missed the Hmong community and Portland had more Hmong people, so we had to move. We continued our school and then moved to Fresno, California where the largest Hmong community lives. Though English was a hard language to learn we learned enough to survive in America.

When we first arrived in America, my parents could not work since they did not know how to operate machines or to speak English so we were on Public Assistance. In Oregon, the cash aid program pays less than California. There were ten of us in the family eligible for Cash Aid, Food Stamps and Medi-Cal. I do not know how much we got but my parents said that after paying the rent, utilities and laundry, we had no more money left to spend.

We did not have a car so we walked almost everywhere we had to go. If we had to go far we took the city bus. We rarely took the bus though because we could not afford the bus fare. My parents had to be frugal. We could not even buy clothes; we had to go get second hand clothing that cost us nothing. There were some Sundays that we couldn't even go to church because we could not afford the bus fair. My brothers were too young to drive and we had no money to buy a car anyway. We would see other people that had more money and material things that we could not have. It was so hard to think that we made a great decision coming to America yet we were enduring all of these difficulties.

When my oldest brother got married we had to pay a bride price. At the time, it was five hundred dollars but we had no money. Our relatives had to help my brother so that he could get married. After he got married, he and his wife went to work. They saved up a little money and bought a commercial van. It was the only vehicle that could carry the ten of us. We did not complain that there were not any seats in the van. We sat on the floor of the van and were very pleased to have a ride.

It did not take as long to figure out that we did not want to live like our parents. Since we had the chance to go to school, we wanted to do better. My second brother and I got our Associates degrees. My third brother got his PhD in Economics and the rest of my youngest siblings got high school diplomas. Each of us are now employed and bought our own homes. We live in a new country trying to meet our needs and to be financially secure.

When we left Laos and Thailand to come to America, we had to learn and relearn a new language and a new way of life. It took so much energy out of us. Many times we wanted to give up but something told us that if we did not try, we would not survive. We thrived because we had no choice. We are one the many mini tribes that no longer has their own country since we had to move from one place to the next. There were many that gave up, unlike us. We wanted to see what the world had to offer. If you ask those of us who are here and have succeeded, we would say that the sky is the limit. Here is to America, the land of opportunity!

My name is Va Her Vang. I was born in Laos but I am not sure what city I was born in. My parents had me at home in the mountain so there was no birth record of me. I was the ninth child of the twelve children born to my parents. Then, my birthday was any given day until we applied to come to America. In order for anyone to come into the United States of America, my parents had to pick a birthday for me, so they picked April 2, 1968. I have been married to a wonderful husband for twenty-five years with six children and four grandchildren.

Update from the author: My life has remained the same since I wrote the story. The story was written about when I was growing up and how it was moving to America. Now, I am taking one day at a time to enjoy my life, my family and those adorable grandchildren. Here is to LIFE! Cheers!

The Roundabout Way to Becoming Me

by Doreen J. Garrigan

~

The Question

It began with a question. I was making my way to my favorite lunch table to relax for a few minutes and to enjoy the company of my fellow teaching colleagues. My girlfriend Kim was holding a red game card in her hand. She said to the table, *"OK everyone, next question... What is the one thing you've done in your life that you wish you could erase?"* There was a considerable pause among my colleagues when I blurted out, *"I have one."* All six sets of curious eyes turned in my direction, waiting for me to share my one erasable life choice.

"I wish I could erase my choice to date another man, during my separation, rather than work on my marriage."

Six years of therapy, numerous life coaches and many roads traveled had led me to share the one part of myself that I am not proud to admit. The truth is, I didn't just date another man; I let my marriage crumble and fall apart simply because another man (a much younger and very attractive one) paid attention to me when I was lonely and struggling with my life. What began as an emotional affair while my husband still lived in the home quickly became a "relationship" once my husband moved out. I allowed myself to get caught up in a whirlwind, without a single word spoken about my actions and their impact on the future. When I wasn't with my two daughters, I was with this man, living a lie while my husband stayed faithful until our divorce papers were signed.

To complicate matters, my "boyfriend" broke up with me the same week my divorce was final. I then got the devastating news that my "boyfriend" had been cheating on me with a close friend of ours. To say that I hit rock bottom would truly be an understatement. I felt as though I was drowning in despair with no lifejacket to save me. There are days I don't remember; how I got to work and maintained appearances is beyond me. By the second week post-breakup, I was in therapy trying to learn how to breathe again. My marriage was officially over and the man I thought loved me had moved on, quickly and publicly, with my friend. My friend's response when I confronted her was, *"Did you think it was going to last forever? Doreen, you need to find someone your own age and in your own situation."* I wanted to claw her eyes out. It took many therapy sessions to move away from the pain they had caused me. Once I made the shift, truly great moments started to happen.

It was only after my life went careening out of control that I realized that there was a drastic need to change. I needed to get my head out of the clouds, be honest and responsible for the pain I had caused others and myself, and, most importantly, get myself on the right track. My marriage ended in divorce but my life didn't have to crumble away like the vows. Only after I did some serious work and honest self-examination with a licensed therapist did I start to see a future so very different from the one I created during and after my marriage.

Erin Go Brah

My therapist and I had narrowed down my major life issue to the fact that I had never done anything on my own without family approval. Being raised in a very strict Irish-Catholic household with few individual privileges, I navigated adulthood choosing to please family and friends over pleasing myself. I didn't know how to stand on my own and make my own choices without the approval of my parents. Being a people-pleaser had resulted in two failed marriages and a string of bad choices.

It was time for me to do something very personal, just for me. I chose to go to Ireland for eight days. I chose Ireland because I had always dreamed of visiting there. While I researched my trip, I realized for the first time that I was doing something completely new and exciting without a man by my side. I was still working through the pain of my divorce and the betrayal by my friend and ex-boyfriend, but now I had something to look forward to.

Ireland was incredible. My favorite spot was a manor house, Walton Court, in Oysterhaven, County Cork, about 30 miles outside of Kinsale. While staying at Walton Court, I befriended the owners, a charming English couple named Janis and Paul. We dined together, enjoying Argentinean wine and French cuisine. I found the couple worldly and very engaging. I inquired about the French workers they had caring for their organic gardens. They told me about a work program called WWoOFers: Willing Workers on Organic Farms. For free room and board, people volunteer from all over the world to work the organic gardens and farms in Ireland and to travel on their days off. A light bulb went on in my head: What an incredible way to get back to the country I had fallen in love with. I was organizing my return before my feet touched down on American soil.

Before I left the Emerald Isle, I spent my last night in Dublin, in a castle/hotel in a district called Clontarf. I decided to commit to my normal routine while visiting. I headed to a pub to have dinner and pretended to read something very interesting so that I wouldn't look like I was desperate for company. As usual, others noticed that I was dining alone and asked why I didn't have a dining companion. This particular evening, I was invited over by a charming group of "professionals" including an accountant, a social worker, a mortician and a government worker.

One of the ladies pointed to a man next to us and said, quite seriously, *"If you had three days with this man, you'd marry him."* She introduced Mark to me and for the first time in a long time, I was without words. He was beautiful: 6'2", black hair, piercing blue eyes and an Irish brogue straight out of Belfast. It was nearly 2 a.m. and the pub was closing. The others at the table were discussing the morning's business ahead. I had a good walk back to the hotel ahead of me and I realized I was alone in a foreign city, after midnight, without a taxi readily available. Mark offered to escort me back to the castle. I said yes.

Our walk back was awkwardly romantic, exciting and also bittersweet because it was my last night in Ireland. My flight left at 8:30 a.m. and I knew I was going to get very little sleep. When we came to the castle/hotel, I was at a crossroads. I could invite this very charming and very attractive man (with an accent that made my knees weak) back to my hotel room and probably commit several cardinal sins or I could say goodbye and move on, grateful for one of the most exciting nights in a very long time. Mark was interested in coming to my room but he was a complete gentleman when I declined.

This trip was about me learning how to live on my own. That meant not turning to a man to ease my loneliness or my anxiety about being alone. What awaited me when I returned home was a beautiful email from Mark telling me what an impact I had on him. We conversed for two years and shared many wonderful life moments via email and phone calls. I never did see him again.

The Reluctant Gardener

It didn't take long once I returned home to realize that one trip to Ireland wasn't going to be enough. I was a different person upon arriving home. Ireland changed me. I kept saying to myself, *"No one can take this experience away from me, no one."* My ex-boyfriend and former friend were now engaged, after dating only five months. My ex-husband was being transferred to Japan for the next three years. Not only was I a single woman, but I was going to be a geographic single mother as well. My life was looking very different than it had a year prior. Would I be able to handle the continuing changes? With my new-found personal power, I embarked on creating additional positive changes in my life. First on my agenda was getting back to Ireland.

I emailed my English friends, Janis and Paul at Walton Court, and inquired about working at their manor for the summer. They responded with an enthusiastic yes. It took a lot of shuffling around to arrange places for my daughters to stay, but by October, 2003 my trip was confirmed. I was going back to Ireland for five weeks to work in the organic gardens at Walton Court. I was ecstatic. When I told friends and family they looked at me as though I was crazy! I didn't know the first thing about gardening. *How was I going to live so far from home? How could I leave my daughters for that length of time? What kind of mother was I?*

Landing in Ireland felt like coming home. It was exactly as I remembered it. At Walton Court, I had my own "chateau," complete with a kitchen and bath. It was in the main kitchen that Janis shared with me her love of French cooking. It was also the beginning of my education in the Slow Food movement. Janis and Paul educated me on organic foods, the indecency of raising American cattle and the movement worldwide to salvage certain indigenous foods from extinction. I absorbed everything they taught me, like a sponge. Paul and Janis teased me about being American. They said I wasn't meant to live in America; that I was meant to live in Ireland. I was beginning to believe it myself.

My "Soul Mate"

Chris, the head gardener at Walton Court, introduced me to the world of organic gardening. We spent most mornings in the poly tunnel greenhouse, working on 5 different varieties of tomatoes. We spent afternoon hours in the garden, weeding potatoes, asparagus, and strawberries. Chris lived simply, with no bank account and only enough clothes to fit in his backpack. Chris taught me how to garden, and it was during our late-night conversations that I really learned that there is a big world out there, full of people with vastly different opinions.

If someone is fortunate enough to meet a "soul-mate," then I think you could say that their life is complete. I'm not talking about the sort of "soul-mate" in romance movies on the Lifetime channel. I'm talking about the kind of person who changes you, from the inside out. Chris did that for me. He affected me in so many wonderful ways. Chris became my best friend and it was obvious to Paul and Janis that we had a close friendship.

Evenings were my favorite part of the day. Chris and I would join Paul and Janis in their kitchen around 8:00 p.m. Dinner conversation went on for 2 or 3 hours, usually accompanied by 1 or 2 bottles of wine. After dinner, Chris and I would go back to my chateau and talk into the early morning. We discussed things I would never think of discussing back home; you name it, Chris and I talked about it.

Mid-way through the summer, Chris and I began to become more romantic. When he began backing away, I got upset. I didn't understand why he was resisting. He came back to me when he heard me crying and shared with me his very private secret: Chris was suffering from the advanced stages of a Venereal Disease. He'd become infected with a former girlfriend who lived in the United States. She transmitted the disease to him during one of her visits. By the time she told him about her diagnosis, Chris was already past immediate help. He never realized how serious the disease could become.

That night, I learned how to love someone on a completely different level. Chris and I never had sex or even explored other avenues for sexual pleasure. We didn't want to risk my health. We continued to spend every waking moment with each other, venturing off to Cork for day trips on our days off. He constantly spoke about me living my dreams and never giving up on myself. He told me how precious and beautiful I was and how he wished it could be different for us. My last night at Walton Court, Chris slept with me. He helped me pack and walked me to the cab. I cried all the way to the airport. I was again leaving the one place I loved more than any other. *Why was I leaving?*

The Invitation

During my stay in Ireland, I ventured to Scotland for 8 days, enduring a lengthy bus tour. I was one of three 30-something singles on the bus: An American man and an Australian woman, Kym, rounded out the trio. We became inseparable as Kym (from Sydney) became my travel confidant. Together we explored late night discos in Edinburgh and Glasgow, making the most out of the Scottish nightlife.

One day, over a very traditional Scottish lunch of lamb pie, I was talking to Kym about the American tradition of Thanksgiving. The conversation ended with an invitation for Kym to visit me and my girls for Thanksgiving. Why I invited someone I'd only just met was beyond me, but for some reason, it made sense. She enthusiastically agreed.

Kym came to visit and stayed with us for just under two months. Our friendship grew to one of sisterhood, built on mutual trust and respect. My daughters fell in love with her and adjusted with ease to having another adult in the house. Kym didn't have children of her own and was nervous about the baby years slipping by her. One night over dinner Kym said to me, *"This is what I want. I want what you have. You have your children and you have love in this home. That's what I want."*

For many months after her return home, we discussed ways to get Kym back into the United States permanently. We had a hard time with the separation. I felt as though I had lost my best friend and sister. Time went by and Kym resumed her life in Sydney. I did see her again, in Las Vegas in 2006, when I was Maid of Honor in her Elvis-inspired wedding to a wonderful man named Matt. She remains one of the most special people in my life. We may not speak over the phone as often as we'd like, but we remain committed to staying in each other's lives.

Lessons

From my travels abroad and the truly unique and uplifting people I've met along the way, my life lessons have come down to a few: It is absolutely okay to be alone. It is absolutely okay to make decisions for you and you alone. The world is not going to stop because you decide to fulfill a dream or reach out to try something new for yourself.

I was once terrified of being alone. I associated being alone with not being worthy. Not having approval from family or from a man in my life left me feeling shaky and full of doubt. I didn't know how to navigate around uncertainty. I didn't know how to relish the comfort of a quiet, dateless Saturday night. I let others tell me what I should be doing, all the while knowing that my life was not moving in *my* direction. I said *"yes"* too many times when I should've had the confidence to say *"no."* It took traveling across the Atlantic Ocean, pulling weeds for five weeks, having one of the most intimate relationships without even kissing, dancing my way through Scotland and finally finding true sisterhood with a genuine friend to know myself.

It's been five years since my last trip to Ireland. I have since traveled to Greece and to Turkey (where I fell in love again and this time it was very real). The summer of 2009, I went on a trip to the "Land Down Under," Australia, to see Kym.

I am now at a point in my life where I can look back and not feel as much pain for the decisions I made in my marriage. It takes two to unravel a relationship. I have taken care of myself, both emotionally and spiritually, since the divorce. By seeking professional help, I was able to ask for forgiveness from my ex-husband and daughters and then to start anew.

I was asked that day, at the lunch table, whether I could or would do things differently. All I can say now is that I would not want to hurt my daughters or my husband. Truthfully, I would not change the past six years, because today I love who I am and where I have been. More importantly, I look at my future with confidence, knowing that I will be just fine, without fear or anxiety because I am single or alone. I may have taken a more difficult road, but the roundabout path led me to find who I truly am. That, quite frankly, is priceless.

~

Doreen J. Garrigan resides in Virginia Beach Virginia with her two daughters, Lauren and Rachel. She is a Gifted Resource Teacher with Virginia Beach City Public Schools. In July 2009, Doreen co-led a delegation of high school students with People-to-People to Australia. She snorkeled in the Great Barrier Reef, rappelled off a 90 foot cliff in the Blue Mountains and surfed at the famous Manley Beach. She also got to spend a wonderful evening with her dear friend, Kym.

~

Reflection Points

Only in growth, reform and change,
paradoxically enough, true security can be found.
— Anne Morrow Lindbergh

From the authors in their words

- *Once I made the shift, truly great moments started to happen.*

- *My life lessons have come down to a few: It is absolutely okay to be alone. It is absolutely okay to make decisions for you and you alone.*

- *I understood that my children did not deserve that life. I also understood that he would never change. I put together the love for my sons and the courage that I needed to leave him.*

- *No one really knows what life might throw at us. One day, we think that life will be the same...Then, change strikes without warning.*

Questions to contemplate at the threshold of starting over

- *Have you ever started over before? What happened that led you to that decision and how did it go for you? If you are considering starting over, what are the pros and cons? What barriers must you overcome? What supports and resources do you need?*

- *Is starting over worth the risk(s) that you might face? If you are not sure, what are some alternatives to starting over?*

- *What are your trusted friends and loved ones saying about this potential decision? If you have not told them, why have you kept it from them?*

- *What is your head telling you that you must do? Your heart?*

CHAPTER 14

Identity and Rediscovery (Moving on)

When I speak of change,
I do not mean a simple switch of positions
or a temporary lessening of tensions,
nor the ability to smile or feel good.
I am speaking of a basic and radical alteration
in all those assumptions underlining our lives.
— Audre Lorde

At some point, you might find yourself questioning if you are where you want to be in your life or if you are doing what you want to do. These common reflections often occur at significant developmental, social or interpersonal turning points, such as at mid-life, the end of a marriage, children leaving home, the onset of a serious medical diagnosis or at retirement. Some refer to this as a 'mid-life' crisis, but it is much more far-reaching than middle-age. Changing course in life is not uncommon at all. In fact, feelings of restlessness or the need for "soul-searching" can often lead women to life-changing transitions.

Finding meaning or purpose and affirming your identity are turning points usually associated with much forethought and consideration, and they are often triggered by discontent. In "Ending the Tyranny of 'Supposed To,'" author Margo Pierce confronts the realization in her life that she was acting out of an obligation to others rather than meeting her own needs: *"While fulfilling those obligations, I worked hard to convince myself that it was supposed to be enough."* Margo discovered that the years she lived according to others' expectations were, in fact, *"suffocating." "Unexpectedly cut loose from the quintessential "supposed to" after 18 years, I was surprised by the depth and breadth of the unwanted yet willingly chosen influences that controlled and directed my life."* Her discontent led Margo to the awareness that her life was not the way she wanted it to be and she needed to make changes for her own good.

An awareness of your situation can be the impetus for change, but for most women, change only comes after considerable contemplation and prioritizing of needs, wants, desires, possibilities and options. Margo reminds us of the dilemma: *"Being guided by an internal sense of what is right and best...is a much harder way to live."* Moving forward does not always come easily, even if you know what you want to do.

Another author in this chapter, Karen Ander Francis, faced a radically life-altering turning point as well. However, Karen's transformation did not come until after a traumatic auto accident in which she broke several bones, including her neck. During her extensive and uncertain recovery, Karen realized, *"We have inside us all we need to make healthy, life-giving choices for taking care of ourselves."* In her essay, "Winter Solstice," Karen recounts how life can change in an instant, leading to re-thinking everything that had brought you to that point. Ironically, Karen's auto accident occurred one evening on her way home from giving a presentation on the importance of self-care and the power of saying "no." In her painful year-long recovery, Karen had much time to reflect and to focus on her own self-care. This unexpected pause and shift in her day-to-day routine helped Karen rediscover her meaning and purpose. She was able to reconnect with what she wanted and needed by listening to herself.

Cynthia Perry Colebrook initially questioned her instincts when she and her husband were contemplating a life-changing decision to sell their home in the suburbs and live on a sail boat indefinitely. In "Topaz," Cynthia tells about her 10-year ambivalence with this issue and how she wrestled with the prospect of making such a considerable change in her life. Her essay incorporates a letter she wrote to her children telling how she and her husband came to their decision. Cynthia recalls, *"Right then and there, we made a conscious choice to go with the momentum, and to deny resistance and doubt."*

Moving forward on a path of rediscovery sometimes involves a leap of faith and trust that you will be okay, no matter what happens. All three of these women experienced significant uncertainty, all three made changes, and all three affirmed that they had made the right decision. As Margo realized, *"I could and did choose differently."* Now she is living the life that she wants. Even though it is undeniably challenging at times, she is living life on her own terms. Cynthia and her husband are living on the boat and loving it: *"In the end, once the decision was made, we called it our seamless transition."* Karen pursued her path of rediscovery through her healing. She knows now, "*At times when I need a pick-me-up I can remind myself that I have some options.*"

Recognizing your options and trusting yourself are crucial to moving on in life. You just might discover that you have been on the right path all along. Or, as these three women have demonstrated, it is possible to transform your dreams into reality and to be true to yourself along the way.

TOPAZ

by Cynthia Perry Colebrook

Reflections from Women Writing Contest Selection

~

Grappling with the decision to sell our house and live aboard a sailboat was a process that took my husband and me ten years. In the end, once the decision was made, we called it our seamless transition.

It took a lot of effort, however, for us to bring our degrees of readiness into alignment. Sometimes my husband would come home from business travel and say, *"Why are we still in Cincinnati? Let's get a boat!"* I would place my hands on my hips and respond, *"Well! I'm a leader here, and this is where I work and have community!"* Other times, I'd say to him, *"Come on, let's do it!"* and he would resist, saying, *"But we've been building our garden soil for almost twenty years, how can we give it up?"*

My own decision-making process came to a head at a writing retreat which I had shared with the same women for years. That February weekend I decided to write a letter to my daughters to explore some pros and cons about the move.

~

Dear Augustine and Priscilla,

You two know, probably better than anyone else, that we've been talking about the decision to sell the house for a long time. You've even given your blessing to the idea, and yet, part of my hesitation has been concern about your loss of your childhood home. So, not wanting to project my fear of your loss upon you, I'll try to identify my own issues.

I used to fear the loss of community, and yet, the experience a couple of years ago of commuting to work in another city helped me to recognize that it's more a matter of gaining additional communities than of losing one. I like the stimulation of new scenery, new sensory input and new patterns.

I love the notion of being debt-free, of living a simpler life with less overhead, yet I fear being economically irresponsible. I fear that going toward a life that just satisfies Daddy and me in the short term does not responsibly address the long term, such as retirement needs or the possibility of disability. Essentially, we are not looking to build wealth (which also translates to building your inheritance); we are looking to work only enough to support a simpler lifestyle.

When we talk about living on a boat, many people express concern for my discomfort or inconvenience in such small accommodations. That doesn't worry me because of our years of living in a tipi and in the "little house." I know my body is older and less resilient, but so is Daddy's, and I believe we can make sure that we have a comfortable bed, a place to stretch, and time to exercise.

I do have fears about my competence on a boat. I simply don't know very much about nautical protocols, charts or navigation. But, I know enough to be humble, and I don't think I'm too old to learn new tricks. I can learn the technical stuff and I can defer the maintenance stuff to Daddy.

I crave being in nature a majority of my time. I am nurtured and sustained by the rhythms of the seasons, the cycles of the tides and the moon. I am inspired by these things, and I believe that the immediacy of each day's influence will beneficially impact my writing. I'm hopeful I will find adequate time for reflection, the inward-turning time that I know I need.

As you might imagine, I have my fears about totally changing the construct of my life to live so fully in close proximity with Daddy. He and I have talked about this, and Lord knows, you two have been witness to the struggles of our relationship, to the frequent clash of our styles, the impact of the fact that we are both strong-willed and fond of argument. Yet, you also know, in a true and honest way, the extent of our love.

My heart does still skip a beat when he comes in a room (unless, of course, I'm furious with him), and I am still willing to follow his lead. The separations we have observed over the last few months when he has been away painting have re-enforced my personal growth. I am stronger, more independent and confident. And so, when I choose now to follow his lead, it is a conscious choice, based both upon my own sense of self, and on the favorable experiences of following him in the past.

When we went to West Virginia to be homesteaders on a farm in the mountains, that lifestyle was certainly never a conscious goal of mine. Back then I was unable to conceive of a future, to even consider goals, entrenched as I was in surviving parent loss. Teddy had a dream of building a camp in the woods, so we set about finding the right property in the right region of the country, with virgin timber and a source of fresh water. I learned how to use tools to fell trees and grub stumps, to put up a house and rive shingles for a roof, to grow food and put it by for the winter, to cook and heat my house with wood. Through all that, I learned faithfulness about the right order of things, about being embedded within nature's scheme. I gained tremendous inner strength knowing that I could provide, with Teddy's help, the basics of food, water, shelter.

As we consider this next step, I draw upon these lessons to inform my choice, and I add to it the factors present in our lives now. I think I am more fearful of getting stuck in suburbia than I am of moving into the unknown.

We look around at elderly couples at church—pillars of the community—and realize that, without too much trouble, we could become one of them. I like being someone with a leadership role who contributes to a community's life but, in many ways right now, I am bored. I'm keen for something new. I know that wherever we end up following "the boat period," I can re-invest in community life to whatever extent I choose.

I worry about being homeless, uprooted and always on the move. How will I get my mail? What will be my address? Before Daddy and I were married, while traveling on the scooter in Europe, we experienced how un-free and unsettling a trip is when it does not have a core itinerary. While the boat will be a home, and home is where the heart is, I am concerned that the vagaries of our work and an unknown schedule could be similarly unsettling. However, during the last couple of weeks, we've both started to feel that it's time to make this move.

Now, the prospect of sorting our belongings into piles of "store, take, sell or donate," of fixing up the house and yard into show-able condition, of organizing the myriad details of our lives in order to adopt a different lifestyle, seems exciting instead of onerous.

I very much want to hear your reactions to this letter. Do either of you hold emotional attachment to the place? How hard will it be for you to let go of it? Writing this has helped me to let go. Thanks for listening.
Love, Mama

~

When I read this letter and other pieces to my writing friends at the retreat, they heard more conviction in me than I realized I had. When the weekend concluded, we assembled for the traditional group photograph, and it took me by surprise when they organized a second grouping to exclude those of us who would not be at the fall retreat. I felt kicked out of the nest.

Still, I thought about what I had heard myself say: *"I am more afraid of getting stuck in suburbia than I am of facing the unknown."*

A couple of weeks after returning home, I received a phone call from a friend of one of my writing sisters who said, *"I hear your house may be coming on the market."* I hung up the receiver, turned to my husband and said, *"I think this train has already left the station. We'd better get on board!"*

Right then and there, we made a conscious choice to go with the momentum, and to deny resistance and doubt.

We spent a couple of months eagerly finishing up projects around the house and researching the real estate market. On a Monday in late April, the house was listed with a realtor; we got an offer on Tuesday and a contract on Wednesday. After a couple of weeks of inspections and counter-offers, both parties agreed to a closing on June 30. The buyer gave us two weeks to move out, so we packed everything up and put it in storage. Then, we went on a two week boat-buying trip.

The options had been narrowed down by my husband's online shopping. While we packed, two of our choices were sold, and our sense of urgency increased. We drove straight to Annapolis in order to look at many different makes and models of sailboats. Then, we traveled to a few locations in New England to inspect specific boats on our list. Getting aboard a Norseman 447 confirmed that the design and layout would meet all our criteria, but she was a "project boat," and we could not take on time-consuming repairs. We needed a boat that was in good shape so that we could get underway safely and continue to serve our clients. The one that we really wanted was in Newport, but she was out of our price range and we fretted that if we visited her, we would fall in love and no subsequent boat would compare.

Then we remembered that we had agreed to have faith and to "go with the flow." So we drove to Newport, met with the sales agent for the seller, and got aboard the boat which had always been at the top of our list. She was spectacular, but she seemed so big and out of reach. Friends with a lot of cruising experience came to inspect her with us; they endorsed our choice and boosted our confidence. The agent called the seller to say that he had "bona fide Norseman buyers" and he counseled the current owner to lower his price, which he did. We had the boat hauled out of the water for a survey, signed papers, drove back home for our things, returned to Newport, and on August 11 moved aboard our 45' sloop, *Topaz.*

In less than five months we had traveled through a daunting decision, a seamless transition, and into a completely new life style. It took writing, communicating, and believing to make it happen. We sail between Maine and Florida, and now, almost five years later, I can truthfully say that it gets better all the time.

Cynthia Perry Colebrook is a writer, poet, and consultant to not-for-profit organizations. Her poetry has previously been published by The Monroe County Poet's Collective and the International Library of Poetry. She has had two solo appearances and one group appearance with her selected poems and short stories on PBS station WVXU on the program, "Women Writing for (a) Change - On the Radio" 2002-2003. She and her husband have two married daughters and five grandchildren. Having cruised in the Bahamas in the winter of 2008-09, they remain happily open-ended about the duration of their "boating phase." To view pictures of the boat "Topaz" which inspired this turning point, Cynthia and her husband invite you to his website at www.theodorecolebrook.com/id2.html.

Ending the Tyranny of "Supposed To"

by Margo Pierce

To Chris, for her silence and her unwavering support.

When my husband walked out, I was supposed to try to save our marriage. That's what I said to myself and that's the message that was tactfully delivered by some well-meaning people. But the truth of the situation—that there can be no relationship without trust—pulverized that "supposed to" with an intensity that was as startling as it was freeing.

Unexpectedly cut loose from the quintessential "supposed to" after 18 years, I was surprised by the depth and breadth of the unwanted yet willingly chosen influences that controlled and directed my life. I sat on a narrow strip of beach called Brackett's Landing in Edmonds, Washington, and came to grips with that silent and sinister tyranny that had ruled my life.

I don't remember anyone explicitly telling me that I was supposed to get married and have children and a station wagon to haul people and things to and from baseball practice and swimming lessons. But that's the world in which I grew up. It was a routine of carpooling with the neighbor kids who went to the same school and summers playing with those same kids in sprinklers or riding bikes. Nothing really had to be articulated.

I went to church with my family.

I went to college.

I married the man I had dated for several years.

I had a job with all of my income going into a joint checking account.

I had a mortgage and the use of two cars in an attached garage.

On the surface it appeared as though I had a comfortable, even idyllic, life. But I chafed under the "supposed to's." I only vaguely recognized it and didn't see this as the source of my discomfort. There were rebellions. Most were small—I worked for non-profits, eliminating any hope of a six-figure income—but there was one glaring exception: I didn't want children and I didn't have any.

Despite my occasional restlessness, "supposed to" kept my life running smoothly. I was the good daughter, the good wife, the good sister, the good aunt, the good employee; and while fulfilling those obligations, I worked hard to convince myself that it was supposed to be enough. Everything around me implied that I was ungrateful if I wasn't content with the amazing life I enjoyed.

I sat on the beach and reviewed all of this and more with my toes in the sand and my eyes on the Olympic Mountains. At some point, I saw the pattern of "supposed to" behind the façade of a wonderful life. After getting past my shock, a depressing sense of shame settled over me. *How could I, who was supposed to be smart, have allowed this to happen? Why didn't I follow those rebellions to their source and stop all of this sooner?*

The answer was simple and hard to admit – love. I made my choices based on what I thought I was supposed to do when you love someone. That realization gave me a way to see past the wreckage of my former life and to consider possibilities of freedom from the "supposed to's" that no longer had any influence.

If I wanted to drive out to Ruby Beach on the Pacific Ocean, all I had to do was get in my car; there was nobody to check in with or to cook for. So that's exactly what I did. It was the beginning of the end of the silent tyranny of "supposed to" in my life.

The practical reality was a big adjustment. Finding an apartment was equal parts exciting and terrifying; I thought I had an idea of what I could afford, but when I was married I never paid the bills because I was told I never did it "right." What kind of financial trouble would I get into if I miscalculated?

Standing in a store in front of rows of towels, I didn't know which color I liked because for so long I wasn't supposed to have a preference; I was supposed to simply agree. I always compromised on things like that. I left, stunned and empty-handed, not wanting to choose until I knew for sure what I wanted in my bathroom. The answer emerged in time.

When I placed ceramic canisters filled with flour, sugar and brown sugar on the counter of my apartment, I relived the day almost five years before when I had defiantly placed them on a kitchen counter for the first time. Our house was *supposed to be* a showplace – everything in a pre-defined place and no clutter in sight. Throw pillows were acceptable when carefully positioned but nothing, absolutely nothing, was to interrupt the expanse of the kitchen countertops. The blender was in a cupboard, as was the recipe box and everything else my husband thought ruined the look he hoped to accomplish.

To me, the kitchen looked sterile, unused and unwelcoming. I wanted pictures from my nieces and nephews hanging on the door of the fridge and a cookbook propped open, ready to be used. But day after day I put away every single dish and scrubbed off the silver-gray marks left by pans on the surface of the white porcelain sink. It wasn't worth the questioning that would follow, *"Was this left out for a reason?"* or the mini-lectures, *"Everything looks so much better when it's clean. I know you like to be able to find things when you're baking, and this way everything is in its place when you need it."* So I went along.

But one day I found a set of canisters that I liked. They looked as though they were made by a potter – perfectly round but with ridges under the glaze and a wooden top that made a satisfying "thwoop" as the seal was broken. I decided right then that they were going to sit on my kitchen counter. I was giddy with the thought. After I got home and did the deed, I called my sister, triumphant with the news of my rebellion. She was silent.

Her unwillingness to celebrate with me wasn't going to mar my excitement, but it did register. Later she told me that she remembered that conversation, in more detail than I, and explained in a hesitant voice that the incident made it clear to her that something was profoundly wrong in my life. If she had told me that at the time, I would have brushed off her concern with a cheery response. Her silence was more powerful and stayed with me, helping me to learn when I was ready.

For a very long time, looking at those canisters and other habitual behaviors—like hanging all of the clothes in my closet in the same direction—roused the old "supposed to's." Over time they lost their power to influence my thoughts and feelings because I was creating a life in which they could not thrive. I could, and did, choose differently.

The contrast of who I was and who I have become is startling and exhilarating. Making comparisons keeps me grounded in the choice to live without "supposed to." The highlight of my travels in my "former life," driving to Canada to see Shakespearean plays, was replaced by a trip to Mongolia, which included time in the Gobi Desert. My wardrobe of suits and high heels has been replaced with hiking pants, oversized flannel shirts and gym shoes.

The resume carefully built over 10 years in marketing and communications sits abandoned in a drawer as I build a new career and portfolio as a writer. The thrill I felt when I was able to add a successful promotions campaign to my list of accomplishments is overshadowed by being banned from death row when a prison official didn't like an article I wrote after an interview with an inmate. There has yet to be anything more satisfying than winning the right to go back to interview another prisoner.

Never would I have imagined the life I have now. Those pre-packaged strictures were a false sense of security that suffocated any choice and challenged the belief that I was doing what was best. As long as I did what I was "supposed to" do, everything would eventually turn out OK, as it had for others who followed the same directions.

Being guided by an internal sense of what is right and best for me is a much harder way to live. It requires thought, vigilance and constantly addressing, not ignoring, the hardest questions of living, all the while surrounded by the old "supposed to's."

Nothing is automatic, which can be difficult when I find myself alone and facing a difficult decision. But the freedom to choose from limitless possibilities is becoming familiar enough to feel less daunting. After experiencing the difference between making thoughtful choices and accepting the imposed standards in the form of "supposed to," I can't go back.

Margo Pierce is a freelance writer in Cincinnati, Ohio. A full-time journalist for the past five years, Margo currently writes a monthly column for Streetvibes. With more than 250 articles in print, she has also published one non-fiction book. Margo is working on her first novel researching a non-fiction book about human trafficking of U.S. citizens into the modern-day slave trade. Since her divorce, Margo has embraced her independence and freedom as a means to pursue new and ever expanding passions in personal and professional endeavors including social justice and advocacy work. Margo invites you to visit her website at www.writerdiva.com.

Winter Solstice

by Karen Ander Francis

~

Yesterday was winter solstice. It was also the third anniversary of the day my halo came off. "Halo" is a euphemism for a titanium neck brace and vest which renders the broken neck and upper body immobile so that delicate vertebrae can heal.

Solstice, a most ancient of days, reminds us that the light returns to the world after a season of encroaching darkness. In the Northern Hemisphere, the Earth slowly tilts away from the sun in the 90 days after the autumnal equinox. On winter solstice our planet is at its farthest point from the sun as it turns again toward the source of its light.

Shortly after the autumnal equinox three years ago, I was nearly killed in an automobile accident on a two-lane highway in the Amish country of north central Ohio. Since then, this period between equinox and solstice has become a living metaphor, a celebration of light and a returning to my own life.

~

The solstice brings a rich history. From the mists of antiquity people have huddled around fires as days shorten and nights lengthen, listening to mythic stories of light's return. In ancient Celtic lands, an itinerant bard stayed the winter in the village where he found himself when the cold, dark season set in. He told reassuring stories of light's promised return.

Scandinavia's saga of the classic clash between the forces of darkness and light was re-enacted at the opening ceremony of the 1980 Winter Olympics. Jews celebrate Hanukkah and Christians celebrate Christmas all around the time of the Solstice. It is no coincidence that these celebrations call on the everlasting power of light over darkness.

Born and raised in the Christian tradition, I especially enjoy the four-week period of preparation before Christmas called Advent. It is a season of readying our hearts for the birth of Jesus—the Light of the World who overcame the forces of darkness. That is the Christian story, added two millennia ago to the more ancient tales of the struggle between light and dark.

Throughout Advent I gradually decorate my home, bake traditional holiday recipes, and prepare gifts for loved ones. As the days dwindle to darkness, I infuse my life with increasing numbers of lights—white fairy lights, multi-colored lights, and candle light. I bring out special bright-red dishes and mugs, each adorned with an image of a dark green tree trimmed with white candles. For four weeks I engage the metaphor of preparing for the return of the light by recalling the stories of the triumph of light over darkness, of good over evil. Each year, like countless ancestors, I ponder anew the season's significance and reflect on it in relation to my own life.

~

The accident occurred on September 25, 2005 when I was returning from a women's retreat where I had talked about the importance of self-care and the power of no. *"The word no creates a holy vacuum into which a resplendent and life-giving yes can enter,"* I'd said.

It was a talk I've been asked repeatedly to give to women's groups, from "church ladies" to business women. Most of us habitually say yes when we really mean no. Sometimes the outcome becomes resentment toward the person we have agreed to help. *"Resentment is like taking poison and expecting the other person to die,"* I explain to laughter as heads nodded in recognition.

I remind the audience that women often arrive at adulthood well-trained to put the needs of others before our own. This can inhibit us when it comes to making decisions for ourselves. I ask the group to think of times when someone asked them where they would like to eat out. A common response is, *"Oh, I don't know, you decide."* Then, when the other names a restaurant we don't like, we go anyway in order to avoid hurt feelings. I tell my audiences that "No" is an answer and women are allowed to say it.

Then I go on to say that "no" begins a process of elimination: a process of illumination, of shedding light on our own wants and needs. I confide that I, too, sometimes have difficulty naming my wants and needs. In responding to this challenge, I have learned the importance of listening to the small voice that resides within me and sheds light on even my most mundane choices.

Giving an example from my own experiences, I tell the audience that at times when I need a pick-me-up I can remind myself that I have some options. Does my body need a nap? Will reading a chapter in that new novel give me the break I need? Do I want to walk in the fresh air?

"When we listen, we hear the voice of our soul guide and direct us," I explain. *"We have inside us all we need to make healthy, life-giving choices for taking care of ourselves. Learning that we have choices and then making a choice is empowering— we just need to become quiet and listen. Then our soul's voice can help us eliminate dark places in our lives and point us to the places where we find the light of life."*

I recollect with the audience that Jesus gave us the Great Commandment to *"love your neighbor as yourself,"* stressing that he did not tell us to love our neighbors until we resent them, that he did not command us to become doormats. Once again they nod and laugh.

In Christianity the emphasis has always been on the neighbor, but a close look reveals that Jesus says to love others as yourself. Only in doing that can we have the energy and selflessness needed to truly love and serve others.

~

My broken neck was just one of many injuries that I incurred in the accident, including two broken legs, a crushed ankle, and several broken ribs. The neck injury was the most serious. My spinal column was broken in three places at the C-2. This is the tiny little vertebra with the big job of joining the skull (with its precious cargo of the brain) to the spine.

When I awoke after two days of being asleep, my head was in a vise— literally. The titanium halo, screwed into my head, front and back, would remain there for 12 weeks with the halo vest strapped tightly to my upper body. I wondered to myself how I would tolerate this bulky contraption for three months.

After the doctor delivered this news and left the hospital room, I counted the weeks on a calendar. My finger landed on December 25, Christmas. I knew he would not remove it on the holiday. However the Wednesday before Christmas was Solstice. I whispered a prayer of hope that the halo would come off on that day.

Following five weeks of hospital rehabilitation, I was discharged and sent home with in-home physical therapy and nursing care. From September to November, as the light faded from the sky and rehab dragged on, my spirits darkened, too.

The halo had become a real nuisance. I tried to convince my spinal trauma orthopedist to surgically fuse the vertebra. Surely neck surgery would be better than wearing this thing. He refused and told me we would know more when the 12 weeks were up.

On a Sunday afternoon in December the phone rang, disrupting my nap. Reaching for the phone from the hospital bed, I was surprised to hear the voice of the medical secretary. It was, after all, Sunday.

"The doctor has reviewed your latest x-ray and would like you to come in on Wednesday. He thinks he will be able to remove your halo." I couldn't believe my ears: my neck was mended. My hope was going to be realized: my halo would be taken off on the Solstice.

As New Year's Day 2006 approached, a resolution slowly emerged. One year later I found this resolution scribbled on a page in my day-timer: *"I will no longer waste my energy on anyone or anything that does not bring me life."* That's a very big no. When I looked back over 2006, I realized that I had been living this promise even though it had slipped from my conscious awareness. I was very happy to find the note. It was the first New Year's resolution I ever kept.

Throughout nine long, dark months of rehabilitation, I struggled to take my life back, one small task at a time. Gradually, it dawned on me that energy is my life force. It is like money. I can squander it or use it for things that nourish and sustain me. With my resolution of 2006, I vowed to limit my spending to relationships and activities that enhance and increase my energy.

Three years later, this resolution still guides me as I weigh choices and say yes or no. I have learned to trust that my soul's voice will faithfully lead me to light and life.

The 2005 accident nearly claimed my life. The third anniversary of this accident brought with it an overarching sense of significance. To Christians, as to the ancient Celts, three is a sacred number. As I reflected during the trinity of months between equinox and solstice on this traumatic, life-changing event, I pondered the lessons learned and wrapped in silent contemplation certain existential questions: *Who am I now? How do I want to live now?*

Such questions confront us at all of life's turning points. Trauma is a turning point—and its third anniversary has resurrected these questions for me.

The accident and rehabilitation put a spotlight on the advice I often give to other women to increase attention to our own self-care. I have become very aware of how vulnerable I am. I have learned that life can change in a split-second. I have come to appreciate how important it is to enjoy the experience of being human.

Prior to the accident I sang in a community chorus, and I loved to raise my voice in harmony with others. I have missed performing. Dayton, Ohio, my home town, is also home of the Bosnian Peace Accord. In tribute to this event, a group of private citizens established the only International Peace Museum in the country. When I learned last fall that one of the museum's founders had also been the catalyst for the Dayton Interfaith Peace Choir, I promised myself that I would join rehearsals after the holidays.

The choir participated in an interfaith Solstice Celebration and I attended as a way to mark the anniversary of my halo removal. The celebration gave me a chance to listen to the folks I would soon join in song. Since I already knew several of the singers, they gave me hugs of welcome. As news traveled through the ranks that I would be joining soon, others came up to me after the concert to add their welcomes.

This new activity, along with others I enjoy, brings new light to my life and renews my energy. As the planet turns toward the source of its light and its very life, I am reminded once again to turn toward the Light that overcomes darkness. This New Year's Eve, I raise my glass to Life!

Karen Ander Francis has been writing a spiritual memoir throughout her adult life as an aid to inner healing. She is the author of The Soul Friend: Spiritual Direction with Adults Abused as Children. As a contributing editor to Pathways for Spiritual Living, she wrote a column called "Sophia's Table." In addition to being a writer, Karen enjoys her work as a corporate communications consultant, group facilitator, and spiritual director. Karen can be reached at innerwork@fuse.net.

Reflection Points

Follow your instincts. That's where true wisdom manifests itself.
— Oprah Winfrey

From the authors in their words

- *Never would I have imagined the life I have now... The contrast of who I was and who I have become is startling and exhilarating.*

- *I am stronger, more independent and confident...I'm keen for something new.*

- *When we listen, we hear the voice of our soul guide and direct us... Learning that we have choices and then making a choice is empowering—we just need to become quiet and listen.*

Questions to contemplate at the threshold of rediscovery

- *When you sit quietly by yourself, do you experience restlessness or dissatisfaction with your life? If so, what is it about?*

- *If you are facing a life transition or feeling unhappy in your life, listen deeply to your own inner voice. What is it telling you?*

- *Are you at peace with the person you have become? If not, what can you do to be at peace with yourself and your choices?*

- *Consider this message from The Dalai Lama about inner peace: "As human beings we all want to be happy and free from misery. We have learned that the key to happiness is inner peace...When we feel love and kindness toward others, it not only makes others feel loved and cared for, but it helps us also to develop inner happiness and peace." What is one thing you can do today to feel this inner happiness and peace?*

CHAPTER 15

Women and Lasting Impressions

She was the cornerstone of our family
and a woman of extraordinary accomplishment, strength and humility.
She was the person who encouraged and allowed us to take chances.
— Barack Obama, describing his grandmother Madelyn Dunham

Some of us do not have to look far to find incredible women who have influenced our lives. President Barack Obama was fortunate to have several remarkable women at his side while growing up and as a husband and father raising two girls, including his mother, grandmother and wife, Michelle. His love, respect and enduring admiration for these women in his life is apparent in his words and his actions. His quote about his grandmother highlights the significant and lasting impression that women can have on our lives. This chapter examines the very different ways that women have affected the writers' lives.

Most of the women described in these essays have shaped lives for the better but a few of them have left some residuals of suffering. In the essay and tribute entitled, "Paula," author Vickie Andresen Sedillo shares the painful story of her mother's mental illness and subsequent suicide. Vickie begins her essay by reflecting on the illness which struck her mother when Vickie was growing up, "*Schizophrenia is cruel that way. It stole her from me–my sweet mother who sang along with the radio and danced with my dad in the kitchen and taught me to love reading.*" Vickie did not have the opportunity to know her mom very well before the onset of the schizophrenia, and her sense of loss is profound. Vickie's mom left her a lasting legacy of love as well as the painful memories of the turmoil of schizophrenia.

Vickie's essay is not about her mom, however. The woman who inspired her and who helped to raise Vickie is her step-mother, Paula. Vickie reflects on Paula's influence in her life, particularly during the difficult times with her own mother: "*Paula was there to put my self-confidence back together, as she had done a hundred times before.... This was the woman who, despite the aches and pains that go with being the step-mother of a teenager, had taught me to laugh through adversity."* Vickie shares the horrific experience of cleaning up her mom's apartment after the suicide, made bearable because Paula was there by her side through the ordeal. Although Vickie's mom left a lasting impression, it was Paula who was Vickie's lifeline.

Some of the women in our lives are role models inspiring us to do better, as Paula is for Vickie. Some women are caretakers showing us unconditional love and acceptance. Some are pillars of strength teaching us how to be strong, independent and able to stand up for ourselves. Others are important in our lives simply because of our relationship with them. They are our mothers, grandmothers, daughters, sisters, aunts, teachers or mentors. The connections with these women often turn out to be our foundation when we become mothers, caretakers and mentors.

In her essay "Traveling the Matriarchal Path," Kelli Kirwan addresses the foundational roles of the women in her family. She begins with the transformation of her family after her father's unexpected death and the subsequent profound grief of her mother who, as family matriarch, was unable to lead the family during that time of grieving. Kelli felt the absence of both her father and her mother at that time. She also recognized the impact of the generational passing and shared her concerns about taking on the role of family matriarch: *"Before I know it, the responsibility of bridging the generations between my mother, my daughters and my granddaughters will be passed to me."* Kelli reflects on her mom's critical role as *"... the pivotal person connecting our generations."*

The thought of carrying on after her mom is gone brought up many emotions for Kelli, as it does for other women when they face the passing of the matriarchal torch. She realized, *"I am confident that when the day comes, I will stand shoulder-to-shoulder with my sister as we step into the leadership roles that our Mom and our Grandmother fulfilled before us."* Kelli's essay offers a glimpse at how the presence and absence of the women in our families can affect us.

In a very different way, the essay "Hand Me Down," also looks at the relationship of mother and daughter and the influences left behind. Author Karen Kidwell tells a coming-of-age story rooted in her experiences with her mother during early adolescence. Karen and her mother would regularly sort through 'hand-me-downs' to supplement Karen's junior high school wardrobe. *"It... was an adventure we took on as a mother and daughter team – it was quite a bonding experience really."*

Karen reflects on the ritual and on how her mother was able to transform the hand-me-downs into a wardrobe. *"She was a master of frugality and saved money by stitching up numerous outfits for me. These were things that I loved about her."* However, one day the unexpected words of her mother left a shocking and lasting impression on Karen. Karen's essay provides another look at women's influences and impressions. For Karen, as with many women, the impact is unforgettable.

The following essays, though very different in content, remind us once again of the common bond among all women: we move forward because of the doors opened by the women before us and together, we create a bridge for those women who will follow us. We carry the legacy of our foremothers and pass on the torch to our sisters and daughters. We are all a part of a tapestry of unique and wonderful women. We all leave a legacy in one way or another.

Hand Me Down

by Karen Kidwell

ᔓ

From the hallways of junior high I had learned that hand me downs (recycle not becoming a favored term until much later) were a topic of scorn. I heard younger sisters complain and solicit pity on this score but did not participate in the conversations. No, not even for good gossip was I tempted to risk the raining down of their disdain. I knew better and so kept my little secret, my mental cache. For about a year, I had been the joyful recipient of cast-off, grown-up riches. My older and worldly almost-cousin, Lorraine, periodically collected whatever fabulous clothes she had tired of and set them aside especially for me.

I knew, even if my friends didn't, that I had fallen upon treasure, but I didn't know that answered prayers could become so bitter-sweet.

My idolized Lorraine and her parents lived about 50 miles away and my parents frequently visited them for the day on a weekend, with me in tow. Often Lorraine would be home, usually getting ready to go out later with special friends (in a car). She would invite me to her room to chat, smile at me, close the door and I would listen to her talk in total awe of her exciting dating life.

I loved everything about her: Her perfectly coiffed and shiny hair (it was artistically arranged even when smoothed over rollers), her many lipsticks, and her wonderful long red fingernails. I was permitted to sit on the bed with her as she did her make-up. I watched as she explained the benefits of – and proceeded to demonstrate – her Maybelline eyelash curler. After two layers of coal-black mascara, I was enthralled to see her slender wrist flex as rubber and metal squished together and pushed an eyelid back into the top of the socket, revealing the white of her eyeball. Heaven. Who could have imagined that such a tantalizing device even existed?

My father didn't waste his hard-earned money on the frivolities of fashion. I didn't know if my cousin's family had a lot more money than my family did, or if Lorraine's parents were much more generous and willing to spend family money on outfitting their only child. (I had overheard my parents talking and refer to Lorraine as being "spoiled".)

The cast-offs were clearly expensive even to my untrained eye. The clothes, which came stuffed into a bag, might have rips or snags or even an occasional stain. Sometimes the contents disclosed a hodge-podge and could deliver a rolled up ball, which opened to reveal a single, soiled sock. Other times I had to hunt for the imperfections and would find the garments suspiciously not out-grown. Then I guessed Lorraine really was spoiled – I would never have been allowed to toss away a good sweater out of boredom or some tiny flaw. My mother was talented at letting down a hem. Well, maybe my aunt just didn't like to sew.

I was feeling a bit smug on this particular Saturday. My mostly flat chest had recently graduated from sleeveless T-shirt to cotton training bra. It was late morning, my father and brother were out somewhere and my mother and I had been working in harmony. For extra space we decided to plow through my new stockpile while sitting in the hallway. The paper bag of clothes sat on the floor and my mother had dragged out my old wooden school chair to sit on. She was a little overweight and too big for the chair but that just added gaiety to the scene.

It began with a crumpled, snap-front gym shirt we rejected and continued on to other lack-luster items. We worked our way through the colors and the pieces. Not everything fit so only a few things went on the "keep" pile.

About halfway down the bag, out came something that looked promising as I focused on the fabric – a white polished cotton with beautiful sprays of purple and lavender and green lilacs strewn over it. (I am still fond of wearing purple with green.) My mother opened the folds to reveal a to-die-for summer dress. The neckline was rounded (up not down!). The smooth torso buttoned in the back (most girl's stuff was cleverly designed like this then) and was attached to a lightly gathered skirt. Lavender ribbon adorned the top and the fabric seemed silky to the touch with its polished sheen. It yielded one more truly amazing feature – spaghetti straps. My eyes glazed over with the vision of so much grown-up gorgeousness on my bare-shouldered adolescent body. Except for a broken strap, the dress looked brand-new.

My mother looked at me with a small smile watching my reaction. She just never knew what would turn up in a Lorraine discards pile. I want to credit my mother here; she never tried to do a sneak preview first or censor any of the clothes before I saw them. Deceit was not a part of my mother's repertoire. This *trying-on activity* was an adventure we took on as a mother and daughter team – it was quite a bonding experience really. It hardly ever ended with me in tears.

My mother was unsure but I refused to acknowledge her hesitancy. I immediately began talking about how we might repair the ripped-out strap. (This was in the midst of a 2-3 year period when my mother was an industrious seamstress. My father always kept her on a severe "household budget" with no bonuses for frills or holidays. She was a master of frugality and saved money by stitching up numerous outfits for me. These were things that I loved about her.)

My mother smoothed the dress and held it up. I began anticipating a possible rejection of this find.

She cast a glance back into the bag and picked out another plum. It was a perfect little shawl that matched the dress. The flowered lilac print was on one side and a fully-reversible polished purple was on the other. This would be my salvation. I could wear the shawl with the dress and my bra straps wouldn't even show!

My mother at last conceded with a plan to sew purple piping on the dress and create new straps from the trim, with ties at the top. I determined that the sundress did in fact fit and sighed with relief. Victory.

As she rummaged to the bottom of the bag, out came a folded square of soft corduroy. When my mother shook it out, it was a slim green skirt also known as a "tight" skirt. Absolutely verboten as part of my earlier wardrobe. I desired it. I craved it. I would have genuflected in front of it, had I been Catholic. After so successfully maneuvering the spaghetti slope, I felt emboldened and confident. This was not just a new horizon, this was an article specifically outlawed by name in times past. But I was on a roll. I was sailing, feeling light and even feeling a little smart-alecky.

"It's a tight skirt," I managed. *"I can try it on, can't I?"*

I pulled it on over my head already savoring the taste of forbidden fruit. It was a bit of a wriggle tugging it on as I walked to the mirror. I noticed the deep kick pleat in the back and the zipper on the side as I smoothed it down over my camisole and my hips. I zipped it up, then reverently ran my hand down both sides of the velvety corduroy. *"It fits,"* I said. *"Can I wear it Mom, please? It's just what I want. Dad won't care because we don't even have to buy one. I have my brown pullover I can wear with it."*

She looked at the skirt dubiously and told me to turn around to let her see the back. As I came around to face her, I felt my hopes begin to chill. This was a different battle, this meant too much growing up, this was a more intense permission than the lilac dress. Somehow the skirt smacked of sex. (This word was still rather foreign to my vocabulary and I barely understood what it meant, but I felt it.)

"I don't think so, honey."

"But Mom, it's great. Everybody in my grade wears them. I think I'm old enough now."

"Well maybe and maybe not – but you can't wear this skirt."

"But why not? Why can't I? It's perfect, Mom. Mo-om!"

"It's, well, it's just, you have a fat can, honey."

Oh momma, what a shock—and what a jarringly inelegant delivery falling on my tender pre-pubescent ears. My own mother, who loved everything about me, from whom I'd grown up strong and cautiously confident with a nurtured belief that she thought me perfect. My very own mother had called me FAT.

I hear her words again now and see they are really so like her. She never swore, and had a quite simple vocabulary and speaking style. So when she did attempt her very rare "off-color" remarks, they sounded as unpracticed as they were – and came off as naively crude.

In the hallway I am almost dizzy as the meaning of her words takes root. *I'm not too young to wear a tight skirt, I'm too fat. No wait, my can is too fat. My CAN? Am I a giant tin of tomato soup?* I look at her first in bewilderment, then disbelief, and finally acceptance. She looks back at me – her eyes hold firm with hazel honesty.

I unzip the skirt and pull it off. *"Okay,"* I say. The victory of the lilac dress is already stale. My mother starts folding the things I've tried on and sorts them into careful stacks. I dress again in my old Saturday clothes, walk to my room and close the door. I sit on the bed dry-eyed, dazed, and attempt to digest this new reality. I place my hand on the small wrinkle of my stomach and abruptly sit up very straight.

While this trauma has set me back, it has also edged me forward in my journey to becoming a young woman. Here is proof that I am in fact budding. My body has budded me smack into an awareness of the albatross of fat. Even in the shadow of laying on this ultimate insult, it is an injury I will begin to perversely savor.

In the next few weeks I will assimilate the painful adjective as it applies to me and, of course, will go on a diet – my first. I will begin to devote some part of every day to the notion that I am fat and cannot improve my status until I have become thin and thinner and pencil-thin.

I look at myself as I was then and realize I was not fat, but I wasn't skinny either. Later I did grow into generous hips. Maybe I would not have looked any worse than the other girls at school; or maybe I would have undergone the palest ghost of uneasiness walking down the chalk-smelling halls in the soft, clinging skirt. My mother believed me uncomely and perhaps saw what I had not – that she had passed along to me some hand me downs of her own.

It will be a long time comprehending that these new demands I will live by are artificial, extreme and self-loathing. But even then, I will bow to the belief that I must subscribe to survive.

Karen Kidwell has lived on the Eastside of Seattle, WA, for 25 years and is employed as a technical writer. She enjoys being outdoors as much as possible and considers her two, much-adored Standard Poodles as part of the family. Karen is fascinated by fiction writing - both reading it and creating it.

Update from the author: Karen continues an unrequited search for meaning in the arenas of style and eclectic jewelry. She has disciplined herself to never become more than several pounds overweight but considers her life one long diet.

Traveling the Matriarchal Path

by Kelli Kirwan

~

It was the wee hours of the morning as I loaded five of my six children into my big green Yukon. It was a gray morning and I had a three hour drive ahead of me to get to the Raleigh airport, and then two flights before I would land in San Antonio, Texas, where my sister would be waiting to pick us up. My husband was en route from Iraq on emergency leave and would arrive a day or two later in Texas. We were all heading to my family home to be with my mom and to bury my dad.

It began to drizzle as I headed out of the small town we lived in, home to the Marine Corps Air Station where my husband was assigned. The windshield wipers beat out a rhythm, seeming to chant, *"Daddy's Dead, Daddy's Dead"* over and over. It was almost like they were trying to convince me of what I still found difficult to even consider. I pressed on, knowing that I had a long day ahead and an even longer week once I arrived in Texas. My ten-year-old daughter, Rebekah, was already there with my mother. It had been my daughter's hysterical phone call the morning before that alerted me something bad had happened.

Mom called soon thereafter and confirmed what I had already guessed. She and Rebekah had driven up to the house, set back on three acres, when they saw that my father had fallen off the tractor he was driving. He had suffered a massive heart attack. He had most likely died before he hit the ground.

It was one of those moments that I can point to and say, *"That's when life changed."* Mostly, these moments were happy: my wedding, the birth of my children and the first day of kindergarten for our children.

Growing up, my family made sense to me. I knew my role and my place in the family. I was the oldest daughter and granddaughter. We visited grandmother and grandfather every summer and we spent most Christmas holidays with them. My father was in the Air Force and my mother stayed home and managed every other aspect of our lives. My life now was much the same as what my mother had modeled in my earlier years.

I grew up in a good family; not a perfect one, but a really good one. It was the kind of family that no matter where you went or what happened, you could always go back home. Everyone fulfilled their role. It was always a soft place to land when the rest of the world was just too hard. There have been plenty of times as a teenager and young adult where home was a haven for me. Even after I was married, because we moved so much with the military, "home" for both my husband and me was always my parent's house. Their home was safe and stable.

My grandparent's house was like that too. These were the two places where I could get help or advice, or just show up for dinner. It didn't even matter if other family members I clashed with were around; they were supposed to be there too. It was how my world had always been. Even after I married and had children of my own, my role in the family was still secure.

I saw a slight shift when my grandfather passed away. Christmas moved to my mother and father's house and it seemed natural for that transition to take place. My mom was still the pivotal person connecting our generations and we still had grandmother. I was a middle woman in my family. I had daughters behind me and two Grandmothers before me. I wasn't alone and I wasn't in charge. It was comfortable for me and it made sense.

Then with my father's death, it all changed, and I found myself listening to the chanting windshield wipers and driving five children to an airport three hours away.

My father was only 59 years old. He was in his prime in his role as Grandfather. It was too soon for him to leave us. My two youngest children, ages 1 and 2, would never know him other than through our memories. That's not the experience I had growing up and it was certainly not the experience I wanted for them.

෴

I found myself standing on a sidewalk in the backyard of my family's home, not sure if I should go after my mother or leave her alone. I was unsure of my role. I was the oldest, but not by much. My mother and grandmother were both unavailable to take the lead due to their grief and their age. That left my sister and me, but I don't know that either of us was prepared or wanted to step into that leadership role within our family.

It was our habit to look to my mother to make big decisions and take control of the situation. It was somewhat uncomfortable stepping into that role because Mom wasn't necessarily relinquishing it, and it wasn't in our family DNA to go around our mother. So, stepping in and taking over was out of the question. My sister Kerri and I tiptoed ever so slightly into her place, temporarily, watching our mother with every step. We were walking on eggshells and not wanting to push decisions, but decisions had to be made. I stood shoulder-to-shoulder with my sister and walked behind my mother as we took care of the arrangements, solved problems as they came up and fought the urge to throw stools across the room.

The next two years didn't prove to be any easier as my mother began her own journey of grief and rediscovery, much of which she needed to travel alone. My sister and I stood on the sidelines and just watched. During those days I felt like I had lost both of my parents that August day—my father to death and my mother to grief.

There was no maternal leader in our extended family and now I had to become the grown up. Even though the world saw me as an adult (I was in my thirties with six children and had lived far from home for the past 15 years), I had yet to see myself as one of THE adults.

I didn't want to step into my mother's role. It was not because I didn't want to grow older or to be a grandmother one day; it was the reality of being THE Grandmother. Stepping into my mother's role was bringing me closer to becoming the family matriarch, with no other women in my family to go to for advice, comfort, or approval when I had big life decisions to make.

~

It's been almost four years since my Dad passed away. Soon I'll be watching my oldest daughter graduate from high school and move back to Texas to go to school and to be near my mom. I see her moving forward in her life and getting closer to eventually becoming a middle woman in the family. I'm also becoming a little more comfortable with my role as "upper management" in the maternal pecking order. Time has a way of helping you get used to the way things change.

I want to be a good example for my daughter as she walks this path behind me. Before I know it, the responsibility of bridging the generations between my mother, my daughters and my granddaughters will be passed to me, and I'm okay with that. I am stronger because of my mother and I'm not alone. I am grateful for my sister. We are taking this journey together as we move up the ranks of women in our family, making the transition together.

Mom is beginning to wake back up and becoming her old self once again, but she's different. She's a little weary from her journey and from facing life without my father, but she's engaged again in her role as Mother. I'm not finished learning from her yet. I still look to her for guidance, comfort and approval. I have faith that when the day comes for me to take her place, the foundation she's built and continues to strengthen will be my support. I am confident that when the day comes, I will stand shoulder-to-shoulder with my sister as we step into the leadership roles that our Mom and our Grandmother fulfilled before us.

Kelli Wade Kirwan grew up in the United States Air Force as the daughter of a gregarious pilot. While attending Texas A&M University over 20 years ago, she threw caution to the wind and married a young United States Recon Marine. Since then, they have welcomed into their family 4 boys and 2 girls and soon, a son-in-law. Still part of an active duty family, Kelli offers Family Readiness support as a volunteer to the Marine Corps. In her professional life, Kelli works for The Bowen Group providing conference logistics and content support for various Department of Defense websites.

Update from the author: Life has continued moving on and I'm growing more comfortable in my emerging role as a matriarch. Mom also has found her way and continues to teach my sister and me by her loving example. The heaviness of grief has left us, still visiting occasionally and sometimes unexpectedly. It's more familiar to us now. The difference is we know how to honor grief and then move beyond it, leaving us with fond memories, a few tears, and lots of laughter.

Paula

by Vickie Andresen Sedillo

By the time the news came that Mom had died, she had been dead for years. Not her body, but whatever it was deep inside that made her my mother was long dead. Schizophrenia is cruel that way. It stole her from me–my sweet mother who sang along with the radio and danced with my dad in the kitchen and taught me to love reading. She disappeared one confusing summer, leaving behind someone who looked like Mom, but it was never her again. The world went just a little slant that summer, and it was a long time before I could walk without stumbling.

I didn't know the woman who had lain dead in her apartment for two months in the autumn Arizona desert heat before anyone found her. I had not heard from her in several months, and I think I was the last person from the family to have heard from her at all. I'm not sure how I feel about that. She always put a lot more on my shoulders than I could bear. It was a relief to know that cleaning up after her suicide was the last burden of hers that I would have to carry. It was also a relief to know that she was no longer suffering.

I really had no idea what to do. I knew I had to make phone calls. My husband Phil was away at sea, somewhere between our home in Texas and Key West, Florida on the USS Avenger, so I couldn't call him. I sat in front of my computer desk with the phone in my hand, numb in every part of my body. I couldn't cry, though I was shaking. First I called the police department in Mesa since the Ingleside cop who came to tell me had given that number. I was shocked to get the voicemail of a homicide investigator—later I would be told that she had shot herself, and the use of the gun sent the case to his department. Then I notified the Red Cross, to get word to Phil.

Without thinking, I called my step-mother Paula next. I had to call her at work, which felt somehow wrong to me, but I really didn't know what else to do. *"Mom died,"* I told her very bluntly. I couldn't find the words to say it any other way. It turned out to be the right thing to do by calling Paula. She dropped everything to fly to Arizona and meet with me. She had no obligation to do this. My mother had rarely said anything kind about her, and only occasionally spoke to her at all. Paula was a witness to my difficulties dealing with Mom, the Schizophrenic. When Mom cruelly told me she did not think I would ever make it in the Navy, Paula was there to put my self-confidence back together, as she had done a hundred times before. Mom was often cruel to me in my teen years.

When we finally got to Mesa, it was the first week of December and the rest of the world was getting ready for Christmas. We all bunked at my husband's uncle's house a few miles from Mom's apartment. His wife, Valerie, turned out to be woven of the same tough cloth that made Paula. Phil's Dad came down from Flagstaff to spend time with Phil and our girls, while Paula and I and Valerie went to sort out Mom's belongings.

Paula took charge from the very beginning, aided by a very capably by Valerie. I went where they pointed me and did what they told me to do. Without going into too much detail, the apartment was a horror. Not visually—it was neat as a pin and unremarkable–save for the rectangle of missing carpet in the living room, covered tactfully by blankets. There was also a rectangle cut out of a sofa cushion. My mind soared away at full speed imagining her there with the gun to her head. I was trying to reconcile the position of the shape on the floor with the cutout on the cushion before finally realizing dully that the cleaning crew must have moved the sofa. Beyond that, the apartment was so plain I felt sad for Mom.

The horror was the smell. The police estimated that when they found her, around the 22nd of November, that she had probably been there since sometime between the last week in September and the first week in October. The first trip we dashed in, grabbed a box of papers, a lock box, and Mom's purse, then made a run for the car.

The next day we were more prepared: painters' masks, Vapo Rub for under our noses, and Valerie with a can of Lysol in one hand and a spray bottle of fabric refresher in the other. This is how we went in. Valerie had the truck at the ready, and we started putting everything of Mom's into boxes and trash bags. I knew I could never bring myself to use her dishes, even though they had been the same dishes we had used in my childhood. My heart broke just a little more when I dumped them all into a bag without ceremony.

The smell had permeated all of the furniture, and we figured that any appliance that might heat up would probably also revive that smell for a long time. We kept a pair of oak barstools, and I gave the oak table and chairs to Valerie for her breakfast nook. Paula also convinced me to keep a stack of knitted afghans, a box of pictures, and the hand-written book of

Mom's recipes. Everything else got hauled to the dump. We did it all in one day, with no help from the men.

This is not to say that the guys wouldn't have helped, had we asked them to help us. Uncle Johnny, however, had gone an eloquent shade of green the first time he smelled the papers that Paula and I carried through the house to the back patio, where we would sit out in the cold to sort them. Phil looked pale and apprehensive every time we mentioned going to the apartment. So, with Valerie as our cheerleader, we carried on very well without them.

Some images stand out from this time. I can see very vividly the fly that was on the wall when we first walked in, a horrible black-and-white striped thing with red eyes. Occasionally I will see one around the trash bin at home and I still feel close to coming unhinged every time. For a while I would burst into tears so Phil took the trash out for two years to spare me.

I can see Valerie with her mask on, holding up her bottles of air freshener and spraying them in alternating squirts as she went past us. I can hear, as I see this, the three of us laughing like a trio of mad women at how incongruously hilarious she looked, spraying away at that impossible smell.

I can see Paula at the end of a long day, pouring half a bottle of fabric refresher into the top of a large capacity washing machine at the Laundromat. We had gone there to wash the afghans. Her hair was a mix of soft white and brown and grey, and her face was still. Then she looked up at me and smiled as she handed me the bottle to dump into my machine.

I can see her too, cigarette in hand as we pieced Mom's life together out of a mess of papers—some dating as far back as her divorce from Dad, other weird lists of disparate objects that we found all over the apartment. She sat with me while I read through all the court papers from their divorce, the accusations and counter-accusations and what finally led to an end of it: me turning thirteen and declaring I wanted to live with my father. Mom gave up my sister, too, on the grounds that without me, she had no babysitter.

Strangest of all, I can see a green recliner in pristine physical condition, perched on top of a pile of trash at the landfill. We laughed ourselves sick imagining someone wondering why on earth anyone would get rid of an excellent recliner—until he got too close. Perfect on the outside, when you looked at it, but hiding a nasty truth that made it something else entirely.

It seemed a perfect symbol of my poor mother after schizophrenia stole her away.

A man who lived on the floor above Mom's was shocked when I told him she was schizophrenic. It turned out he'd been kind to her, always stopping to chat and occasionally giving her an Applebee's gift certificate, where he was a manager. I remember that he smelled sweetly clean when he hugged me and told me he was sorry. I cried when I thanked him for caring about her.

When everything was said and done, and I left the keys for the landlord, Phil took us to the Grand Canyon. It was stark and lifeless just then, the trees bare of leaves and the ground patchy with snow. We got there late in the day, just in time to watch the sunset in a blaze of red and gold that lit the canyon stones with the promise of another day. As we sat there, Paula pointed out that it would be a great place to lay Mom's ashes. She laughed when I told her that it wasn't nearly so peaceful in summer, but we both understood what she meant. Peace in a place so beautiful it made the heart ache, that is what my poor mother deserved.

It was then, I think, that it hit me. I had believed for a long time that I had been motherless since I was eleven or so. But right there beside me in the cold crisp air whirling up from the canyon floor was another mother: Paula. This was the woman who, despite the aches and pains that go with being the step-mother of a teenager, had taught me to laugh through adversity. This woman had dropped everything to be with me when I needed her, without having to be asked. She'd gone into the most horrible event of my life with me, and helped me close the door on Mom's empty apartment.

Paula shares with me that last indelible image before I did close that door: a vast expanse of beige carpet, spotless but for the rectangle in the middle of the living room, with a couple of old blankets laid on top.

~

Vickie Sedillo is a native of Michigan, a six year Navy veteran, a mother of three and wife of a retired Navy Chief. She has lived in South Carolina, California and Sicily, but she and her family make their home in South Texas. She is currently a graduate student at Texas A&M University–Corpus Christi where she is studying English literature and writing.

Since the events of her essay, Vickie and Paula have endured the loss of Vickie's cousin Mary Lynn Anderson Babb, who was murdered by her estranged husband January 9, 2007. They are working on an extensive compilation of essays for Mary's son, Sam.

Reflection Points

A woman is the full circle. Within her is the power to create,
nurture and transform.
— Diane Mariechild

From the authors in their words

- *This woman had dropped everything to be with me when I needed her...*
- *I am stronger because of my mother...*
- *... she had passed along to me some hand me downs of her own.*
- *I'm not finished learning from her yet. I still look to her for guidance, comfort and approval.*

Questions to contemplate about women who have left lasting impressions in your life

- *Who comes to mind when you think of women who have influenced you?*
- *What is/was it about people that influenced you?*
- *How have you been an influence to other women or girls?*
- *How have you been an influence to men or boys?*
- *What will be the lasting legacies you leave?*

CHAPTER 16

Acceptance: Finding Peace Within and With Others

"Forgiveness is the key to action and freedom."
— Hannah Arendt

Most women want and try to find a sense of inner peace. When women do not have peace with others or within themselves they often suffer greatly. This common thread was woven into many of the stories that women shared about their lives. It is a universal yet very personal struggle. Yet, many women discover that peace has been within their reach all along.

Feeling peaceful within and with others can have a transformative effect on women's lives. Not surprisingly, this serenity does not arise from getting what we want, but from acceptance and forgiveness of yourself and others. However, reaching a peaceful place can be filled with many obstacles and does not come easily.

The women in this chapter write about three very different experiences which caused them much emotional pain and suffering. They also faced significant barriers to realizing their peace and to moving on. In the essay, "Extra Baggage," author Michelle M. Bessette describes a series of ups and downs that accompanied her many roles as a mother, military wife, college student and more. As she reflects on her personal journey of finding balance, Michelle recalls, "*A deep sorrow took root within me. I felt more alone than ever.*"

Laura Morey also writes about a period of withdrawal and isolation in her essay, "Thank you, Midnight." Laura notes, "*Circumstances, disconnection and an internal disquiet had all motivated me to create a wall between myself and the world around me.*" Laura was a college student at the time and trying to come to terms with both a significant loss in her life and her own identity in the world.

The theme of feeling lost or disconnected was present as well in Tamara Bastone's essay, "A Letter to My Mother." Tamara, whose mother left her when she was two years old, recalls, *"For years, I had unanswered questions about why you decided to leave me."* The unanswered questions and feelings of disconnect and emptiness were all obstacles to realizing peace for these women. They also shared a common need to search for their true selves, for answers and for their place in the world.

Each of these women describes an all too common characteristic shared by many women: a critical, hurtful inner voice that causes women to question their value and worth. At times, these negative and harsh self-judgments can lead to self harm or destructive behaviors. *"Was I that unlovable that you had to leave?"* asks Tamara Bastone in her essay, "Letter to My Mother." *"I often travel on self-inflicted guilt trip,"* writes Michelle. Over time, these women realized the destructive nature of their critical thoughts and they were able to find their way through them.

Like many women, Laura suffered greatly before she was able to reach out for help. She became depressed and used alcohol as a way of coping and escaping her feelings. *"Drinking was useful to me because I could hang out with my friends and the feelings of inadequacy and difference would go away. I didn't have to think and I didn't have to feel."* Laura found a way to escape her suffering but alcohol turned out to be even more harmful than facing the source of her pain.

Some women experience significant uncertainty, obstacles and painful emotions before they get to a place where they can recognize and let go of their self-criticism. *"I tried leaving it behind, but instead it acted as a sneaky stowaway and hopped on board in silence, ready to follow me wherever I went,"* notes Michelle. Acceptance often brings relief and the certainty that there is a light at the end of the tunnel, where hope and calm exist. Laura, reflecting on her struggle to accept her sexual identity, says *"I was finally getting to that truth that had always been there but had been ruthlessly shoved away."* Finally, she was able to accept who she had been all along. For Laura, peace came with acceptance.

Healing and peace can also come from forgiveness of self and/or others. Tamara beautifully describes this sense of peace: *"... calmness covered me as if a small space of grace had opened in the midst of all of my grief and anger."* She goes on, *"I realized...I am resilient, I do matter, I am worthy, imperfections and all, and I am loveable. I can forgive, let go and let be."* Similarly, Michelle found solace in forgiving herself and letting go of some of the guilt and ambivalence she carried: "*The shadow once cast over my heart had finally lifted...*"

These women were able to find their peace with others and within themselves. Likewise, when Laura accepted herself, she was able to find her true love in life: "*With her I've found something that I've always sought: the peacefulness and rightness of just being myself with someone.*"

You carry peace within yourself. As Tamara Bastone reminds us, "*This place could be called forgiveness...*" All you have to do is open your mind to the possibility and accept that you deserve to be happy. Forgiveness and compassion are the keys. Both peace and torment can take up space in your head and in your life. The question is which door do you hold open?

Thank you, Midnight

by Laura Morey

ↀ

In late summer 1985, I looked out the screen door of my family's ranch house to see our 20-year-old cat, Midnight, sitting on the front porch. Earlier in the week when I had returned from school, she'd wobbled her way to greet me, so frail and in pain. We'd held a family conference the day before and had decided that in three days' time we would take her to the vet to end her suffering.

I don't remember exactly what I was thinking as I looked at Midnight, but I do know that I was having a hard time wrapping my mind around it. I was nearly twenty four years old and no one close to me had ever died. Midnight was more than just a cat, she was my sounding board, protector and really the only non-judgmental being in my immediate family (except perhaps my youngest brother). She also offered affection. We didn't hug in my family or show any overtly strong emotions other than yelling in anger. We weren't a cruel family, just remote, disconnected, and, with the exception of my mother, angry. Midnight would sprawl in my lap for hours, purring her contentment. I could talk to her without fear of being labeled weak or "too sensitive." When we were younger she would follow us to wherever we'd play and sit and watch over us; once she even ran off a German Shepherd that had us cornered. She was loyal and consistent, and if she was a bit intolerant of childish rough play, we forgave her the sharp claws.

Now we were going to kill her.

I understood the necessity, but despite my long-practiced detachment, I was struggling to understand what it would mean to no longer have Midnight in my life. So, I stood there watching her as she placidly sat on the porch. I heard my brother's car pulling up when I saw this blur of black streak from the porch, landing just in front of the front tire of my brother's blue, '75 Toyota. In slow motion her body rolled under the tire and then rested, partially under it because by then his car had stopped. I think my brother realized that something was wrong (was that me screaming at him to move his car?) and he rolled forward enough so she was no longer under the tire. My controlled, carefully constructed self melted into a sobbing, incoherent mess.

~

Midnight's death was one of the single most significant events of my life. Before it happened, I had been a mere shell of the person I would become. I had friends and party pals and even some fairly close friendships with men and women but I'd had no lovers; there had always been a part of me that I held back. Circumstances, disconnection and an internal disquiet had all motivated me to create a wall between myself and the world around me.

I'd had one significant relationship—if you could even call it that—with a guy in high school, which lasted about one year. Due to a hesitation I couldn't explain, we'd never had sex. Raised Catholic, I was taught that sex was only for married people and only to make babies at that, but I really didn't buy into the whole religious thing. I would like to think that I was being noble, knowing that I didn't love him and that it would hurt him, but I'm not so sure I can give myself that much credit. So, even though Robert had all these perfect things going for him—my parents loved him, he was from money, he had his pilot's license and he was in love with me—it still didn't feel right to sleep with him. More than once I'd found myself trying to figure out what was wrong with me: I had everything a young woman could ever want in Robert, but I felt nothing beyond mild affection.

In college I would occasionally date guys, but none ever stirred a passionate enough response to merit further dates or consideration. I was studying graphic design at a top school and course work was very demanding, so I used that as an excuse for not having more interest in guys. I don't think anyone thought I was too strange, but I felt weird, like I was out of step with my peers and somehow lacking.

In the winter of 1985 I decided that I didn't want to be a virgin anymore so I deliberately set out to find someone to help me. I met a guy in one of my classes and we went out a couple of times. One night we ended up back at my apartment and got naked. We were kissing and *he* was getting turned on and it was all very interesting, but I was focused more on the Pink Floyd song and the cigarette I was craving. I had a crystal-clear moment when

I realized that what I was doing was ridiculous, that I was on the verge of sharing an important part of myself with a guy that I cared nothing about, someone who mildly excited me at best, and why? *Because I was ashamed – I was still a virgin?* I did a tactical retreat, helped him get off (it was the right thing to do, I wasn't uptight about the sex part and wasn't insensitive to his predicament) and sent him on his way.

I then decided not to date any more, at least until I was out of college. I was disgusted with myself and increasingly worried that something was seriously wrong. Instead of looking deeper, I stuffed it all into my deep-down place, and buried myself in school and partying. I had been drinking alcohol since I was sixteen, and partying with friends was a social activity that I indulged in quite frequently. Drinking was useful to me because I could hang out with my friends and the feelings of inadequacy and difference would go away. I didn't have to think and I didn't have to feel.

It wasn't until Midnight's final act of independence on that autumn day that my comfortable shell began to crack, allowing a pervasive sadness and longing to seep into my carefree life. That's when I met Casey.

Two weeks after Midnight died I went back to New York City for a co-op job, having found a living arrangement with three other students in a Hoboken apartment. Casey and I shared a room. We hit it off immediately, and she quickly became the focus of my world. During the day we each worked hard at our jobs but at night New York was one big playground. We would find the bars with the best happy hour specials (and free food) and spend our time surrounded by friends, both known and newly made. Late in the night, we would walk, taxi or take the subway back to the World Trade Center, ambling aimlessly through the mostly deserted corridors below the towers, eventually making our way to the train that would take us back to Hoboken.

Our apartment became a social hub. On any given evening, friends—male and female—could be found hanging out, engaged in thought-provoking, philosophical discussion. I thoroughly enjoyed this new and dynamic way of being, free from the typical gossip and chatter. The most astounding thing about Casey and her friends was that they were physically affectionate: they actually hugged each other, and because I was there, they hugged me. This was so new that I had no idea how to act, and I was perpetually embarrassed. Casey never made fun of me; instead, she showed only kindness, affection and understanding. As I learned how to hug, it filled me with warmth and, somehow, soothed the sadness and deepened the nascent connection to feelings first opened by Midnight's death. I still didn't understand the true depth and root of those feelings: I had fallen in love with Casey and didn't even know it.

I started getting a clue when I went on a weekend trip upstate for a Halloween party with some friends. The entire time I was away, I missed Casey terribly. The day we were to return we visited Woodstock. I was sitting in a grassy field in my car on a sunny autumn day, impatiently waiting for my friends to finish shopping when I had a very sensual fantasy involving Casey. Within moments my brain had categorized it as abnormal and crushed it. I was actually able to pretend that I had not experienced the fantasy and its implication, even as I was filled with the wonder of it.

Days later, I began having panic attacks. The first occurred in a Hungarian restaurant in the East Village. As soon as my food was served I felt like I was going to puke, or pass out, or quite possibly die. I had no idea what was wrong, only that I desperately needed to escape. The train ride that night under the Hudson River was a terrifying combination of hyperventilation and detached surrealism. By the time we got back to the apartment I was in my own world, completely unaware of what was going on around me. I remember catching glimpses of myself in lucid moments, thinking, *why am I in this place?* I was lying in another roommate's bed, with Casey beside me, holding me while I cried. I cried for hours. I didn't know where I was. I became convinced that I was going insane.

The rest of the school quarter was a confused mess of drunken nights, whirling images and thoughts just on the edge of consciousness, panic attacks and jealousy. I wanted to talk to Casey, or anyone, about what was happening but I had no idea how. I was so terrified of being despised for how I was feeling. To make matters worse, Casey was becoming more flirtatious with me; this while she was sort of seeing a guy. As December arrived (and with it the end of the quarter when we'd go home) she would sit on my lap, kiss me on the cheek, and want to cuddle.

One particularly alcohol-laden night she even blurted out that she wished I was a man so she could come over there and "kiss me senseless." I had no idea what to do with that. I remember leaving—humiliated because I was convinced that everyone at the table knew that I wanted her to kiss me, and hurt and angry because it took her being drunk to say it. I was beginning to understand that even though she might feel something, she would never act on it, reinforcing feelings of shame at my abnormality. As I found my way home that night, I pointedly attempted to tell myself that everything was fine, that what I thought had happened hadn't really, and that I didn't love Casey *that* way.

My carefully controlled façade was history and my subconscious self was determined to run the show. I could no longer lie to myself. Even so, I was unable to name the "it" that was dying to come into the light so the panic attacks continued, growing in intensity and frequency.

When I returned home for holiday break, I was run down and had the flu so my parents sent me to our family doctor. I told him that I was experiencing panic attacks and he offered Valium. There was no suggestion that I try to get to the root of the issues or that the panic attacks may even be related *to* issues. I was stunned and disappointed; he was going to write a prescription for a sedative—to a college student who had admitted to abusing alcohol. I said no as I had enough unknowns in my life and didn't need another. Since he counseled a sedative, I actively chose the one with which I was most experienced, knowing/hoping it would not always be needed.

At the beginning of winter quarter 1986, Casey was living with a new boyfriend but we were still involved in a weird push/pull full of mixed messages and I was self-medicating more heavily and more frequently. To keep from having panic attacks in my classes, I started taking a big plastic cup to class, nearly half-filled with vodka. I'd sip on that and it would take the edge off, allowing me to function. Knowing that I was a total mess and that this was not sustainable behavior forced me to tentatively begin to look into other options.

By the beginning of spring quarter 1986, I was in therapy. Before my first session I was a wreck of nerves and panic; but, I knew I had to go because I couldn't continue the way I'd been. I had enough self preservation and instinctual knowledge to know that if I didn't do something I would probably end up killing myself. The first time I had a thought about suicide, I was in the bathtub. I was lying in the tepid water, stoned and crying, wishing I had never met Casey, obsessing with detached horror on my exacto knife, visualizing it slipping beneath the skin of my wrists. That scared me like nothing before and I immediately got out of the tub and made the call to set up the appointment.

The first words out of my mouth when I sat down with my therapist were, "*I think I may be a lesbian.*" Speaking the words, however qualified, to another human being—words that I hadn't even fully said to myself—gave me a cascade of relief and rightness. I was finally getting to that truth that had always been there but had been ruthlessly shoved away. It gave me hope that I was going to somehow get through the fear, the shame and the attendant drama. I finally started to learn how to listen to that part of me that was deep within, to begin to understand, and to accept that it was okay to love myself.

∾

Update from the author: Casey and I never became lovers but we did remain friends for many years. After a few years of therapy and several relationships in my twenties and early thirties I met a woman who is now my life partner. We have been together for nearly twelve years and own a home which we share with two cats and a dog. With her I've found something that I've always sought: the peacefulness and rightness of just being myself with someone. In her arms I am calm and soothed. I am loved.

I would like to comment on the alcohol abuse as I believe I am very lucky that I'm not an alcoholic. I do not advocate using it the way I did, because if I had whatever that "thing" is that makes a person keep on drinking well past the party's end, I would not be the person I am today – striving to be connected and present for my life.

∾

Extra Baggage

by Michelle M. Bessette

~

The waters of the Mississippi River are restless this morning. As I drive across the Government Bridge into Davenport, I watch the river surface as it splashes and sprays, tossing and turning its bitterly cold water all about. I suppose the wind is what creates havoc across this majestic waterway, but I don't notice any at the moment. I am too busy concentrating on how this visual display of restlessness resembles a familiar feeling within me. I can barely describe it, except that it seems to have taken up a permanent residence inside my soul, comfortably nesting itself in a far off place just outside my reach.

I was hoping this feeling would have vanished a few months ago when my family was moved to my husband's new duty station. I tried leaving it behind, but instead it acted as a sneaky stowaway and hopped on board in silence, ready to follow me wherever I went. I was not happy at all when I saw it pop up a few weeks after our arrival.

I need to think for a minute. I lower the volume of my car stereo blasting the *Hairspray* soundtrack, one of my few sources of joy these days. There must be a logical explanation why I carried this extra baggage halfway across the nation. My mind begins racing, jumping from one thought to another. Random memories and 36 years of life experience whirl through my mind. I create a mental outline, a very rough draft of personal milestones. My noisy, ongoing inner monologue needs direction—maybe coffee will help. I hang a left at the next light and drive through Starbucks. It didn't take me long to map out the local coffee houses recognizable by the circular green mermaid, a comforting reminder of my Pacific Northwest home. An overpriced mocha is hardly the right thing to purchase, especially when our nation is in recession and our family budget is tight. I set my not-so-guilty conscience aside as I sip my nonfat, no whip, peppermint mocha. I scribble a few ideas onto some nearby paper before I drive away.

My mind wanders to the year 1998. It was a difficult one and certainly my year to grow up. A newlywed at 25, I had just moved to Germany with my soldier husband and his young son. One month after arriving, my husband deployed for six months and I was thrust into the role of full time single step-parenthood. Luckily his son was little enough, and loving enough, to forgive many of my mistakes.

But by the time my husband came home, something had seriously changed inside of me. I had resentment in my tone and anger in my disposition. We fought with words that were sarcastic and hurtful. I also came to realize just how naïve I was. One of the most difficult lessons I learned was that our love for one another would always be overshadowed by a world focused on its mission, one where marriage and family came second to one's service.

A decade has passed since that eye-opening year. I've come to develop a much better understanding about supporting the mission of my soldier, although my heart still aches in his absence. And even though my personal and professional sacrifices may not be as obvious or as noble as my husband's, they still exist. It weighs on us both, knowing that I chose to put my dreams on hold to support his career and raise our family; but love, friendship and appreciation for each other keeps us focused on what is yet to come.

Professional sacrifices remind me of my current status: a stay at home mom. Parts of it I enjoy, like when I watch my kids walking home from the school bus, disheveled from a busy day, or the peaceful midday hours when the house is still and I can think in peace. Other parts I loathe: the housekeeping part, for example. I am not and never claimed to be a domestic goddess and thankfully my husband understands this. Cluttered house or not, I view my time at home as a luxury. I know that I want to contribute financially to our family and yet I am overly focused on what I *don't* want when it comes to working outside the home.

I often travel on self-inflicted guilt trips because long ago, I promised myself (and my husband) that upon my completion of college I would gladly return to the full-time workforce. Two of these college years had been completed before I even met my husband, my third while living overseas. So why did it take me so long to finish my last year? I recount the aforementioned sacrifices, all which helped delay the fulfillment of my promise: raising a busy stepson, birthing twins, moving between duty stations, buying a house, working full time, baby number three (surprise!), returning home to care for four kids (daycare was too expensive) and taking an occasional substitute job. All this occurred throughout my husband's multiple field exercises, random temporary duty assignments, trainings, promotional boards, and two separate year-long deployments since 2003. Phew! No wonder it took so long. I have to catch my breath just thinking about it.

I redirect my thoughts from my daily state of unemployment to 2006, a pivotal year for me, when I received my acceptance letter from the University of Washington. My excitement for autumn quarter to arrive quickly dissolved when we learned that my husband was going to be deploying to Iraq for his second tour. He left in the middle of spring quarter 2007 and I continued on with a brave face, completing my degree after a hectic summer quarter. In my reminiscent state of mind, I realize how much I miss attending school. It served as my coping mechanism, my escape from a chaotic home life where I was living as a pseudo-single mother. I was able to recapture the individuality that had eluded me while fulfilling my roles of wife and mother.

I recall how life at home began to worsen after he deployed. My 30-minute commute home from school quickly became the most dreaded part of my day. I hate to acknowledge it, but the truth is I never wanted to go home. My oldest was a large part of this frustration because he needed his dad as much as I did. My younger ones were still very impressionable, and the dog – well, that's another story.

After one particularly bad day, I knew I needed outside help. I went to the doctor, reciting a seemingly ongoing list of daily stresses and was quickly given a prescription for antidepressants. I prayed it would counteract the often uncontrollable rage erupting inside me. It helped all right – maybe too much. I felt numb, an unexpected side effect for someone as emotional as myself. My typically passionate self seemed to disappear and I began caring less about life around me. I stopped berating my kids and let up on my own imperfections. A feeling of indifference soon developed toward my husband which also stemmed from the resentment of being left alone once again.

Just after the 2008 New Year, the unexpected death of our children's grandmother brought my husband home to a wife who didn't seem to care whether he was there or not. While mourning for her, painful memories of my own mother's death resurfaced. A deep sorrow took root within me. I felt more alone than ever. My focus on applying to graduate school was blurred, I was running a household alone, and the one person who should have been here for me was going to be leaving as quickly as he arrived. The poisonous effect of the antidepressants on my thoughts and behavior prevented me from letting him into my heart. After the funeral, he departed for Iraq with a feeling of hopelessness which I helped create.

One month later my husband received orders to go to his next duty station in Illinois. There was an Army base in Illinois? This became the turning point in our relationship. We took this opportunity to talk more openly about our marital commitment. We communicated deep concerns and strengthened our friendship a little more each day. We agreed to weed out negative influences in our lives and focused our attention on each other once again. We even considered going to marriage counseling upon his return. By the time my decline letter from graduate school arrived, I had a new perspective on our impending move. I recall feeling a sense of relief because it seemed to be the result of divine intervention.

After an arduous 16-month tour, our June reunion was full of joy as well as a bit of apprehension. We worked hard at salvaging our nearly 11 year marriage, succeeding with each day that passed. Our first big family vacation was that summer to Disneyland. It served as a celebration of his safe return home and a new beginning for the two of us.

It turned out to be a memorable summer for many reasons. One reason especially was that I stopped taking my antidepressants. The shadow once cast over my heart had finally lifted after nearly two years. No longer going through the motions (my ode to Buffy), I felt alive again. Passion for life returned and my emotions swelled. I had missed the old me, from the feisty side to the weepy, sappy side. I welcomed myself back with a renewed level of devotion to my husband and our children.

But what does it all mean? Slow realization and serious reflection have made the answer more clear: the contemplative mindset I have been living in for three months has kept me from moving forward in life altogether, doubting my abilities and clouding my confidence. I need to learn to let things go. I really don't intend to dwell on things—it just happens. It's in my nature to be reflective.

Still, one of the biggest struggles for me is that I have a difficult time finding balance. I continue with an all-or-nothing approach regarding my budding professional life and established personal life. I suppose this is normal for many women, when one aspect of your life improves, the other areas may suffer. When I begin working outside the home, will my personal life suffer once again? That is up to me. I must remind myself to be cognizant of the fact that life can be balanced in a healthy way, and I can enjoy all the things I love to do.

Weeks have passed but I clearly remember how I felt driving across the bridge that day. The restlessness within my soul has settled more and more. I feel lighter with each new day because I am learning to let things go. On my way home from lunch, I am aware of the serenity of the moment. The river is calm and so am I. The reflective surface mirrors the peaceful riverbank scenery. *Yes* is the word I say to myself as I drive forward, smiling. I'm finally moving in the right direction.

Update from the author: Writing this story was very therapeutic. One could say that my "extra baggage" is finally getting unpacked, albeit bits at a time. Married life (12 years now) is better than ever because of our communication level. I especially thank my husband for encouraging me to complete this story so it would be submitted on time. I'm working part time and am hoping to return to the University of Washington for a Masters degree one day.

Letter to My Mother

by Tamara Bastone

To Rachel, Rich, Phillip and Sarah...Thank you.

~

Dear Mother,

As I sit here in my garden on my 50th birthday surrounded by roses, lavender, and rosemary, and allowing the beauty to fill my senses with calmness—I'm reminded of a dream I had many years ago. That dream made this peaceful place possible, not only in a physical sense, but in a deep, soulful way. This place could be called forgiveness and I have this precious garden to thank.

There was a time when I couldn't forgive you. For years, I had unanswered questions about why you decided to leave me. The longing to know you, to see you, and to touch you was unbearable. You see, I was so very young when you left, only two years old. I don't even remember you but my soul remembers you. She grieved for you.

One day she was tired of grieving and she appeared to me in a dream. Young and vulnerable, she led me by the hand to a gate. I couldn't see inside. The tall juniper hedges were thick and blocked my view. She unlatched the handle and gave it a gentle push. Her face was beaming as she turned to me and gestured with her hand for me to take it all in. And I did. I was looking at one of the most beautiful gardens I had ever seen. Lush, inviting, warm, and nurturing...just like a mother's arms. In the middle of the garden was a cottage like the kind you see in an old English picture book, the roof covered with pink climbing roses, lavender spilling out of every crevice of the sidewalk leading up to the slightly ajar door.

When I woke from this dream, calmness covered me as if a small space of grace had opened in the midst of all of my grief and anger. I never in my life experienced anything like it. I never had a garden before but I knew I had to create one.

So, Mother, my need to create a garden became a driving, unrelenting force in my life. At times I felt such urgency, as if I might die before the garden was in place. I would get up and out of bed by 4am, flashlight in one hand, a potted rose in the other, in my robe surveying my small plot. Where should I put the rose? The placement had to be perfect. The soil had to be perfect. After planting my plants, the care had to be perfect. I bought the right plant food for each plant and fed them. No plant or rose could show any signs of disease or bug infestations. Years were spent putting in walkways and bubbling fountains only to have them ripped up and redesigned to meet some perfect picture I had in my mind. Nothing I did was ever enough. I found no time to just sit in the garden and allow the incredible peace to permeate my life. There was too much work to be done!

You are probably wondering Mother, what my garden looks like today after the many years of sweat and labor. Sometimes I wonder if you have a garden. If you sit there in the evening drinking in its beauty and thinking about the daughter you barely knew. You must imagine from this letter that my garden is a picture of perfection. Much like how I had imagined that if I was a perfect daughter you would have never left me. I would have experienced all those joys my friends had with their mothers: baking cookies, Girl Scouts, listening to endless dramas about boys. Do you know what I wished for the most? I wanted to have you brush my hair. I would ask myself over and over "was I that unlovable that you had to leave?"

For the first five years of my garden's life, I would allow no imperfections. If a rose showed a black spot, it came out. When certain bugs set up home on a plant, I would rip up the plant and toss it into the rubbish pile. Then, I would search endlessly for a replacement…the perfect one, guaranteed to never fail or to disappoint.

I know what you must be thinking Mother, that all of this must have been exhausting. You are right. I didn't realize how exhausting it was until I went to move a huge potted shrub and the pot shattered. The shrub was laid bare on the deck. The roots totally exposed to the July sun. I felt that I had to save this shrub. I had nurtured it from a tiny seedling I found in the garden. I had dug it up, watered it, fed it and over the years watched the shrub grow taller and taller. I couldn't just let it die. I struggled to get the shrub into another pot, rushing around the yard to find any left over bags of soil to cover the roots. Hours later, the shrub was safely in its new home. Two days later my back gave out while lifting a very light blanket. I had severely sprained my entire back.

Months of being immobile taught me a great lesson about life and perfection. I watched helplessly as the weeds settled in, diseases ravaged my roses, and creatures made off with my heirloom bulbs. No more, I thought; the garden is finished, over. I hardly ever looked out the window or wandered into the garden.

One day when I was pulling my car up into my driveway, I noticed a dozen red flowers greeting me. They were the special bulbs that I thought were long gone in the stomach of some rodent. I walked over to the back gate, swung it opened and to my total surprise the garden was in full bloom. Roses tumbled into the lavender, taking a risk to be wild, without a care in the world. I stood there quite in awe of the whole scene.

On that day, I learned how utterly resilient nature can be. How, after a rose is speckled with leaf disease, she just sheds them and puts out new growth. Bulbs will multiply under the ground so that they can withstand a few losses to varmints. A bird's disturbed nest will be rebuilt and ladybugs will descend on a bush making a wonderful feast of the insects which sucked the plant dry. Everything, given time, grows stronger. I began to see the real beauty in my garden, warts and all. I began to see the real beauty in me, warts and all. As my back began to heal that summer, so did my soul....and my heart. I realized, as in nature, I am resilient, I do matter, I am worthy, imperfections and all, and I am loveable. I can forgive, let go and let be.

So, Mother, my garden taught me forgiveness. At 50 years old, I am now able to forgive and to accept myself. And in turn, I am able to forgive and to accept you along with the decision you made so many years ago. You really did do the best you could at that time in your life. Now, my garden is a peaceful, comforting oasis. It is magical, nurturing, unpredictable, wild and so utterly loveable... like me. I think about that long ago dream of a rose covered cottage surrounded by beauty and peace and I wish the same for you...peace.

Peace and Joy,
Your Daughter,
Tamara

Update from the author: On July 1st 2009, my garden celebrated its tenth year of imperfect existence. Now, I happily share it with the voles, moles, weeds, abundant blooms, butterflies, birds, my husband, Rich and my thirteen-year-old feline friend Lucy. When I am not gardening my small patch of heaven here in Chesapeake, VA, I am helping my husband run our mail order business and creating mixed media art for clients.

Reflection Points

All of the wonderful things you are looking for—happiness, peace and joy—can be found inside of you. You do not need to look anywhere else.
— Thich Nhat Hanh

<u>From the authors in their words</u>

- *I finally started to learn how to listen to that part of me that was deep within, to begin to understand, and to accept that it was okay to love myself.*

- *Yes is the word I say to myself as I drive forward, smiling. I'm finally moving in the right direction.*

- *At 50 years old, I am now able to forgive and to accept myself. And in turn, I am able to forgive and to accept you...*

- *I wish the same for you...peace.*

<u>Questions to contemplate at the threshold of acceptance and peace</u>

- *Is there a need for forgiveness for yourself or someone else? If so, what do you need to do to make it happen?*

- *Do you love and accept yourself as you are? What do you love about yourself?*

- *What does it mean to you to have inner peace?*

- *What are you doing to nurture and sustain gratitude in your life?*

- *As you live today, in this moment, are you at peace?*

- *How can you demonstrate acceptance of yourself and others?*

In Conclusion: Lessons Learned

When you have come to the edge of the light you know,
and you are about to step off into the darkness of the unknown,
faith is knowing one of two things will happen:
there will be something solid to stand on...
or, you will be taught how to fly!
– Author Unknown

In Conclusion: Lessons Learned

The women in this book experienced some very different turning points–some were life-changing decisions and some involved a different way of looking at the world. Whatever their situation, the women found a way to cope with the challenges that life presented and to make decisions that were right for them at that time in their life. *They learned that no matter what was put in front of them they would eventually find a way to face it, to survive and to move on with their lives.* This is the common thread linking each of their stories. It is also the bond that connects these women despite their diverse experiences, backgrounds and beliefs. The following lessons learned are some of the universal connections among women facing turning points in their lives.

~

Facing a turning point can be an opportunity for change or growth.

The women in this book discovered that life's turning points can become doorways to transformation. For many of the women, their turning point led to new opportunities, changed perspectives, strengthened relationships, peaceful resolutions or a greater sense of self.

The turning points also opened doors for the women to move forward in their lives. Most of the women found themselves at decision points: they could stay in the past or find a way to move on. Their decisions made all the difference in their lives. As one of the authors reminded us, "*The way we react to the unexpected can be equally as important, if not more so, in determining what happens next.*"

~

There are at least two sides to every dilemma or situation.

One insight that was present in all of the stories is that there are choices in every situation. However, the options are rarely black and white. The choices we all face in life are complex and often clouded with uncertainty. The complexity of women's lives and the diversity of circumstances, experiences, beliefs, values, perspectives and individual strengths add up to countless possible outcomes for responding to similar situations and dilemmas.

Usually there is no definitive right or wrong answer, just different perspectives based on the individual and their experiences and values. This was another theme that was evident throughout the book. For example, the chapter about children included stories from women who have tried desperately to become mothers and from a woman who made a decision to not have children. The chapter on love and loss included a story from a woman whose husband had an affair and an essay from a married woman who questioned whether she had fallen in love with a married man. In the chapter on faith, one woman wrote about the importance of God in her life while another woman reflected on why she left her religion. For some women, the path was clear, while for others it was not. Each of these women faced significant life decisions. Each had to make a decision that *they* could accept for themselves in their lives, even if it conflicted with others.

We all face difficult decisions and turning points. The diversity of experiences and of the choices made by the women in this book offered a wide range of perspectives and opinions. Perhaps there were some choices that you did not agree with because they differ from your values, beliefs or world view. Hopefully, you were able to read about these women's dilemmas with empathy and compassion even if you did not agree with their decisions.

Including such a diversity of experiences and perspectives in the book was not intended to persuade. The intention was to allow all of the women to be heard, in their own voices, even though others may not share their perspectives or agree with their decisions. It is my hope that readers will be able to appreciate and respect the difficulty of the writers' journeys and that reading these stories will demonstrate that we are more alike than we are dissimilar. We may choose different paths, but we all face common turning points and similar life circumstances. As another woman shared, *"I always believed that you have choices in life and the most important choice you make is how you choose to perceive and then deal with what life sends your way."*

~

Obstacles are inevitable.

Some people face life's challenges and crises with an ability to transform and to grow from their experience. Others have a more difficult time getting over the obstacles, learning from their experiences and moving forward. At times, we get stuck at the threshold and at times we may turn back to what is familiar, even though it may be risky or harmful. Some of the obstacles to moving forward explored by women who contributed to this book include:

- Attachment to the past and holding on to the feelings left over from the event or associated with the other person (e.g., anger, hurt, resentment, grief, loss...);
- Anxiety, apprehension or uncertainty about the future or about change (fear of unknown);
- A lack of adequate information or resources to make the decision or take the next step;
- Limited support and feeling alone;
- Recognition of the consequences or the potential negative impact of the decision; and
- Doubt or negative self-talk which undermined or influenced the decision (e.g. feeling hopeless, cynical, guilty, unworthy...).

These are common barriers to change or moving forward when facing a turning point. They can be so powerful and intimidating that they can get in the way of confronting the situation or making a decision. For many women, overcoming these hindrances was a significant move toward taking charge of their lives and taking the next step.

~

Healthy coping and resilience are imperative to moving forward.

Most of the women in this book wrote about extremely challenging times in their lives: the death of loved ones, chronic illness, infertility, parenting, career moves or life-changing decisions to start anew. Although their turning points were quite different, each of the women eventually found ways to face her situation. Many of them discovered that connecting with other women, writing about their experiences or practicing their spirituality were helpful ways to deal with their dilemmas.

These women were able to gain perspective and find ways of coping with the tidal waves of uncertainty, apprehension, doubt and fear. It is not our falling down but our ability to get up that makes all the difference. This allows us to move beyond the crisis or the dilemma. These women found ways to transform their challenging circumstances into resilience, growth and healing. One author summarized it this way, *"It gave me hope in a way that I thought would never be possible again."*

Many of these women's stories reflected their resilience. No matter what, they persevered, they found strength and they kept putting one foot in front of the other. The author of "Remembering Mary," Paula Andresen, reflected on her experience of losing a loved one to murder:

> *"I believe attitude and perspective is everything and is essential for survival, let alone moving forward. If you face life's challenges, looking for that window that opened after the door closed, (instead of feeling trapped in the room with no way out) the possibilities are endless. My personal journey is a case in point–never in a million years would I have ever dreamed I would be trying to do what I am working on. But I am. I'm trying to make some good come from a tragedy. It really would have been much easier to just wallow in my grief, locked in that room, but I saw that opened window...and look how far I have already come."*

Women want to have a purposeful or meaningful life.

A significant way of coping for several of the women was to connect or reconnect with their sense of purpose and to live a meaningful life. Some of the writers found their calling in their careers or dedicating themselves to service. Some found deep meaning in their faith and their spiritual practice. Some discovered the importance of being a positive influence on others because they were inspired by women who influenced them. It was a priority for them to make a difference in the lives of others. For these women, the turning points in their lives, often unexpected and unwanted, created opportunities to gain new perspectives, realize their purpose or find new meaning in life.

We all want to know that our lives matter. With this desire comes the awareness that we are important and that we can make a difference. This recognition does not always come easily. Many women struggle to find themselves and their place in life. When the women contributing to this book realized their purposes, doors opened for them. The possibilities, options and choices as well as their potential were illuminated. The authors shared through their essays how and when they found meaning or purpose in their lives, whether on their own or with the support and the influence of others.

~

Women need and benefit from a connection with others.

Another common thread woven through these women's stories was their connections with others. Everyone needs to know that there are people who care about them. Support and companionship with others are tremendous resources for dealing with life's turning points. One writer describing the critical importance of connections concludes, *"I was not alone on this journey after all."*

These connections can be found in a variety of places with many different people in our lives including family, friends, partners and colleagues. Some women have also found ways to connect with others through the Internet. Regardless of where or how we find people in our lives, we need them. Many of the writers related their reactions to finding and losing connections in their lives. These women learned that a connection with others was integral to their sense of meaning and fulfillment. Their happiness increased when they had healthy relationships.

Their discoveries are consistent with the current research on happiness: women who have solid friendships and/or partner relationships are more likely to report being happy than women who do not have these kinds of relationships. Furthermore, women who have support and connection with a group of women report increased satisfaction as well as enhanced self esteem. As one writer summarized, *"I learned that my life and my friendships are more important than I ever imagined."*

~

It is most helpful and desirable to have peace within your self and with others.

Several women reflected on finding peace within themselves as well as with other people in their lives. Peace comes from acceptance: knowing that you are okay and that you will be okay no matter what. Some of the women in this book struggled during their turning points because they doubted themselves, criticized themselves, or questioned whether they could ever find happiness or love again.

Many women are searching for happiness and peace. They often follow paths that they mistakenly believe will lead them to true happiness or fulfillment. They spend lots of money, time, energy and effort and they search in many places only to finally discover that the peace they seek is actually within themselves. Some of the effective pathways to peace in this book include:

1. **Gratitude.** Some of the women found peace by connecting with and expressing gratitude. They were able to discover the good fortune in front of them rather than seeking it elsewhere.

2. **Compassion.** Many found peace and joy through expressing compassion and loving kindness toward others. When people are compassionate and generous, they experience an increase in their own happiness and self esteem.

3. **Forgiveness.** Some found freedom from their own suffering when they forgave themselves and/or others. Forgiveness allowed them to be more loving toward themselves and to let go of the destructive feelings of anger, hurt or resentment that they carried toward others. Forgiveness allowed them to move forward with a free heart.

The search for peace within is a very personal endeavor, but we can benefit from what the women in this book (and many others) discovered: Your journey will be more rewarding if you look within rather than outside yourself for peace. True happiness will emerge if you are living a compassionate life—no matter what your profession, how much you earn, or where you live. If you looked deeply within each of the women's stories, you learned that this was the most significant lesson of all: *When one door closes, it is the one that you open that can make all the difference. However, you must open the door to compassion for yourself and for others before you can realize peace within yourself.*

Many of the women in this book found their turning points to be transforming events in their lives. Like so many other women facing challenging decisions or significant life events, they found strength, resilience, courage and the support needed to move forward. In the final analysis, these women realized that even in the most difficult of circumstances, compassion, hope, forgiveness, or peace can be found.

Attributes for Quotes

We want to acknowledge and thank these individuals for their words of wisdom found in our book:

Alcott, Louisa May (1832-1888) An American novelist best known for the novel *Little Women.*

Angelou, Maya (1928–) An autobiographer, poet, educator, historian, best-selling author, actress, playwright, civil-rights activist, producer and director; one of the most honored writers of our time.

Arendt, Hannah (1906 –1975) German-Jewish political theorist who escaped from Europe during Hitler's reign.

Beecher Stowe, Harriet (1811 –1896) An abolitionist and author of *Uncle Tom's Cabin* in 1852.

Bloom, Amy (1953–) Writer nominated for the National Book Award and the National Book Critics Circle Award.

Buck, Pearl S. (1892-1973) Writer and humanitarian winning Pulitzer Prize for the novel *The Good Earth* in 1932.

Buddha (est. 563-483 BCE) Named Siddhattha Gotama, Buddha was a spiritual teacher who founded Buddhism.

Cross, Amanda (1926-2003) Pen name for Carolyn Gold Heilbrun; wrote academic, feminist works and mysteries.

Cummings, e.e. (1894-1962) Named Edward Estlin, a poet (over 2900), painter, essayist, author, and playwright.

Dalai Lama (1935–) The 14th Dalai Lama (born Lhamo Dhondrub); the Tibetan Buddhist spiritual leader and statesman; he is a prolific author and humanitarian; awarded the Nobel Peace Prize in 1989.

Diana, Princess (of Wales) (1961-1997) Humanitarian and supporter of numerous charities around the world.

Dickinson, Emily (1830-1886) Prolific poet (over 1800) known as a powerful author in American culture.

Frank, Anne (1929-1945) A Jewish-German girl whose diary about hiding during the German occupation in World War II is a best selling book of all time; killed at age 15 at the Bergen-Belsen concentration camp.

Frankl, Victor E. (1905-1997) An Austrian psychiatrist, neurologist and Holocaust survivor whose parents and wife were killed at concentration camps during World War II; author of *Man's Search for Meaning* in 1963.
Goldberg, Natalie (1948–) Author; recent work: *Old Friend from Far Away: The Practice of Writing Memoir.*
Hillesum, Etty (1914-1943) Jewish writer; her letters/diaries from 1941-43 were published posthumously in 1981.
Keller, Helen (1880 –1968) Author, political activist and lecturer; she was the first deaf blind person to earn a Bachelor of Arts degree when she graduated from Radcliffe College.
Kemp, Gretchen (1909–?) Recognized for significant contributions to the field of journalism and as an educator.
Kennedy Onassis, Jacqueline (1929-1994) wife of the 35th president of the US; later became editor at Double Day.
Lessing, Doris (1919–?) An Iranian-born British writer, pen name Jane Somers; oldest person to receive the Nobel Prize in Literature in 2007 at age 88.
Lorde, Audre (1934-1992) Caribbean-American writer, poet and activist (civil rights, anti-war and feminist). She described herself as a "black, lesbian, mother, warrior and poet."
Mansfield Murry, Katherine (1888-1923) New Zealand-born short fiction writer; pen name Katherine Mansfield.
Mariechild, Diane Contemporary American author with a focus on women and Buddhism; recent works include: *Mother Wit* and *Open Mind: Women's Daily Inspiration for Becoming Mindful.*
Milner, Marion (1900-1998) English psychologist, pioneer of introspective journaling; pen name Joanna Field.
Morrow Lindbergh, Anne (1906-2001) Writer, poet and aviator; author of several books including *Gift from the Sea.*
Mother Teresa (1910– 1997) born Agnesë Gonxhe Bojaxhiu; Catholic nun who devoted her entire life to care for the poor, sick, orphaned and dying; awarded the Nobel Peace Prize in 1979 for her humanitarian work.
Nhat Hanh, Thich (1926–) Vietnamese Zen Buddhist monk, teacher, prolific author, poet and peace activist; nominated by Dr. Martin Luther King, Jr. for the Nobel Peace Prize in 1967.
Nietzsche, Frederick (1844-1900) German philosopher who wrote on religion, morality, philosophy and more.

Obama, Barack (1961–) 44th President of the United States and the first African-American President; a community organizer before a lawyer and then US Senator; author of *Dreams from My Father* and *The Audacity of Hope*; awarded the Nobel Peace Prize in 2009.

Oliver, Mary—(1935–) Well known American poet; won the Pulitzer Prize for Poetry for her collection *American Primitive*; the quote used in this book is from "Blackwater Woods."

Roosevelt, Eleanor (1884-1962) First Lady 1933 to 1945, stateswoman, humanitarian and civil rights advocate.

Rumi (1207-1273) Persian poet, jurist, theologian and mystic known as Jalāl ad-Dīn Muḥammad Rūmī.

Saint Theresa of Avila (1515-1582) Spanish mystic, Carmelite nun and writer of the Counter Reformation; canonized in 1622 and named a Doctor of the Church by Pope Paul VI in 1970.

Senesh, Hannah (1921-1944) Palestinian Jew born in Hungary; executed in 1944; she volunteered to parachute into occupied Hungary for the British Army; wrote numerous poems that were turned into Hebrew songs.

Shinoda Bolan, Jean–A psychiatrist, Jungian analyst, author and speaker; Some of her works include: *The Tao of* Psychology and Goddesses *in Everywoman.*

Tempest Williams, Terry (1955–) Author, environmentalist; her quote is from *Finding Beauty in a Broken World.*

Walker, Alice (1944-) Novelist, short-story writer, poet, essayist, activist and author of several works including *The Color Purple*; winner of the Pulitzer Prize and National Book Award.

Wheeler Wilcox, Ella (1850-1919) Author and poet; her best-known work was Poems of Passion.

Winfrey, Oprah (1954–) Multi-award winning talk show host, actress, television producer, literary critic and magazine publisher; she was ranked the richest African American of the 20th century; the most philanthropic African American of all time and has been called *the most influential woman in America*.

About the Reflections from Women Writing Contest

Sugati Publications announced the *Reflections from Women* writing contest for women writers to submit entries for consideration in this anthology. There was no limit on the number of submissions an author could submit and no cost to enter the writing contest. However, only the top 10 essays and poems submitted among all of the contest entries were accepted for publication in the book. The recipients are recognized in the book next to their essay or poem as a selection from the Reflections from Women Writing Contest.

The women's writing contest was open to any adult woman writer (previous publications were not necessary). The topic of the essay or poem was required to be related to the focus of the book and based on a personal life story, turning point, major decision or life changing event. All entries were acknowledged by the author as original, non-fiction and based on the author's personal experience. Fiction was not accepted for this anthology.

It is important to note that the other essays and poems in the book were received and considered through a traditional manuscript review process and they were not submitted nor reviewed for the writing contest. In order to be considered for the writing contest, the author was required to designate their entry as such.

The writing contest submissions were judged and selected by the book editor, Terri Spahr Nelson and by a co-owner of Sugati Publications, both of whom are published authors. The selections brought a diverse collection of writing styles as well as a variation in content to the book. Congratulations to the authors whose entries were selected for publication as a part of the Reflections from Women writing contest!

The Non-Profit Agency Recipients of 35% of Book Profits

In keeping with the spirit of this women's anthology, Sugati Publications is committing 35% of all profits from this book to five non-profit women's agencies that provide assistance to women. The five agencies were chosen from among several other very deserving agencies. The final selections were based on votes and input from the authors and the public. The donation amount to each agency is based on their service area (global, national and local). We want to acknowledge and thank the organizations chosen as the recipients of the partial book profits. We encourage our readers to visit their websites to learn more about these agencies and how to be of assistance. We are grateful for all of the good work that they do on behalf of women in their communities, in our nation and around the world. Thank you!

Global organization (10% profits)

The Global Fund for Women "is an international network of women and men committed to a world of equality and social justice...The Global Fund makes grants to women's rights groups based outside the United States working to address human rights issues that include: ending gender-based violence and building peace; ensuring economic and environmental justice; advancing health and sexual and reproductive rights; expanding civic and political participation; increasing access to education; and fostering social change philanthropy." www.globalfundforwomen.org/cms

National organization (10% profits)

Rape, Abuse, Incest National Network (RAINN) "RAINN is the nation's largest anti-sexual assault organization" offering education, legislative advocacy and victim services through two national hotlines (by phone and online). www.rainn.org

Local, community-based organizations (5% profits each)

The Beginning Over Foundation is a community-based organization in Easton Pennsylvania offering "education, support, advocacy, housing and hope to those touched by domestic abuse." Their goal is to help shelter and protect families in crisis and support long term solutions. www.BeginningOver.org

Washington Area Women's Foundation "one of the fastest growing women's foundations in the nation providing both grants and operational resources to non-profit organizations serving women and girls." They have provided over $4.1 million in grants to over 100 leading community-based organizations. www.thewomensfoundation.org

Women's Legal Resource is a community-based advocacy organization in Los Angeles, California that provides assistance to victims and information regarding state and federal laws. "Women's Legal Resource is a nonpartisan organization that supports the efforts for Domestic Violence Reform and Family Law Reform." www.womenslegalresource.com.

About Terri Spahr Nelson

Terri Spahr Nelson is a national consultant, educator, author and psychotherapist. She has 30 years of experience in mental health and behavioral sciences specializing in women's issues with victims of violence and trauma. Terri has served in many consultant roles, including as a Subject Matter Expert for the Department of Defense on their Sexual Assault Prevention and Response Program; Chair of the military subcommittee of the National Task Force to End Domestic and Sexual Violence; and consultant on the National Agenda on Violence Against Women.

Ms. Spahr Nelson is also the author of several publications and articles, including the book: *For Love of Country: Confronting Rape and Sexual Harassment in the U.S. Military* (2002, Routledge); an essay in the edited book *Abuse Your Illusions* (2003, The Disinformation Company, Ltd); and several trauma booklets from Sugati Publications including: *Coping with Sexual Assault: A Guide to Resolution, Healing and Recovery* printed in English, Spanish, Braille and Large Print. Her most recent publication *Coping with Trauma Work and Vicarious Trauma: A Guide for Professionals and Volunteers who Work with Victims of Trauma, Abuse and Disasters* was co-authored with her husband, Dr. Patrick Nelson. In addition to her publications Terri has facilitated programs and retreats for professionals on vicarious trauma and for women on a wide range of topics. She maintains a part time psychotherapy private practice and is a volunteer and activist for peace, social justice, and healthcare issues. You can contact Terri Spahr Nelson at: **tsnelson@reflectionsfromwomen.com**

About Sugati Publications 

Sugati Publications is a small, independent publisher (a subsidiary of Sugati, LLC). The publications division has two branches: 1) booklets for the general public and for professional audiences with a focus on trauma, sexual assault and other violent crimes; and 2) trade books for the general public and for academic or professional audiences. The premier trade book for Sugati Publications is *When One Door Closes–Reflections from Women on Life's Turning Points*. It is also the first in a series from the *Reflections from Women* collection. Additional book titles will be forthcoming from Sugati Publications. To order our publications or for manuscript submission guidelines, go to: www.sugatipublications.com

Other titles available from Sugati Publications:

Coping with Trauma Work and Vicarious Trauma

Coping after a Violent Crime:
A Guide to Healing and the Criminal Justice Process

Responding to Sexual Assault in the Military:
A Resource Guide and Policy Overview

Coping with Military Sexual Trauma:
A Resource for Veterans and Their Loved Ones

Coping with Sexual Assault:
A Guide to Resolution, Healing and Recovery
Adult, English; also in Braille and Large Print
A Guide for College Students; A Guide for Teens;
A Guide for Professionals and Volunteers

Enfrentando La Violacion Y El Abuso Sexual
Guia para facilitar el alivio y la recuperacion

"Sugati" comes from the ancient Pali language and refers to a happy destination.
May you find peace on your journey.

To contribute to future books in the Reflections from Women series

Do you have a story to submit for an upcoming edition?

We want to hear from you. We will look forward to reading your essay or poem and considering it for a future edition in the "Reflections from Women" series. Please note, due to the high volume of queries, we request that you first refer to the publication guidelines at www.reflectionsfromwomen.com. We are also requesting only one submission per author please. We will respond to all queries but cannot publish all submissions. Thank you for your interest!

Topic areas for upcoming books:

Reflections from Women at Mid-Life

Reflections from Women on "Lessons to My Children"

Reflections from Women on "The Moment I Knew"

If you would like to have a personal essay or poem considered for future publications, please visit the website for updates and submission guidelines at:
www.ReflectionsFromWomen.com

Sugati Publications
www.sugatipublications.com

"When one door of happiness closes, another opens;
but often we look so long at the closed door
that we do not see the one which has been opened for us."

Helen Keller